The Co-Creator's Handbook

An Experiential Guide For Discovering Your Life's Purpose and Building a Co-creative Society

by
Carolyn Anderson

in collaboration with
Katharine Roske

© Global Family® 2008
Nevada City, CA USA

Additional copies of this book can be obtained for $22.00 plus $4.00 shipping and handling. For each additional book, add $1.00 for postage, except for bulk orders or bookstore purchases, for which discounts are available. California residents add 7% tax. Overseas: contact us for rates. You may use check, VISA or MasterCard. (See order form in the back of the book or on our website: www.globalfamily.net.)

Send your order to:

Global Family
11689 Lowhills Road
Nevada City, CA 95959 USA
(530) 470-9280
(805) 456-0640 fax
e-mail: connect@globalfamily.net
internet: www. globalfamily.net

ISBN: 978-1-883208-01-1

Library Of Congress Control Number: 2001126274

The Co-Creator's Handbook: An Experiential Guide for Discovering Your Life's Purpose
and Building a Co-creative Society,
By Carolyn Anderson with Katharine Roske
Edited by John Zwerver
First Edition 2001
Second Edition 2008
Nevada City, California
Printed on Recycled Paper in the United States of America

Graphics by Una Hager
Book Design by Maverick Designs
Cover by Trina Brunk

Global Family is a non-profit, international network of individuals and groups who are dedicated to experiencing unconditional love and the birth of a new co-creative society. Our purpose is to support a global shift in consciousness from separation and fear to unity, love and cooperation.

The Co-Creator's Handbook is an exciting sequel to the very popular guidebook, *The Rings of Empowerment*, which has been used by groups in businesses, churches, and community organizations all over the world. With almost twice as much material as the original book, *The Co-Creator's Handbook* builds on the information and processes of *The Rings of Empowerment*. It adds a wealth of new and updated materials, based on the evolution of Global Family's work over the past two decades.

What others have to say about *The Co-Creator's Handbook:*

We cannot heal the Earth by acting from feelings of fear and isolation.
To build a sustainable and meaningful future, we must learn to tap into our inner
creativity and then join with others in a spirit of compassionate service.
The Co-Creator's Handbook is a book by pioneering social architects who practice
what they preach. This book provides an inspiring map for the journey
from discovering our inner creativity to developing a supportive and
synergistic community and then to practical and cooperative actions in the world.

Duane Elgin,
Author of *Promise Ahead* and *Awakening Earth*

I believe that working in groups creates transformational synergy, that we can travel
faster and deeper together than we can travel on our own. Through the evocation of
one another, we expand the base of our concern, developing an enhanced relationship
to our planet and intensifying our recognition of its needs as well as our willingness
to respond creatively to those needs. Working in community, each person holds the
dreams and excellence of everyone else in the group, so that should we descend into a
period of depression or despair, our excellence and dreams are held by the group until
we return to a healthier mindset. And if we can do this for each other, we can hold as
well our collective dream for the world's future.

Jean Houston,
Author of *Jump Time* and
A Passion for the Possible

Dedication

This book is lovingly dedicated to our children and grandchildren and to all future generations of our global family—"the sun-eyed children of the marvelous dawn" —with deep appreciation for leading us across the threshold into a new world of unity and love.

All grace to the One known as many: God, Yahweh, Allah, Brahman, Great Spirit—Creator of all things and of which all things have been made. May each of us move beyond separate labels and beliefs to experience the love that pervades all that is.

Acknowledgments

If Providence shines upon us, we may have the experience of being touched by a person of such immense depth, love and wisdom that we are changed forever. Barbara Marx Hubbard has been one of those people in our lives. Her pioneering work with the Core Group Process has laid the foundation for this Handbook and inspired people around the globe. Her friendship and guidance has touched our hearts and expanded our awareness. No words can fully express the gratitude we feel for this remarkable woman! We acknowledge Barbara and her Foundation for Conscious Evolution for the innovative work they are doing to shift consciousness on the planet.

Our sincerest gratitude to John Zwerver, Carolyn's beloved husband and co-creative partner in Global Family and the editor of this book. His devotion, tireless patience, and attention to detail in pulling together all the pieces of this complex puzzle are awe-inspiring and deeply appreciated.

Katherine's devoted husband Makasha and our dear friends Rich and Marie Ruster spent countless hours envisioning and sharing their wisdom and insights with us. We love and appreciate them very much.

Special thanks to Marion Culhane for her vision and commitment in co-founding Global Family, for her on-going support and inspiration, and for being the kind of sister that only the fortunate few can claim as kin!

We are indebted to Tim Clauss for years of devoted service to Global Family, for his invaluable contribution to birthing Core Groups around the world, and for co-creating many of the "tips," principles, and exercises in this Handbook. We laud his talent and generosity of spirit and treasure his friendship.

Deep appreciation to our Hummingbird Ranch community in New Mexico for modeling the Circles of Co-Creation and serving as a living laboratory for the Core Group Process. Special acknowledgment goes to the late Alexa Young for contributing numerous inspiring quotations, Trina Brunk for her lovely cover design, and Una Hager for the exquisite graphics that grace the introduction to each Circle.

Jean Houston, Nick Arjuna Ardagh and Amayea Rae have been most generous in sharing a number of their experiential exercises with us. May their kindness and selflessness be returned in surprising and meaningful ways many times over!

And to those who contributed directly or indirectly to the original *Rings of Empowerment* book—Marian Head, Carol Schultz, Donna Curtis, and Anne Monnin—we acknowledge you as true social pioneers. Thank you for helping to lay a foundation that is building a new global, co-creative society. We appreciate the fine work and spirit of our new friends Charlie Abernathybettis and Anne Adden at Maverick Design, for lending their talents and creativity to the layout of this Handbook.

Finally, we thank those generous benefactors who share the vision of this book and supported Global Family financially so that this dream could become a reality. They include Ralph Huber, Sherry Everett, Barbara Marx Hubbard, Janice O'Brien, Margo King and John Steiner, Ann Johnson, Sara Senet, Glenn and Marian Head, Joan and Lance Goddard, The Foundation for Conscious Evolution, and others.

This has truly been a co-creative endeavor, and we are deeply touched by the support we have received from so many people who mean so much to both of us.

With love and appreciation,
Carolyn Anderson and Katharine Roske

Table of Contents

The Call

This is an invitation to participate in perhaps the greatest adventure of all time…birthing a new world…a co-creative society.

Just as many of our ancestors often traveled great distances to be able to fully express their beliefs, ideals and thirst for freedom, we, the social pioneers of our time, are being called from within to manifest a new culture that reflects and embodies the expanded awareness that we are experiencing in our lives.

The old forms, structures, and institutions no longer serve our collective needs as we step across the threshold into a new millennium. At this auspicious time in our evolution, there stirs within the hearts of a growing body of humanity the yearning to discover and model new social forms which honor unity and diversity and call forth each individual's full creative potential.

As our consciousness shifts from separation and fear to unity and love, we desire to join with others in co-creative endeavors that embody the values and virtues of trust, respect, equality, cooperation, equanimity, generosity, integrity and compassion.

This is a new horizon…a journey into uncharted territory. Many have come before who have pointed the way, responding at moments when the cry from the confused masses echoed around the world. The great masters, saints, and prophets have exemplified what is possible. Most have walked a solitary path, being misunderstood and sometimes even persecuted.

At this time of the Great Turning, we move beyond the path of crucifixion into resurrection. No longer must the pioneers of our age walk alone. As Thich Nhat Hahn so eloquently expressed, "The next Buddha may not be an individual, but an enlightened community."

Millions of courageous individuals in towns and villages throughout the world are opening to a greater reality, by responding to a cry in their hearts to take the inward journey to "know thyself." This creative minority is now sufficient in number to shift the tide.

Emerging from an early wave of social pioneers, *The Co-Creator's Handbook* is a response to the need for a transformed society. This Guidebook offers processes, tools, experiential exercises and understanding necessary for awakening individuals to their full potential and birthing a co-creative culture. It is the evolutionary imperative of our time to join in teams, create and maintain a field of love, align collectively with Spirit, and bring into manifestation the new social forms that embody an awakened consciousness.

This invitation goes out to all pioneering souls who are awakening to their spiritual nature, all who are responding to an inner call, all concerned with the absolute well-being of life. It is a call to collaborate in birthing a co-creative society in service to the highest good of all.

On behalf of all life and future generations to come, let us embark on this transforming journey together.

Foreword

By Barbara Marx Hubbard

There is emerging a new humanity that holds within itself the seeds of a radically new future, one that has been envisioned in the great mystical traditions of the human race—the new heaven and the new earth, the new Jerusalem, beyond death, beyond scarcity, beyond the illusion of separation between humans and the divine.

It is my sense that we are living through a period of quantum transformation, and that on the other side is this radically new future which has been envisioned, yet relegated to the purely mystical or the afterlife. This future is actually the energy field of the next stage of human evolution. It is now unfolding in our midst, not as life after death, but as life after this stage of life. Revelation is unfolding in evolution.

The processes in each of the Circles of Co-creation described in *The Co-Creator's Handbook* offer us a way to create these fields of energy. They can help transport us into this new state of being, which has been held in the hearts of humanity since the beginning of time. I realize this might seem like a merely poetic statement, but I believe it is *really* true.

We might cast our eyes backward only briefly in evolutionary history to our pre-human ancestors—Australopithecus africanus, merely 2 to 3 million years ago. We can follow our rapid rise from Homo habilis, Homo erectus, Homo Neanderthal, and 200,000-50,000 years ago, to Homo sapiens, the creature that knows it knows.

It was only about 5000 years ago that the great avatars emerged—such as the Buddha and Christ. They experienced their divinity. They had a direct experience of the prime directive of the process of creation, which is to be one with that which is creating us. They were the first of these newly emerging beings. But very few of us were able to access that state of consciousness—it was not yet time. Religions formed to hold the precious experience and teachings of these advanced avatars. Gradually, science and democracy emerged, placing actual tools of radical material and social transformation into the hands of humanity. . .but without personal access to the awareness of that deeper source or pattern of creation to guide us. On the contrary, secular scientific materialism posited that there is no pattern, no design, no purpose or greater meaning in evolution.

The critical moment of transition to the next stage of evolution finally occurred when human intelligence matured enough for the mind to penetrate into the heart of nature and discover one of the invisible technologies of creation, the atom. When Einstein discovered that $E=mc^2$, the second chapter in the history of our world began. We began to understand the very processes of nature which are creating us, and became capable of directly affecting those processes ourselves…still without awareness of the deeper design of evolution to guide us.

The new chapter in the history of the world might be called the Second Genesis. For with this understanding the still self-centered creature human is gaining the power of co-destruction or co-creation. We can blow up worlds and build new worlds. We can create new life forms or make monsters. Into our hands is being placed powers that we used to attribute to our gods. It has been said that we were created in the "image and likeness of God," and lo and behold, God-like we are becoming!

However, we clearly are not wise "gods." We are still cut off from the Source of creation by a limited self-consciousness and self-centeredness. Most of our institutions, nations, and even organized religions are founded on the principles of separation, competition, scarcity and egoic self-protection.

It is becoming ever more clear that self-centered humans with this degree of power, in our current state of consciousness (rapidly escalating to include biotechnology, nano-technology, quantum computing—literally powers to transform the material world) will not long be viable. We are facing a choice—either extinction or conscious evolution. This amounts to the evolution of evolution itself, from natural selection to conscious choice. If our species can learn ethical evolution in our generation, if we can attune, like the great seers and mystics of humanity have always done, to the deeper reality itself, we see the possibility of an immeasurable and unknown future—cosmic consciousness, species immortality, contact with other life. If not, we already see the possibility of our own extinction.

Because evolution raises consciousness (a fifteen billion year trend!) and because we are facing the ultimate evolutionary driver in our generation, what is happening, I believe, is that for the first time in human history this new type of human being is "popping" out of every faith, tradition and culture. We might call this new human Homo Universalis. This human is emerging as a new norm, characterized by a deep sense of participating in the process of creation, of being attuned and guided by a higher dimension of reality than the normal self conscious mind. This 'Universal Human' experiences unitive flashes, a sense of oneness with the divine, a feeling of connectedness with all being, and a unique inner code urging us to participate in the evolution of the Self and the world.

I am convinced that this type of human holds the seeds of the future, and that as we come together in new synergistic social forms we can provide a vital contribution to the radical transformation which is occurring due to the rapidly escalating powers to evolve or destroy ourselves.

The Core Groups, as described in *The Co-Creator's Handbook*, attract this emerging Universal Human. Instead of finding ourselves isolated in a dissonant and dysfunctional world, we find ourselves in resonance, in harmony, reinforced in our unitive consciousness, called forth in our unique creativity, supported in our desire to manifest our inner values in projects and programs in the outer world. These groups are cultures of growth for the new humans and the new society, which empathetic, holistic and compassionate consciousness is building, even now.

I don't think it is an exaggeration to say that **by learning how to consciously practice the Circles of Co-Creation as presented in this book, we are making an immeasurable contribution to this quantum jump to the next stage of human evolution—to "heaven on earth." They provide us with personal and social processes whereby we can make the jump together, from the inside out, from our spiritual motivation and unique creativity outward, bringing ourselves into new forms as co-creators of our world.**

Co-creative Core Groups are formative units of the emerging culture. As they connect and manifest action through the chosen vocations of their members, they are even now becoming organic functional elements within the new social body—its healers and entrepreneurs, its communicators, educators, artists, managers, and leaders of all kinds. Even now, networks of human-scale communities composed of such Cores are forming the basis for the cultural reformation of the world.

Taking a deep breath, and jumping across the quantum abyss in our imaginations, we can already see the glimmers of a radically new world. We have developed a society whose organizations are co-creative with the patterns of evolution and with the spirit of creation in each of us. Into this emerging technological and social arena, we can see the young Universal Humans, our children's children, entering into the process of conscious evolution, designing new social systems, and eventually gaining access and guidance over the evolutionary technologies which promise radical new powers, abundant energy, and non-polluting technologies that can liberate us from earth-bound, creature human existence. Even now we find ourselves at the threshold of universal life.

Co-creative Core Groups practicing the Circles of Co-creation are a home base for pioneering souls who are called to make the transition in our own lives, families, work, and communities. By modeling this change personally and socially, at whatever level we are capable of, we are seeding the chaotic culture around us with islands of coherence and alignment with the deeper tendency of evolution for higher consciousness and greater freedom through more synergistic order. We are making the quantum leap ourselves. When we are resonating together in this mode, we are living *in this very moment* in a new heaven and a new Earth. Wherever two or more are gathered in this state of being, the future is present. Now. In this way, we bring the future into the present. We realize the dream and fulfill the promise of all the great mystics of the world.

About The Handbook

PURPOSE OF THE HANDBOOK

This guidebook has been created to support the evolution of individuals and the formation of co-creative groups that have, or wish to develop, a shared purpose or goal. It is a tool to empower you to learn the principles and practices of co-creation and to support you in finding your teammates so that together you can evolve yourselves and the world. **In short, the Circles of Co-Creation facilitate individual and collective transformation.**

If your group has had some previous experience in building trust and attaining resonance, you will get the most benefit from this guide. If not, Section 2 will assist you in starting and maintaining a Resonant Core Group. This book will lead your group beyond sharing and bonding, to the next step, which is co-creation. This Handbook is experiential, not observational, and will allow you to deeply engage at the level of personal experiences and the sharing of your gifts.

The Core Group is not an emotional support group. Its function is connection, not correction—emergence, not emergency. Participants must have attained a basic level of psycho-spiritual maturity to desire to move beyond their personal story and share their gifts with the group.

WHO CAN BENEFIT FROM THIS BOOK?

There are many groups and communities that can benefit from practicing the Circles of Co-Creation: businesses, intentional communities, families, shared households, focused teams, action groups, church and service groups, and any other small group that comes together to experience personal evolution and healing or to support positive change in their community.

HOW TO USE THIS HANDBOOK

We honor the diversity of all traditions and spiritual and religious paths around the world. We feel that the co-creative process described in this book is universal to all humans regardless of nationality, gender, individual beliefs and perspectives. If the languaging used here is not compatible with yours, please translate it in a way that is most comfortable and beneficial for you. For sake of simplicity and consistency, the masculine pronoun "he" is used when referring to a man and/or a woman.

Section 1   Provides an overview of the Circles of Co-Creation and a context for the Core Group process.

Section 2   Provides step-by-step instructions to guide you in forming a Core Group so that you can discover and express your full potential in the world as part of a co-creative team.

Section 3   This is the heart of the matter; it consists of a series of experiential exercises that you can use with your team to fully empower yourselves.

Section 4   Includes sample closing exercises, information about Global Family and aligned groups, and recommended books and music.

To gain the most from these experiences, we strongly encourage each member of your group to buy a Handbook and to read Sections 1 and 2 before moving on to Section 3, the Circles of Co-Creation exercises.

Another advantage to having your own Handbook is that you can make personal notes in the spaces provided. In addition, you are also encouraged to keep a journal to note your insights and track your personal evolution as you go through the exercises.

You will also be given special assignments to complete between some of the sessions and will be guided to assess your evolution through art, writing, and inner reflection.

To assist you in moving deliberately through the material, the Handbook uses the symbol ~ ~ to indicate special places to pause and reflect. It is suggested that you stop reading at this point, be still and feel the truth of your experience or of what has been said.

To ensure a feeling of safety and to support deep communication, please remember that all personal sharing is to be held in confidence by all members of the group.

Please note: You will probably need many meetings to experience all the material provided in each Circle of this guide. Do not rush through the exercises in an attempt to "cover more ground." Savor the joy of building group resonance and the privilege of being fully present to the process of self-discovery and group empowerment.

Most of the exercises in the Circles of this Handbook are meant to be approached in a linear fashion; that is, you can start at the beginning of the each Circle and move through every process or co-create your own version of the exercise.

Circle 5: Honoring the Sacred: Ceremonies, Rituals and Celebration is an exception. We suggest that you go through this chapter before your second or third meeting to become familiar with its contents. You can then use the appropriate exercises as occasions may arise.

Definitions

The following are some key words used in this guidebook and their definitions:

Co: Co in any word means "two things, one to the other joining," as in the words co-creation, community, collaboration, complimentary, cohesion, and cooperation.

Co-creation: Co-participating consciously with the laws or patterns of the Creator; conscious alignment with the essence of others and with nature; Self aligning with Self, vertically and horizontally.

Co-Creative Core Group: A group that comes together around a shared purpose that actualizes the gifts of all members and contributes to the betterment of society. Co-Creative Core Groups usually evolve from Resonant Core Groups. (See below.)

Co-creative Self: The Essential Self expressing in the world.

Co-creator: One who surrenders and aligns his will with the intention of Creation, the universal mind, the designing intelligence, Spirit; one who shares his gifts and actualizes his dreams in synergistic play with other co-creators to bring forth a new world

Cultural Creatives: As defined by Paul Ray and Sherry Anderson, they are those people from every field of endeavor who share the values of service, equality, and compassion and who are committed to preserving and sustaining life and creating a new culture.

Essential Self, Universal Human, the Self, the Beloved: The indwelling divine presence expressing as the individual; the infinite mind, Spirit, life, truth, and love which manifests in human form. The universal, non-egoic, co-creative, authentic self.

Inner coach: The voice of the Co-creative Self; inner knowing or guidance; your guide in co-creating a new culture.

Local self: The limited, self-conscious personality that may feel separate, alone and in control. The ego operating in the world.

Resonance: The invisible field of love in which co-creation occurs; resounding, echoing back and affirming the highest in one another; the frequency that aligns individuals heart to heart, calling forth the gifts and creativity of each person.

Resonant or Resonating Core Group: A group of individuals who establish alignment and harmony and co-create an environment of accelerated growth; a sacred circle at one with the Creator, attuning to the Essential Self in all, experiencing unconditional love connecting them with each other and with all creation; a new social pattern in which individuals become one body with a collective sensitivity to the infinite mind and the will of the Divine. The French word for heart is "coeur", giving meaning to the word "core". Love and connecting heart to heart is the foundation of the Resonant Core Group.

Synergy: The interaction of two or more people that achieves an effect that is greater than what the sum of the individual actions can achieve; the effect that occurs when two or more are gathered in the name of truth.

Section 1

AN INVITATION TO CO-CREATION

An Invitation To Co-Creation

Have you had a sense of knowing, for many years, that society is in the midst of a radical transformation and that you have a part to play in this?

Are you feeling within you a powerful longing for greater meaning in your life?

Are you experiencing a spontaneous surge of creativity greater than what can be contained in your current work?

Are you tired of trying to go it alone?

Do you sense that out of the life-threatening crises of our age—environmental destruction, terrorism, and social inequities—a new way of life is crying out to be born?

If so, you are being lifted up from within by an energy as powerful as the drive for self-preservation or self-reproduction. It is the third great force: the longing for Self-realization and Self-actualization. It is this alignment as our Co-creative Selves, linking with others who share our vision and passion for the possible, that creates positive change in the world.

We call it the urge of co-creation. It is the uprising of human creativity, an evolutionary force that can transform the world. As we collectively move into this new territory, we are finding our way together. There are no maps and few mentors; the only true guides reside within us. We are discovering the process together, following our intuition, and learning as we go.

We are at the threshold of a global renaissance that has only been dimly dreamed of by the visionaries of the human race. **Each of us is awakening to our true nature, as our Essential Self, discovering our soul's purpose, and working together to birth a co-creative culture!**

The Evolution of the Circles of Co-Creation

Rather than being devised, the Circles of Co-Creation have been revealed to and practiced by many groups around the globe. Native people have used a process similar to this for many centuries. However, before the publication of the original *Rings of Empowerment* book, no one had ever described the model or presented it as a whole system so that it could be replicated by others.

The original Rings of Empowerment model came from Barbara Marx Hubbard's understanding of the ways in which humans are now joining in deep resonance for personal and social change. As co-founders of Global Family, Barbara and Carolyn Anderson developed the concept of the Core Group Process and initiated early trainings to share the model with others. Recently, the team that created this Handbook took the processes described in the earlier Rings of Empowerment model and renamed them the Circles of Co-Creation to more accurately reflect the actual processes that occur.

The term "Resonating Core Group" refers to a small group of people who practice relating to each other from a center or core of unconditional love and authenticity. Whether they are called "Core Groups", "Wisdom Circles", or "Listening Circles" —any small group that provides the safe space to relate to others from a feeling/heart place and encourages the full expression of intuitive knowing is a type of Resonating Core Group.

"Co-Creative Cores" evolve from Resonating Core Groups. These are groups that have come together around a shared purpose that actualizes the gifts of all members and contributes to the betterment of society. Unlike groups that focus on personal and spiritual growth but don't take social action in the world, and unlike social action groups that don't take the time to cultivate harmony and resonance among themselves, Core Groups that follow the Circles model call for love AND action. Co-creators choose to use their work and their relationships with one another as THE WAY to co-create the world they choose. Co-Creative Cores are a "quantum leap" in social organization and a new structure for personal and group empowerment.

By seeding our organizations and communities with these synergistic social units, we can become satisfied, actualized humans who are making immense contributions to society. As members of co-creative groups, we can drop the old habits of fear, dominance/submission, unhealthy competition, and separation. In their place, we can experience love, harmony, cooperation, and alignment that will greatly increase our effectiveness in creating a positive future.

AN OVERVIEW OF THE CIRCLES OF CO-CREATION

The Circles of Co-Creation offer a process to assist you in stabilizing as the Essential Self, the indwelling divine presence, discovering your soul's purpose, and joining with others to birth a co-creative society. The following is an overview of this process.

Each Circle presents inspiration, information, and experiential exercises to evolve and empower you and your partners. When all of the Circles are practiced consciously, quantum change occurs and there is a genuine increase in awareness, creativity and fulfillment. Awakening as co-creators, we give birth to a culture that more truly reflects our values, vision, and consciousness.

As you apply the Circles in your own life, you will be modeling the change you would like to see in the world.

Please note: This is a non-linear process. The essential ingredients are the love and awareness each person brings to the group. Creating and maintaining resonance allows each part of the process to emerge spontaneously in perfect timing.

Circle 1:   Awakening the Co-creative Self

Common to all traditions and belief systems is the evolutionary impulse to "know thyself." When someone comes to rest in his essential divine nature, there is an experience of deep inner peace and all-pervading love. For some, this experience is instantaneous—perhaps unexpected. For others, it is the fruition of years of rigorous discipline and religious/spiritual practice. Always, there is an element of grace. To stabilize in this awakened state is a life-long daily practice of vigilance, awareness and remembrance.

In Circle One we recognize that each individual, although on a unique spiritual quest, shares common needs for creative fulfillment and the experience of community. As we shift our identity from self-centered consciousness to the Co-creative Self, we are drawn to kindred souls who share our passion for manifesting positive change. Like the caterpillar, we are moving out of the cocoon of false identity to experience ourselves as butterflies. Participation in a Core Group fosters this awakening, enhances our creativity and fulfills our deep yearning for true family.

Circle 2:   Connecting at the Heart

As we connect at the heart and hold each other in unconditional love and acceptance, an invisible magnetic field of love emerges. It is this resonant field that gives birth to the co-creative process. When we are truly seen, accepted, and acknowledged for who we are, our trust is deepened and we feel empowered.

In this Circle we practice non-judgment, forgiveness, and loving one another as ourselves. We use every incident as an opportunity for reflection, transformation and healing. Our life is our work, as we embody the principles of resonance minute by minute, on a daily basis, in our workplace, our homes and in activities of all kinds.

Circle 3:   Overcoming the Illusion of Separation

Coming together in this field of profound harmony, intimate sharing and safety, our feelings of separation and fear dissolve. We face our shadows and learn a set of communication skills that support alignment with our true natures. We co-coach each other to do and be our best. We create agreements that encourage authenticity and empower each of us as the Co-creative Self. Practicing forgiveness, we dispel the illusion of separation and are able to see and acknowledge the truth and beauty in one another.

Circle 4:   Accessing Our Collective Wisdom

As we rest deeply in the resonant field of love and trust, an opening in our consciousness naturally occurs. The inner voice, the deeper wisdom that resides in each of us is revealed. As our intuitive mind works in concert with our critical analytical intellect, a new synthesis—co-creative intelligence—is born.

When we collectively practice deep listening, we gain access to inspired insights and receive guidance regarding our actions as individuals and as members of a group. Together, we move to a higher frequency of knowing. A dynamic of synergy, synchronicity, and, sometimes, telepathy is experienced, giving birth to our collective wisdom.

Circle 5:   Honoring the Sacred: Ceremony, Ritual, and Celebration

We develop ceremonies and rituals to help anchor and actualize the state of resonance and oneness. We consciously make our relationships sacred—to each other, to the Earth, to all life, and to Spirit. Aligning with the natural order, the cycles of the seasons and the phases of our lives, we take time for retreats, rites of passage, and periods of silent reflection. The ordinary becomes sacred as we breathe meaning into the mundane.

Giving thanks for having discovered our true nature and loving community of friends, we rejoice and celebrate our good fortune together. New games of cooperation, humor and play open our hearts more fully and provide relief from the more serious pursuit of our worldly service. We rejoice in the gift of life and the many blessings that it holds for each of us.

Circle 6:   Expressing Our Soul's Purpose

It is the destiny of each human being to awaken to his divine nature and to discover and express his unique calling. We discover our true place by following the wisdom of the heart and going within for guidance and direction. In this Circle we move from the inner work of personal growth and alignment as the Self to our outer expression in the world. We express our talents and seek to join our gifts with those of appropriate partners to release the potential of each member of the group. Our barometer of success is the sense of joy and fulfillment in coming home to ourselves.

Circle 7:   Discovering Our Shared Destiny

Once we are aware of our unique soul's purpose, we are drawn to others who are aligned with our values, vision, and mission to fulfill our shared destiny. In Resonant Core Groups the shared destiny of the participants is to focus on the healing and evolution of its members. Co-creative Core Groups commit to projects and activities that actualize the unique purpose of all members of the group and allow each person to participate fully and equally. We enter a state comparable to marriage, deepening our intimacy and committing ourselves to be faithful to our partners and our agreed upon actions. Spirit is configuring us into groups and teams so that we can play our parts in creating a new culture.

Circle 8: Attuning to the Design of Creation

As we gain access to our collective wisdom, discover our shared destiny and experience group synergy, a new form of governance emerges: self-governance. Attuning to the design of creation, we allow for decisions and right action to be revealed. Led by the self-organizing laws of nature, we observe "what wants to happen". We naturally desire to make optimum choices which honor our interconnectedness with all life.

We evolve beyond Robert's Rules of Order and parliamentary procedure, as well as consensus decision making, into synergistic cooperative democracy and whole-systems knowing. Revelation joins with thinking to support us in governing ourselves as one living system. True self governance emerges as we stabilize as our Essential Selves, listening deeply to the guidance from within and speaking our truth in concert with others.

Circle 9: Giving Back to the Whole

It is the nature of love to give back, inspiring the offering of one's unique creative talents for the benefit of all. As our lives are fulfilled, we are naturally inclined to serve, bringing the experience of resonance, love and inspired insights to the world. This may take the form of an entrepreneurial venture, a philanthropic gesture, a social reform or a political movement. Win/win practices assure that the magnificence and mastery of each participant is honored and brought forth to benefit all members of the team and society as a whole. Giving back in the form of conscious investing, philanthropy and tithing become part of the new caring economy.

Circle 10: Birthing a Co-creative Culture

As institutions and structures break down, dominance is replaced by partnership. New models are emerging which reflect an integration of feminine and masculine virtues and whole-centered consciousness. The feminine values of sharing, caring, nurturing, and embracing become intimately interwoven with the masculine traits of focused purpose and action in the world.

Qualities of the co-creative culture include conscious alignment with Spirit, service to the well being of the whole, reverence for all creation, deep listening, and the manifestation of our soul's calling.

In order to build a sustainable future, all social pioneers are being called upon to step forward and express their unique gifts in concert with their teammates. As we explore new ways of living, we are birthing whole systems and new structures to express our values, fulfill the destiny of each member of our human family, create community and converge with other sacred circles to build a co-creative culture.

MOVING THROUGH THE CIRCLES OF CO-CREATION

Each of us is a divine co-creator with an authentic Essential Self.

When two or more are drawn to each other, connecting heart to heart, there is formed an invisible magnetic field of love called resonance.

Connecting at the Heart

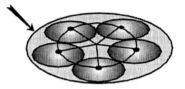

In this caring field of trust, we feel safe to be vulnerable and authentic, thereby overcoming the illusion of separation.

Overcoming Separation

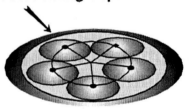

United in resonance, we experience synergy, synchronicity and telepathy. In sacred circles, we access our collective wisdom by opening to higher guidance.

Accessing Collective Wisdom

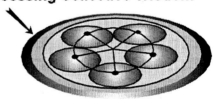

Honoring our connection to the natural order, we anchor our expanded awareness through ceremony and ritual and express joy and gratitude in celebration of the fullness of life.

Ceremony, Ritual and Celebration

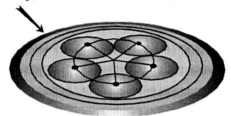

In a field of love, our soul's purpose
is drawn forth into fuller expression.

Expressing Our Soul's Purpose

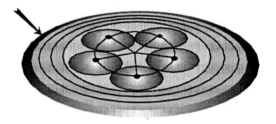

We are called inwardly to rendezvous with our resonant partners to discover
our shared destiny.

Discovering Our Shared Destiny

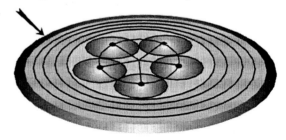

We move beyond consensus decision making into whole-systems knowing
and a new form of governance emerges: Self-governance.

Attuning to the Design

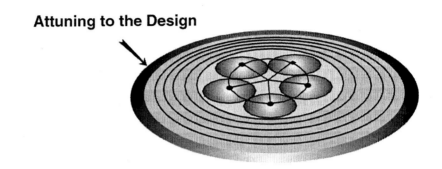

It is the nature of love to give back to the whole by creating sustainable
enterprises and sharing our gifts in service to others.

Giving Back

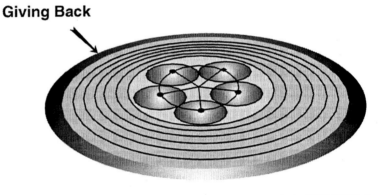

With ease and grace, Core Groups naturally converge with one another,
giving birth to the new world...a co-creative society.

**Birthing a
Co-Creative
Society**

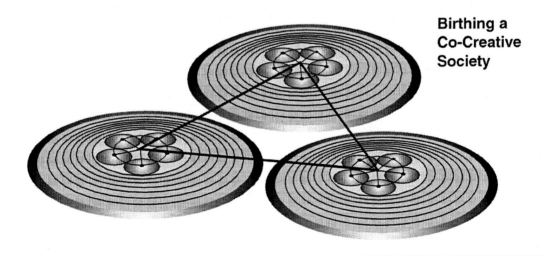

THE CO-CREATIVE WAY OF LIFE

We are living in the most exciting, challenging time in history. Our environmental and societal crises are really a spiritual crisis. Historians will look back on the 21st Century and see it as the time of the great awakening.

Mary Manin Morrissey

After practicing the Circles of Co-Creation, we take what we've learned in the intimate safety of our Core Groups and courageously apply it to all aspects of our lives: our homes, churches, organizations and places of work. As "social pioneers" we are choosing to design new forms that bring forth the best in each of us for the betterment of all.

When groups come together in a field of love, safety, and mutual trust—the creativity, power, and wisdom of each person is liberated. The sense of separation within people that leads to war, crime, pollution, and disorder is healed. As each person finds his place in the body of society, every field of endeavor is taken to a higher level of expression. Thus business, medicine, education, communication, science, and the arts are going through a profound transformation at this time. The pyramid structure is giving way to the circle and ordinary citizens are being empowered to express their full potential. Domination is giving way to partnership. Outer authority is succumbing to inner knowing. Core Groups are emerging to support and empower personal and planetary transformation.

By aligning one group with another, we tap the power and resources available in each Core. Teams link with other teams for the empowerment of all. Eventually, as Cores converge with one another, a sufficient unified field is built, which jumps the entire system to a new level. All of humanity, all life on this planet, shifts to a higher level of consciousness and we evolve into a universal species, capable of healing all sense of separation and co-creating the reality we choose. We grow up and become a mature humanity!

Section 2

HOW TO START AND
MAINTAIN A CORE GROUP

BEFORE YOU BEGIN

Before creating a Core Group, take time to be still and listen to the inner answers that arise when you ask yourself:
- *My purpose for participating in a Core Group is ...?*
- *The people with whom I feel the most resonance are... ?*
- *The groups to which I already belong that might be interested in participating in the Circles of Co-creation process are ...?*

You can begin sharing your interest in forming a Core Group with the groups or individuals who have come to mind from the above exercise. It is important not to convince someone to join the group. Everyone choosing to participate must do so for himself.

Remember that forming a Core Group is like courting. Do not expect that your first group will necessarily be your life partners, any more than your first date will be the one you marry!

It usually takes a few meetings for a group to "gel" and bond. At the conclusion of this trial time period, the group members can state whether or not this group seems to be the right one for them at this time. The members who choose to remain might create a ceremony to honor their participation. You might give your group a name. (See Ceremony of Commitment in Circle 5.)

How many people may attend each gathering? Our experience is that five people is the minimum number for a Resonant Core Group that is focusing on personal healing and development. Eight to ten is a good size to allow for intimate sharing. You will need to determine the best number for your group and purposes. A Co-Creative Core Group that has come together around a shared purpose can be effective with as few as two to three members.

Before the initial meeting, to enhance alignment, individually read the introductory material and Sections 1 and 2. Select one person to serve as facilitator, so that this person can become familiar with the material and experiential exercises before the meeting convenes. Although it's best if the role of facilitator rotates among members of the group, you may find that some people are more adept or natural in this role than others. It's fine to empower those people to fill this role so long as you acknowledge the equality of all participants and avoid any practices that create a hierarchy within your group.

The Initial Meeting(s)

Coming together in the first session to align around purpose and commitment is vital for the success of the group. It is wise to tune into where people are and gently rise up with them. Cultivate resonance with each other and develop empathy. As you get excited, notice if those with you are responding or withdrawing. Ask people questions about what they think and how they feel. Do not judge or reject those who are not attracted. Invite into your Core Group those with whom you intuitively feel an affinity. There are no "observers" in Core Groups. When in doubt, check in with your inner guidance. If people are at cross purposes, the group will not continue.

Effective gatherings of co-creators have the following characteristics:
- Resonance
- Empowerment of each individual member
- A common purpose
- A commitment to each other

An important task for the initial meeting (or meetings, if necessary) includes setting parameters as to time and location and beginning to clarify your purpose for coming together. You may choose to:
- Agree on an initial shared purpose of the group
- Begin to achieve group resonance if the group has not been together before
- Align behind your version of the Co-Creator's Agreements
- Agree on how this guidebook will be used

Some examples of shared purposes for groups initially might be: to support each other as you develop a healing center; to co-create a community event; to love and support each other as you grow and go through changes in your lives; to model new forms of communication and social cooperation as you bring a project into manifestation.

Much of the work of the group may be to help each person find and clarify his life purpose and discover how the shared purpose of the group helps fulfill each person's unique destiny.

Basic questions that will eventually need to be answered include:

- When will you meet? Where will you meet? For how long?
- What is the minimum number of weeks or months the group wants to commit to attending?
- How many times may someone miss (other than for being out of town or having a prescheduled commitment) before it's a clear sign that he is choosing not to fully participate?
- Are friends and visitors welcome?

Allow at least three hours for your first meeting. If you are hosting the meeting, create a safe space—physically and emotionally. Choose a warm, loving, and peaceful environment, free of distractions. Add some flowers. Soften the lights. Play beautiful background music. Unplug the phone. Be sure to have a box of tissues handy, as some of the exercises may provoke deep emotions. Ask your children to give you privacy. If you are attending the meeting, arrive on time and leave on time.

You might begin with the brief attunement or centering practice at the end of this Section.

Initial introductions around the circle are important in building trust. Allow each person to share his reason for joining the Core Group and to describe his personal passion in life.

Then read the Co-Creator's Agreements out loud to each other. Take time to discuss these guidelines after your reading. Agree to lovingly remind each other of these agreements if anyone forgets! **At a subsequent meeting, you may want to re-create or add to these Agreements, so that they are more personal, relevant and meaningful for your group.**

The Co-Creator's Agreements

Be Mindful
My intent is to be myself, to be authentic, and to be fully present.

Realize our Potential
My commitment is to realize my full potential and support others in doing the same.

Follow my Guidance
I agree to attune with Spirit and follow the calling of my soul on behalf of the well-being of the whole.

Communicate with Integrity
I agree to tell my truth with compassion for myself and others and to honor confidentiality whenever appropriate.

Act with Integrity
I agree to keep my agreements and will do my best to follow my heart in making commitments.

Deep Listening
I agree to listen respectfully to the communication of others and tune into their deepest meaning.

Honor One Another
I agree to honor each person's process, acknowledging that everyone, including myself, is making the best possible choice or decision we are capable of in that moment.

Appreciate Our Contributions
I agree to take responsibility for asking for and receiving acknowledgments and for acknowledging others.

Honor Our Differences
I agree to come from a sense of cooperation and caring in my interactions with others, and from an understanding that objectives are often the same even though methods for achieving them may differ. I honor the diversity of all life.

Take Responsibility
I agree to take responsibility for my creations, my reactions, my experience and my relationships.

Maintain Resonance
I agree to take the time to establish rapport and then to re-connect with anyone with whom I feel out of harmony as soon as it may be appropriate.

Resolve Problems Constructively

I agree to take problems, complaints and upsets to the person(s) with whom I can resolve them, at the earliest opportunity. I agree not to criticize or complain to someone who cannot do something about my complaint, and I will redirect others to do the same.

Go for Excellence

I agree to support others and to be supported in participating at the highest level of excellence.

Learn from Experience

I agree to do my best to learn from my experiences.

Accept Imperfections

I intend to embrace and accept the imperfections of myself and others.

Be a Leader

I agree to foster an environment of genuine collaboration in which all people, including myself, feel empowered to express our individual and collective potential.

Service to Others

I am willing to open my heart, still my mind and be in compassionate service to all life.

Re-evaluate My Commitment

I agree to choose and re-choose to participate in this Core Group. It is my choice.

Lighten UP!

I agree to create joy in my relationships, my work and my life.

These Agreements have been adapted from The Geneva Group Agreements, Boulder, CO.

Probably the most difficult decision to make is what to do with out-of-town visitors or interested friends and family. It seems like a contradiction to exclude anyone when a fundamental purpose of the group is to experience unity; however, deep bonding, trust, and sharing is difficult to achieve if the group is continually changing. Most circles have experienced that it's best to close the group to others after the third session and create a special session at the completion of the Handbook to include those who have expressed interest. Other groups keep several places available for newcomers at each meeting as a way to broaden the opportunities for others. Your group can discuss and decide for itself whether or not to admit new members and how this will be done. If you decide to admit new members, it is suggested that you do selected processes from Circles 1 and 2 to help bring the group quickly into resonance.

You will need to establish the Key Roles that follow in this Section for the next meeting before departing. Remember to bring a journal to the next and all subsequent meetings.

Suggested Meeting Format

Gatherings seem to be most effective if they have the following order of activities. These guidelines can be modified by your group, according to your own needs. Also, remember to create a space that is aesthetically pleasing, comfortable and free of distractions. You will want to schedule breaks at least every hour and a half to take care of personal needs and for personal conversations that are a very important part of the agenda.

- Centering or attunement
- Check-in
- Main purpose of the gathering
- Closing

A. Centering or Attunement

Beginning a gathering with some form of centering is an important part of bringing your group together in resonance. Your minds may be focused on conversations with others that preceded the meeting, concerns about getting to the meeting place, or other challenges of the day. The purpose of centering is to reaffirm your connection to Source and with each other and to be fully present. Only by going beyond distractions and centering yourselves can you begin to access the unlimited resources of Spirit. Centering with others has a synergistic effect in bringing about your own sense of well-being and inner peace; you gain momentum and accelerate your own personal evolution. The experiences of others will help to validate your own and support you in taking "leaps of faith" as you follow your inner guidance.

An attunement can take the form of a brief silent group meditation, a guided visualization, or movement to music. You can create your own visualizations that help each of your group members to center or you can use the visualizations included in each chapter of this guide-book. The three major steps in the attunement are: first, to relax body, mind, and emotions; second, to focus your consciousness; and third, to allow time for silence and inner listening.

For people who are experienced in becoming centered, a sound such as that from Tibetan temple bells or heartful music may serve as a cue at the beginning of a gathering to get quiet and connect once again. (A list of recommended music is provided in the Appendix.) It is helpful to quiet the mind—releasing rambling thoughts—by focusing on the breath and visualizing the body as a clear channel for light energy. The ultimate goal of a co-creator is to be centered at all times in all situations. This occurs naturally as the Essential Self takes dominion over the local self.

B. Check-in

The check-in is another important group activity that brings your group into resonance. The purpose is to share with each other where you are physically, emotionally, mentally, and spiritually at that particular moment in time. If just one person is not in alignment, the group will not attain its full power and potential. If someone has some particular concern about the group or other persons in the group, this is a time to share those concerns. An individual check-in may consist of a word or phrase. This is a time for total honesty about what is needed so that you can be fully present and resonant in the group.

The following are some examples of check-ins:

> *"I feel very centered and peaceful. I am glad to be with all of you and am eager to work on . . . tonight."*

> *"I'm feeling anxious. My brother is very ill and I can't let go of my concern for him and be fully present here tonight. I could use your help in sending him positive energy and help in remembering that all is in divine order."*

> *"I feel very positive about what we are about to do but I had a disagreement with . . . yesterday, and I don't feel we can work together until we have reached completion on the issues that were raised between us."*

The check-in may include some details about what has brought you to where you are at this particular moment but the purpose is **not** to tell stories. Generally, it is helpful to limit check-ins to two minutes or less. If you wish, use a timer to regulate the pace of sharing. For groups that are newly forming, allowing a longer time may be important so that you can get to know each other in a deeper way. If your group has been apart for a long time, more time may also be needed. If only a short time has elapsed since your group was last together, one word or sentence may be sufficient.

Discussions in Core Groups are different from ordinary social talk. Its ultimate purpose is to allow the Essential Self to speak. Complaints and negative statements break the group resonance and lower the frequency of the circle, as do gossip and "small talk." Speak and listen from your heart.

As a result of check-ins, your group may decide that you need to address some issues before you can move forward. In the examples of check-ins provided above, the group may decide to take time to address the issue of the person's concern with family illness to bring him fully back to the group. It is important to allow for emotional clearing or release so that each member of the group can be fully present and honored. In this group process everyone is important and every person is needed. If one person is emotionally charged, everyone feels it. Resonance is lost and co-creation cannot occur.

After check-ins, make brief announcements and deal with logistics so that the flow of the meeting is not broken by dealing with the necessary details. A way to keep announcements brief is to make written materials available to be reviewed during the break or after the meeting.

C. The Purpose of the Gathering

Having attuned and checked-in, you're ready to attend to the purpose that is bringing you together. The main content of your meeting may include physical or mental exercises, processes, visualizations, or discussions to develop aspects of the Circles of Co-creation model or to focus on a particular objective. Or, the purpose of the gathering may be to celebrate and play or to conduct a ceremony. The following sections of the guidebook provide very specific content suggestions for your Core Group.

D. The Closing

Another important element of co-creative gatherings is the closing practice or ceremony. Each group develops closings that are meaningful for them. (See Sample Closings in the Appendix.) The purpose of the closing is to reaffirm your connections and to hold and maintain the field of your group until it comes together again. Remember that everything shared in your Core Group is confidential. Do not discuss the details of people's lives outside the group.

The Council Process

To facilitate heartfelt uninterrupted discussions during a gathering, you may choose to use the model of the Native American "talking piece" (or "talking stick") to allow each person to fully share in the group. The purpose of this practice is to remind you that your words are sacred and to honor the sharing of each person in the circle. Use of the talking piece slows down ordinary intellectual discourse and allows deeper wisdom to come through.

Select a sacred object to be used as a talking stick. It can be a treasure found in nature or some other object that has special meaning to you. You may wish to co-create a talking piece as a group and have it present for all of your gatherings. The talking piece may either be passed clockwise around the circle or placed in the center and picked up by the individual who chooses to speak. The talking stick may move around the circle only once or sharing may continue in the circle until all present have expressed "I am complete".

Basic guidelines for council include:

- The person who is holding the talking piece has the right to speak without interruption. He is invited to speak leanly in a focused way and from the heart.

- Everyone listens for the soul, releasing judgment and holding loving presence.

- When another person chooses to speak, he accepts the sacred object from the last speaker or takes it from the center of the circle.

- The speaker takes a brief moment to re-attune and allows the inner voice to speak spontaneously with clarity and simplicity.

- Expressing in silence is always an honorable contribution. No one is ever forced to speak.

Key Roles

In advance of each gathering, it is helpful to designate which group members will take responsibility for the key roles. This provides a structure that helps to actualize your purpose and goals. At first, it is important to rotate these roles so that each person is empowered and has the opportunity to practice all aspects of being a co-creator. As each person recognizes his strengths, the advance assignment of some of these roles may not be necessary. Each person will find the natural place to share his gifts with the group. **The guiding principles of the Core Group Process are that the leadership rotates, responsibility is shared, and Spirit is the ultimate authority!**

A. The Facilitator

The group gives the facilitator the temporary authority to lead with the full understanding that everyone is a leader and each person is a full participant in the process. For any gathering, the facilitator has an important responsibility. He must prepare for the meeting in advance, make any necessary arrangements and plans, and keep the gathering on track for its purpose and mission. In time, you will discover who the natural facilitators are in your group. It is important to remember that, whenever possible, the facilitator is also a full participant in the various exercises of each Circle.

B. The Time-keeper

The time-keeper's responsibility is to stay connected to the dimension of time so that the others can let go of time concerns. Much of what occurs in Core Groups is "out of time" but third-dimensional world concerns may require you to agree on time parameters. The time-keeper may time check-ins or let you know when you need to complete a process and move on.

C. The Nurturer

The nurturer provides for the physical support of the gathering and creates an environment that is comfortable, quiet, peaceful and free of distractions. The tasks may include operating the music system. It may include providing a snack or a meal, or water, or seeing that the temperature and lighting is right for the purposes at hand—or all of the above. Food that is fresh and light such as raw fruits and vegetables and non-caffeinated, non-alcoholic beverages are the best fuels for conscious co-creators.

D. The Heart-keeper

The heart-keeper is the person who keeps his antennae up for situations that are taking the group out of resonance. This person gently reminds everyone when the love energy vital to resonance is blocked or withdrawn. Every person in the group has the responsibility to do their part to maintain the resonance, but in the excitement of the moment, it's easy to move from heart to head and feel separate from one another. The heart-keeper reminds the group to bring themselves back to center and to keep the love flowing. Only when a group is in resonance can it access deep intuition and collective wisdom.

E. The Scribe

The scribe keeps track of what happened, the alignment that was reached, the agreements that were made, and the significant information that was shared. Depending on the purpose of the meeting, a scribe may or may not be necessary.

Staying in Integrity

A. Discernment and Openness

Co-creative love is inclusive, non-possessive, and present-oriented. It fulfills potential rather than holding on to the past. It goes beyond the limits of the family, tribe, culture, and species to the experience of connection to all beings. Each person is empowered by the whole of creation; all creatures are your relatives.

As this creative energy is aroused and the emotional intimacy of a Core Group develops, it is not uncommon for people in the group to be physically and sexually attracted to each other. When in a state of co-creative love, men and women are as attractive as they are attracted. A new charisma often "seduces" others, and you become just as vulnerable. Your past experiences may cause you to associate these feelings with sexual intimacy.

In your group, it is important to bring these issues of co-creative and sexual arousal into an open discussion when it is appropriate. To be truly resonant, every group member must feel in harmony with all the other members of the group. A group in resonance creates a safe, loving, and secure place for all members to express and explore their feelings. Hidden agendas and unexpressed feelings for or between group members will undermine resonance.

If a sexually intimate relationship does develop between members within your group, this is best dealt with quickly, openly, and honestly in a group gathering. This change in relationships shifts the energy within the group and may bring up feelings that block resonance. As you experiment with new relationships, you may want to specifically add loving support for each other to your group purpose.

B. Take Responsibility

For personal and planetary well being, each person needs to own and address his own shadow. One of the best ways to do this is to continually tell your truth with love. Nothing in this guidebook is intended to suggest repressing or denying feelings. Practice returning to center and witnessing yourself, but not at the expense of stuffing and contracting your physical body or your emotions!

It is helpful if each member of the Core Group takes responsibility for his personal conditioning and does not blame others for feelings of fear, guilt, shame, or separation that might arise in the weekly sessions. With awareness, members can use the energy of the group to heal and transform any sense of separation that might occur. Loving connections are maintained with others by taking responsibility for your own thoughts, emotions and actions.

If one member projects his negative feelings onto another member or onto the group as a whole, the facilitator or heart-keeper can step in and bring this to awareness. Eventually, each member of the group should be given an opportunity to tell his truth and fully communicate his feelings, using "I" messages and "tuned-in listening."

When projections occur, take time to re-read the Co-Creator's Agreements aloud as a group, breathe deeply, hold hands in silence and surrender to the power of love.

C.   Separating from a Core Group

There can be many reasons why someone would need to leave his Core Group. Someone might move, change schedules, or simply find that his group is no longer meeting his needs. Society does not give us good models for departing gracefully with good feelings. Many times in our culture, someone separates from a group by:

- Withdrawing from active participation
- Fading away without a complete communication to all group members
- Making the group "wrong" so that the person feels that he has a legitimate reason for leaving. (This may or may not be verbalized to others.)

When it is time for someone to leave a group, it is useful to frame this process as "differentiation" rather than separation. Differentiation is a movement into right relationship based on your soul's purpose and inner guidance, rather than a negative move. It continues to acknowledge your connection to everyone and to all that is, and is handled in a spirit of love and support.

Recommendations for Differentiation

1. Use the Co-Creator's Agreements as a context for your Core Group. Read them aloud collectively before each meeting.

2. It usually takes a few meetings for a group to "gel" and bond. At the conclusion of this trial time period, the group members can state whether or not this group seems to be the right one for them at this time. The members who chose to remain might create a ceremony to indicate that the group is an entity to which they are a member. You might give your group a name.

3. If a group member needs to leave the group for whatever reason, you may want to conduct a ceremony to mark his leaving. (See Circle 5: Ceremony of Differentiation.)

If the group so chooses, a small gift or symbol can be exchanged between group members and the individual leaving.

If the person leaving has any negative feelings towards the group or towards individual members, or if the person is leaving because the group is no longer meeting his needs, it is important to provide an opportunity to share these feelings and to allow for open communication so that all may learn from this experience. Use "I" messages and a talking stick to facilitate the process and to focus on positive growth for all involved.

4. It is strongly recommended that a group never decide to disband unless all members are present. Failure to do this often leads to lingering hurt feelings among the group members who were not present.

Please note that Circle 6: Discovering Our Soul's Purpose, contains additional information about differentiation.

A Sample Guided Visualization
(For use at your initial meeting)

The facilitator slowly reads this aloud, remembering to pause between phrases. You may want to play soft beautiful music in the background.

Close your eyes and be still. . . Take several deep breaths and feel your body relaxing. . . Breathe into any areas where there may be tension or holding in the body.

(Pause)

Be aware of Great Beings of Light who are present with you in the invisible realms. . . Silently call on your own guides and personal teachers to be with you.

(Pause)

Feel a glow spread across your face as you take in a breath and then slowly release it . . . Experience the power of the life force as it flows through your body.

(Pause)

Imagine you are standing in a beautiful place in nature. . . Perhaps there are trees or flowers. . . Perhaps there is water. . . Take in your surroundings: the colors . . . the sounds . . . Sense your oneness with nature . . . Breathe in the fragrance and the beauty of your surroundings.

(Pause)

After awhile you notice a light in the distance . . . The light moves and dances in the wind . . . and you realize you are seeing brilliant colors generated by a group of people.

(Pause)

Feel a quickening of Spirit, a knowing that these beings are like yourself in many ways . . . You sense that they are on a similar path . . . You are drawn to them and you move in their direction . . . As you draw closer, you begin to recognize the glowing faces of people you know and respect.

(Pause)

You hug or join hands with them . . . No words are necessary but you may find yourself in warm dialogue with them . . . A sense of closeness and rapport envelopes you as you reflect on the beauty of friendship.

(Pause)

Gradually you all begin swaying and moving in a beautiful dance . . . reflecting the rhythm of the universe . . . You feel a trust and partnership with each person you see . . . You know in your heart that anything you do or say would be understood and accepted.

(Pause)

You begin to walk towards a path together . . . and, as you walk, you feel an inner pledge of partnership and promise . . . You know that what awaits is a new beginning, a pursuit of knowledge and inner strength never before realized . . . You are filled with the joy of the moment and the vision of a new creation.

(Pause)

Now visualize yourself floating above this group of people . . . You feel the love shared with them as a special gift . . . You make a promise to return to the group again and again to feel their partnership.

(Pause)

Now sense yourself floating back to this time and space . . . Feel the weight of your body being supported by the chair . . . Once again begin to take deep breaths and be aware of the life force within you . . . When you are ready, open your eyes, and rejoin your friends in this room.

Section 3

EXPERIENCING
THE CIRCLES OF CO-CREATION

This section of the book is unique, and should be approached differently from all other sections. It is to be <u>experienced</u> rather than read.

Circle 1

AWAKENING THE CO-CREATIVE SELF

Oh Man!
There is no planet, sun or star could hold you,
If you but knew what you are.

Ralph Waldo Emerson

Our highest potential as a species is our ability to achieve full self-reflective consciousness
or "knowing that we know." Through humanity's awakening, the Universe acquires the
ability to look back and reflect back on itself—in wonder, awe and appreciation.

Duane Elgin

Know ye not that ye are gods?...
...These things ye shall do and even greater.

Jesus Christ

Humanity stands at the threshold of a new dawning.
The challenges and imperatives of our time are calling forth
greater creativity and awakening millions of people
to their true nature and potential.

Like butterflies emerging from the cocoon,
we are awakening as Universal Humans,
capable of co-creating with the divine intelligence of Spirit.

One day we meet someone, or read a book, or have an experience
and something shifts within. An awakening occurs.
Our soul is sparked and we know we must follow inner guidance
and the promptings of our heart.

The Co-creative Self is activated.
We stand poised to give our gifts, share our love,
and fully experience the grandeur of our beings.
We are reborn, and we rejoice in the mystery of this unfolding.

~ ~

Circle 1

AWAKENING
THE CO-CREATIVE SELF

Kneel to your own Self.
Honor and worship your own Being.
Meditate on your own Self.
God dwells within you as you.
Swami Muktananda Parmahamsa

Inside every human is a God in embryo.
It has only one desire...It wants to be born.
Kahlil Gibran

Who am I?
Why am I here?
Where am I going?

For millennia, humans have pondered these questions. Entire schools of philosophy have been created to explore the issues of identity and purpose in human life. Indeed, it appears that self-reflective humans, Homo sapiens, are pre-programmed to "know thyself."

We are all in the process of "waking up" to our true identity. Deep longing pulls us forward, while "evolutionary drivers" in our life—the challenges that call us forth—are driving us into personal transformation. Our old habits and ways of thinking are not working so we search for satisfying alternatives. We experience that we are more than our limited thoughts, emotions, and physical beings—that each of us has a center, a point of contact with Spirit or God.

In a state of expanded awareness, we experience this broader sense of identity. We experience that we are Spirit—that there is no division between "me" and Source. Some call this the higher self. In this guidebook, we refer to it as the Essential Self or the Self. When consciousness moves into action, the Co-creative Self comes into being.

The next stage of evolution is to be at one with that center and act from that inner knowing—to become co-creative with Spirit and the patterns of evolution which lead to higher consciousness, freedom and order. We know that we are spiritual beings having a human experience on this planet. Each of us comes into time, coded with our spiritual possibility. With passion and intention we can birth anything. We are everything and no-thing...pure potentiality...energy manifesting in a myriad of forms—pure consciousness—unlimited and eternal...One appearing as many.

We have always been and will always be the Self. Now it is time to realize this truth. As we awaken from self-centered consciousness and move into whole-centered consciousness, we recognize that we are not in charge. An invisible intelligence is orchestrating a divine dance. As we surrender to this guiding source, we begin to trust and let go. We see that we can allow life to live itself through us—as us—with ease and grace. This takes a leap of faith because at this stage of our metamorphosis process, we are moved to shift our identity from a separate local self to the unlimited Essential Self. We put this purpose first. Gradually, the Self overshadows the local self and the two merge as one. We give up the desire to be special and experience that we are divine.

We are entering a process of birthing ourselves as Co-creators...Universal Humans...Homo Universalis. This takes as much love and patience as raising a child. The self-conscious, waking personality self, gradually comes into conscious cooperation with Spirit to parent the Co-creative Self. We release struggle, effort, and the desire to control. We fall into the arms of the Beloved and relax.

We are preparing for our rendezvous with destiny, an encounter with our own magnificent being. The first step is to connect with the Source of all wisdom, love, and power that lives life in all its forms. We do not have to travel far away or look to any outer manifestation to find this connection. This Source is the center of our own being. We can learn to access it anytime, anywhere through a process of inner listening. As the Self, we connect center to center to all human life and to all kingdoms of nature. Pure consciousness expresses as a myriad of forms. The One manifests as many.

The activities of this Circle are primarily individual, daily practices that keep us centered and aware as the Self. Through vigilance and practice, we learn to release anxiety and turn to our inner knowing. We learn to listen to the quiet place within. We may get ideas from others but we take these ideas to the place of tranquility and let all issues be decided here. We become neutral observers as life unfolds in our presence. "Doing" flows effortlessly from our being.

Circle 1 practices are lifelong and ongoing. Our personal transformation never ends. It is a joy-filled and sometimes arduous journey, requiring commitment and support. The practices in this Circle prepare us to join with others who are ready to co-create. This step of awakening the Co-creative Self is critical to discovering our purpose and joining cooperatively with others. ***The objective of this Circle is to experience ourselves as co-creators, capable of accessing information from our inner source.*** As we dream our dreams and tune into the needs of the whole, the Spirit of creation molds energy and potential into matter, magnetizing to us the perfect people and activities for that moment.

We experience that linking with others, heart to heart, center to center, lifts our energy frequency and deepens our sense of knowing. An inner shift occurs as we tap into the power of creation.   Gradually, we are able to detach from the oscillating circumstances of our lives and become impartial observers… "in the world but not of it." We are born anew—humbled and awed by the Great Mystery and honored to have life live its dance through us, as us.

Suggested Process Sequence

- Open your session with the Visualization that follows—or create your own attunement process.

- Remember to check-in. All members of the group take 1-3 minutes to say how you are feeling and report on any insights or experiences you may have had since the last meeting. (You may want to have a timer for the check-ins.)

- Read The Co-Creator's Agreements aloud.

- Read the Introduction to the Circle. Take a moment in silence to reflect on this. Then share your inspired insights with the group.

- Select one or more of the Experiential Exercises that follow.

- Take a break! Move around and stretch. (Personal conversations can be as important as every other activity on the agenda!)

- Select who will fill the key roles at your next meeting.

- Create a closing that will maintain your heart connection. (See the Appendix for suggested closing exercises—or create your own.)

EXPERIENTIAL EXERCISES

Process: Becoming Centered

Only by going beyond distractions and centering ourselves can we begin to access the unlimited resources of Spirit. Life can flow more easily and naturally as we tap this inner knowing and choose to live from its guidance. It is also our connecting point with others. Through the Self, we connect at the heart to the very source of life and commune as one living body. It does not depend on time, space, or physical form.

GUIDED VISUALIZATION

The facilitator slowly reads this aloud, remembering to pause between phrases. You may want to play soft beautiful music in the background.

Close your eyes. Create an aura of silence around you.

(Pause)

Relax your body, starting with your feet . . . Then feel that relaxation moving up into your calves. . . then into your knees. . . your thighs . . . and your hip area . . . Now, let that feeling of total, complete relaxation move from your fingertips to your wrists . . . up into your forearms . . . then into your upper arms . . . Shrug or shake out the shoulders so that they feel completely free of tension . . . Let that feeling of relaxation move up from your hip area into the lower abdomen . . . Breathe deeply . . . and feel the breath in each part of your body . . . Relax your stomach . . . back . . . and chest . . . As you continue to breathe, release your neck . . . jaw . . . face . . . and scalp.

(Pause)

Feel totally at peace as you continue to concentrate on your breath . . . Breathe deeply and naturally.

(Pause)

This time, as you inhale . . . imagine the Earth's strength and compassion filling you from your feet up through your head . . . Breathe out any negative thoughts and feelings . . . As you breathe in again . . . imagine the love and wisdom of the universe flowing from above . . . through the top of your head . . . and down through your feet to the Earth . . . Continue to breathe out any tension . . . and see your thoughts fertilizing the Earth's new growth.

(Pause)

Place your attention on your heart . . . Allow the warmth of your love for nature, for your family, and for life to permeate your being . . . Feel the utter peace of that love . . . Imagine each breath bringing golden light into your heart . . . Feel the alchemical process of transmutation occurring in your body now. . . warm currents of electrical impulse filling every cell . . . bringing joy and release. . . flooding your physical form and your awareness . . . Experience the Essential Self in every cell of your body now.

(Pause)

Release any sense of age or gender . . . Feel the spaciousness of Self . . . Notice that there is no sense of lack or limitation . . . no boundaries to the Self . . . Relax and experience yourself as peace and freedom for the next few minutes . . .

(Pause for 2 - 3 minutes here)

Now, slowly bring your awareness back into the room . . . Be aware of your body . . . move your hands and feet to re-energize them . . . Take a few deep breaths as you come back to the present moment . . . When you are ready, open your eyes and slowly look around the room . . . Make eye contact with each person in the circle . . . See your Self expressing as others . . . Experience that there is no other!

Process: Introducing One Another

To get to know each other better, your group can pair off and "introduce" each other. In each pair, you can share deep insights about yourself with your partner. Allow about five minutes for each person. Then, when the group comes back together, you can "introduce" your partner. If you know your partner well, you might skip the sharing of deep insights and introduce your partner with your deepest sense of appreciation. After the introductions to the group, the person being introduced can add to, or clarify, what was said.

Process: Characteristics of the Essential Self and the
Local Self (or selves)

The following exercise has many parts. Make sure you have at least 90 minutes to complete all parts of the process in one meeting. Otherwise, you could progress to the section on Inner Listening that follows and cover this material in your next meeting.

The list below describes the differences we experience between the Essential Self and the local personality self, living in the world of duality.

A. Discuss this in your group and co-create any additions or changes.

THE ESSENTIAL SELF	LOCAL SELF
Oneness/ the experience of union	The experience of separation
Detached/ the observer	Attached/ involved
Has no identity/ is no thing	Has multiple identities
Expansion/ no limitation	Contraction/ a sense of lack
Flow/ ease and grace	Rigidity/ efforting
To sense/ to be "in the body"	To be in thought/ operating from the mind
Intimacy/ nothing to hide("into me see")	Defensiveness/ protecting self image
Acceptance of what is	Manipulation/ assertion of personal will
Allowing/ welcoming	Resisting/judging
Now oriented	Future or past oriented
Spontaneity	Control/ Domination
Being love/ overflowing with love	Looking for love/avoiding others
Authenticity	Saving face/ wearing a mask
Acknowledges mistakes/ asks for forgiveness	Blames/ scapegoats/ projects on others
Transpersonal	Personalizing/ victim mentality

_____	_____
_____	_____
_____	_____
_____	_____

B. Make a list of those aspects of your ego/personality that comprise your local selves (for example, the critic, the worrier, the victim, the blamer, etc.)

Local selves are, in reality, thoughts in your mind! For example, feeling like a victim, fear, jealousy, regret and resentment come from the past; worry, anxiety, and concern are negative projections onto the future. Love, peace, and a deep sense of well-being—aspects of the Essential Self—live only in the moment and are accessed by being fully present! At another time you may want to discuss this in your group and tap into your personal experience to see if it's true for you!

_____	_____	_____
_____	_____	_____
_____	_____	_____
_____	_____	_____

Like two golden birds perched on the selfsame tree, intimate friends, the ego and the Self dwell in the same body. The former eats the sweet and sour fruits of the tree of life, while the latter looks on in detachment.

The Mundaka Upanishad

C. Next, with heartfelt music playing in the background, take a few minutes to write a detailed description of your Essential Self. (Select all the qualities that you most admire.)

_____

_____

_____

_____

_____

D. The facilitator slowly reads the following, remembering to pause between phrases, with soft music continuing to play in the background.

Gently close your eyes and allow your body to relax fully . . . As the Essential Self, call forth those local selves that live most strongly within you . . . Reflect for a moment on these characteristics of your personality.

(Pause)

Now, in your mind's eye, bring one of your local selves into your awareness . . . Notice the behavior, the body posture, the facial expression . . . What is this local self doing? . . . How is it feeling?

(Pause)

Step forward as your Essential Self and invite this local self to come into your arms . . . Open your heart to this quality . . . Feel compassion and empathy for the struggle it experiences . . . Feel this local self taking in your love and energy and responding by dropping its need to act up for attention . . . Feel the flow of love between the Essential Self and the local self. . . back and forth . . . healing any sense of separation that might have existed here . . . Now, tenderly, say goodbye to this local self and see it fading into the distance.

(Pause)

Bring into your awareness a different local self . . . Notice the behavior, the body posture, the facial expression . . . What is this local self doing? . . . How is it feeling? . . . Once again, step forward as the Essential Self and invite this local self to come into your arms. . . Open your heart to this quality . . . feel compassion and empathy for the struggle it experiences. . . Again, feel this local self taking in your love and energy and responding by dropping its dysfunctional behavior . . . Feel the flow of love between the Self and the local self . . . back and forth . . .

healing any sense of separation that might have existed here . . . Say anything you need to say to the local self before waving goodbye to it . . . Listen for any response.

(Pause)

Now imagine that all the other local selves are like your children . . . and as a compassionate parent, bring them into a loving embrace . . . With a sense of gratitude, feel this integration occurring at a cellular level.

(Pause)

Envision the qualities of the Essential Self woven into a beautiful invisible cloak that you slip on and can wear all day, every day . . . Take in the beautiful music for a few minutes and feel these qualities emanating from you and embracing you . . . Claim your identity as the Self as you bring your ideal nature into reality.

(Pause for 1 - 2 minutes)

How would you see yourself benefiting by living as this Self in the world?

(Pause)

How could your family, friends, co-workers, and colleagues benefit?

(Pause)

How could your community, nation, and the planet benefit?

(Pause)

Now, take a few deep breaths and, when you're ready, slowly open your eyes and bring your awareness back into the room.

Take a few minutes to write down your insights and share them with the other members of your group.

_____

_____

_____

_____

_____

_____

This might be a good time to take a break or complete this session. You may want to put on some music and dance before moving into a Closing Exercise or proceeding to the next exercise.

PRINCIPLES OF INNER LISTENING

Read aloud and discuss the following principles. In the next exercise, you will put these principles into practice. Inner listening is the foundation to being the Co-creative Self. Agree to practice inner listening when you are alone and with the group.

- To practice inner listening, sit in a peaceful, undisturbed environment that supports you in centering yourself. Close your eyes, relax your posture, and breathe deeply. Play soft music, if you wish.

- Quiet your mind, emotions, and body. Be aware of them from the calm and loving space of the Self.

- Pose a question and open up to inner knowing without investment or attachment to what you experience. Often the first response is the clearest.

- Be cautious of interpretations and trying to figure things out. The truth is simple. Look to the energy of the response, rather than to the content of the response, as a more reliable guideline. As you align with truth, your body will feel relaxed and energized.

- Listen with assurance, knowing that you are being directed even when you are unaware. Be in full observation of everything that is occurring in yur experience. This observer is the Self that you are.

- Accept without judgment whatever you hear, see, or sense. If you desire more clarity or assurance, ask for it. Then act on the guidance you receive.

- If in doubt, keep listening. You will always know the real truth when it comes to you and brings insight and understanding to your world. Perhaps, an immediate response may not be timely or a "non-response" may be important in this moment.

- Go within often and make it a normal part of your life—as though it were a "waking meditation." Avoid "foxhole praying" or only connecting in emergencies when the "bombs are dropping overhead" and you find it difficult to relax and flow as your Essential Self.

- Be open to change, being off balance, the miraculous, and to the impossible (from your mind's point of view) to access your innate creativity.

- Ask for an opening "for your highest good" in any area of your life needing assistance. Let go of expectations. Just be open and ready to receive and learn.

- Envision and affirm answers being given and demonstrated to you.

- Use art, creative writing, visualization, dance, music, being in nature, and other creative forms to assist in accessing inspired insights from the Self.

Process: Listening as the Co-creative Self

GUIDED VISUALIZATION

The facilitator slowly reads this aloud, remembering to pause between phrases. You may want to play soft heartfelt music in the background.

Feel like a sail poised for the wind—open, relaxed, surrendered to this moment . . . There is nothing to do except to relax and let go.

(Pause)

Now, ask yourself a question that is meaningful in your life right now . . . Just take a moment and let a question emerge.

(Pause)

If a question doesn't come, then ask yourself: What do I need to do to bring my life into balance?

(Pause for 1 - 2 minutes)

Allow the answer to come forth freely . . . It may come as an intuition or knowing, or as a feeling, or as a body sensation . . . You may even hear words.

(Pause)

If nothing comes, relax, and be at peace.

(Pause)

In a few minutes, or whenever you feel the time is right, open your eyes and record any inspirations, insights or feelings that have arisen for you.

_____

_____

_____

_____

_____

Next, share your insights and feelings with each other.

Process: The Heart Meditation

For millennia, people in the Eastern world have followed a practice called Tonglen. It was described in the First Century by the Tibetan Heart Master Atisha. He called it "giving and taking on the breath." He urged his followers to give and take alternately and to begin all training with themselves. The following practice can be used privately to open the heart more fully, with a partner or with your entire Core Group.

GUIDED VISUALIZATION

The facilitator slowly reads this aloud, remembering to pause between phrases.

Sit comfortably and close your eyes . . . Take a few deep breaths and relax your body.

(Pause)

Focus your awareness on the middle of your chest, the heart center . . . You might imagine that you are fanning the flames of the heart with each in-breath . . . Feel the flame spreading throughout your body on the out-breath.

(Pause)

Visualize your heart center as a window into the vastness that is your true nature . . . From this place of limitlessness, look out at the world of form . . . Now imagine breathing form back in through the window of the heart . . . Continue to breathe in form and breathe out formlessness, emptiness . . . Radiate presence and love with every exhalation.

(Pause)

Notice any thoughts and breathe them in through the window of the heart . . . Once again, breathe in form and breathe out formlessness . . . Radiate silence that is empty of thought.

(Pause)

Now notice any emotions and breathe them in through the window of the heart . . . Take all the time you need to breathe in emotions and breathe out emptiness.

(Pause for 1 - 2 minutes)

Now continue to do the same with any physical sensations you may be feeling . . . Take all the time you need to breathe in any sensations you are feeling in the body and breathe out warmth, love, and stillness.

(Pause for 1 - 2 minutes)

Continue to absorb with the in-breath . . . and radiate with the out-breath . . . Make no distinction between thoughts, emotions, and physical sensations . . . Continue with this practice until it becomes as natural as breathing.

(Pause)

Slowly open your eyes and continue to radiate love and silence.

After you feel comfortable doing this alone, practice the heart meditation with a partner.

Process: Practicing the Heart Meditation with a Partner

Pair up with another member of your Core Group. Face one another and practice breathing in form and breathing out formlessness for five or ten minutes. If you are able, merge as One, releasing all sense of boundaries and distinctions that arise in the world of form. You may choose to use the Heart Meditation on a regular basis at future meetings. As you progress in this practice, you can use it to send healing energies to specific individuals, situations, or to the Earth.

Process: Connecting Self to Self

The timekeeper can participate and keep track of the time for the following exercises. Allow 30 - 40 minutes for this process.

The purpose of this exercise is to acknowledge and reinforce the timeless qualities of the Essential Self, rather than features of the local self. After a few minutes, the timekeeper signals you to stop and you reverse roles.

> Pair up and sit facing each other. Look deeply into each other's eyes and connect heart to heart. Practice the heart meditation for a few minutes. One of you completes the phrase, *"I am _____"* with different endings, over and over again for two or three minutes while your partner listens. (For example, *"I am a mother"*, *"I am love"*, *"I am spaciousness"*, etc.) Do not consciously "think" about it, just say whatever comes to you.

In this second exercise, you are guided to experience yourself as pure awareness.

> Facing your partner, spend a few minutes centering in the Heart Meditation. When you feel ready, the first person says, *"Tell me about that which is looking."* The second person responds spontaneously. Person "A" repeats the statement after each response: *"Tell me about that which is looking."* Reverse the roles. Repeat the process so that Persons "A" and "B" have two - three turns each. Allow at least three minutes for each person each time. When you are complete, sit together in silence. Allow your eyes to meet as you sink deeply into presence, experiencing the Self, experiencing that all is one—that there truly is only one Self.

When you have completed the process, acknowledge your partner. Then come together and share in the larger circle.

Process: Meeting the Beloved

GUIDED VISUALIZATION

The facilitator slowly reads this aloud, remembering to pause between phrases. You may want to play soft beautiful music in the background. Allow 30 minutes for this process.

Close your eyes. Take a few deep breaths and invite your body to relax completely.

(Pause)

See yourself in a beautiful place in nature . . . Take in the sounds and smells of nature . . . Breathe deeply and let go . . . There is nothing to do . . . Just relax . . . Allow any thoughts to float by . . . like clouds in the sky.

(Pause)

Breathe in and out through your heart . . . Breathe in love . . . radiate love . . . Allow the breath to open your heart ever more fully . . . Feel the love that you are radiating through every cell in your body.

(Pause)

Now allow that love to burst forth and to become a form in front of you . . . This is the Beloved . . . your ideal being . . . This is the person you have been looking for in the world . . . Take a close look at this Beloved . . . Notice the hair . . . the color of the eyes . . . the shape of the body . . . Notice the gender and the clothing.

(Pause))

When you feel safe with this Beloved . . . speak silently to this being . . . Ask any questions . . . express any fears . . . call forth any wisdom . . . Tell the Beloved your needs and aspirations.

(Pause for two - three minutes)

Now listen to the Beloved . . . Allow this silent inner dialogue to continue, as you ask questions and listen to the response of the Beloved.

(Pause for two - three minutes)

Now become the Beloved . . .   See and feel yourself actually merging with the Beloved . . . Look though these eyes . . . feel these feelings . . .   Notice how the body feels . . . Be aware of the grandeur and expansiveness of this being . . .   Slowly, shift your identity and acknowledge that you are the Beloved . . .   That which you have been seeking in the world is who you are . . .   You have come home to your Self . . .   Take in the magnificence of your being.

(Pause for another two - three minutes)

Now shift your identity once more . . .   Take a few deep breaths and focus on your physical body . . .   Be aware of any emotions that arise . . .   Look at the Beloved . . .   Continue dialoguing with the Beloved.

(Pause)

Now, once again, shift your identity . . .   Become the Beloved and merge into emptiness . . . Feel the love that you are . . .   Feel the deep sense of peace that is always present as the Self . . .   Notice that you are not male or female . . .   You have no age and no gender . . .   You are pure awareness . . .   All that is . . .   whole and complete . . .   There is nothing to do . . .   You are it all . . . you have it all.

(Pause)

When you're ready, slowly bring your awareness back to the room . . .   Look at each person in the circle . . .   See the Beloved, the Self, in every member of your group.

When this exercise is complete, some members of the group may want to sit silently, while others may wish to stand and move to the music. Flow with the energy of the group, but refrain from speaking with one another to honor the depth of the experience.

This might be a good time to take a break.

Process: Aligning Body, Mind, and Spirit

When you make two one; And when you make the inside like the outside and the outside like the inside; And when you make the above as the below; When you make the male and the female into a single one, so that the male will not be male and the female not be female— then shall you enter the Kingdom.

The Gospel of Thomas

Our circumstances or the events of our lives are a reflection of the alignment or conflict between our body, mind, and Spirit. Life is a mirror of our consciousness. When we are connected as the Self, life seems to flow easily and miraculously. There is a direct link between inspiration and manifestation.

When we are feeling separate and out of touch, we experience struggle and effort. For example, we may feel conflicted inside or have a pain or have an argument. By sensing the energy present in each of these occurrences, we can begin to discover what is really going on. It is looking beyond the outward appearances to the consciousness that is causing these things to occur. The purpose of this process is to learn to self-correct when our life circumstances do not reflect our ideals.

The facilitator invites group members to write down the following:

1. First, select a circumstance in your life that indicates that something is out of alignment.

_____

_____

_____

2. Now, turn to the state of your body, mind, and emotions. How do you feel physically, mentally, and emotionally when you focus on this situation?

_____

_____

_____

3. After checking in with all three, what is the consistent thread or message? How are your body, mind, and emotions out of alignment with Spirit?

_____

_____

_____

4. Reflect on the choices you are making in your life. How are they affecting you?

_____

_____

_____

5. How are your choices affecting those around you?

_____

_____

_____

6. Now ask the Co-creative Self what you can do to bring balance back into your life. Who might you turn to for support and encouragement?

_____

_____

_____

Share your process and insights with a partner. Then share your intentions in the larger circle. The members of your group can bear witness to your intentions and provide encouragement as you make changes in your life. You may want to ask someone in your group to support you in staying true to your intentions.

Process: Speaking as the Self

Form triads. Close your eyes and take a few moments to quiet your mind and center yourself. Open your eyes, and each of you in turn, speak as though you were your own personal "god" speaking. Imagine living in Greece at the time when "gods" abounded. Speak to the other two "gods" about the human you are lovingly attached to and speaking through. Tell all about the ways of this wonderful human and then share compassionately about areas of growth that this human is engaged in—whether the human is aware of them or not! The other two "gods" are invited to offer any of their "godly" wisdom and insights that might assist the human in living as the Co-creative Self.

Write down anything you wish to remember. Then share with the larger circle.

_____

_____

_____

Select or create a closing for the meeting.

To see myself in everybody and everybody in myself most certainly is love.

Sri Nisargadatta Maharaj

DAILY PRACTICE
(Exercises to be Done Outside the Group)

We recommend that you read *Emergence: Ten Steps on the Developmental Path of a Universal Human* by Barbara Marx Hubbard, in conjunction with practicing the exercises in this Circle to deepen your experience.

Centering Practices

A daily centering practice can facilitate awakening the Co-creative Self. You may find it helpful to stop, breathe, and focus on the Beloved when you feel off center. Slow down and allow the local self to be held by the Essential Self.

Because there are many practices that you can learn and many paths to realizing the Self, each person must take the time to explore and find what is right for him. Whatever path you take, the goal is to be the Self, touching the deeper knowing that is inherent in all humans.

Co-creators are vigilant and learn to spend more and more time in a centered state. You will know the Self by the feeling of connection with others and with nature—a sense of unity with all. Feeling relaxed, aware, and present in the moment, you experience a sense of mental, emotional, physical, and spiritual balance. You maintain witness consciousness—feeling all your emotions with a sense of detachment. You feel free from the ups and downs of self-centered consciousness.

The following may be helpful to support you in living as Self.

- Listen to soothing music, meditate, visualize a place of peace and/or use some stress-reduction techniques to relax your muscles and dissipate any tensions that you are holding in your body.

- Close your eyes to remove the distraction of sight and to turn your mind inward.

- Breathe consciously from your abdomen, this helps to still the mind and creates a feeling of peace.

- Create a sacred space in your home that is private and quiet. You might want to close out other distractions by unplugging the phone or closing the door. Many people find that being outdoors in nature creates the right environment for going within. Soothing music might create the appropriate background for your centering processes and help draw your mind away from other distractions.

- Consciously bring the energy of the Earth and the life around you into your body to support you in your centering.

- Release the energy of thoughts by observing them from a place of neutrality. Do not fight thoughts or judge them. If you engage in battle with them, they will be more persistent. Surrender your agenda and concerns.

- Focus on the blessings in your life.

- Let go, relax, and be.

- Ask and you shall receive. From within you will get the answers to your questions. Ask for insights, guidance, or answers to any question. Be still and patient and allow the answers to come forth freely. Sometimes insights come when you ask, and other times they appear unexpectedly. By sincerely wanting to know, focusing your questions, and taking the time for deep inner listening, the responses will be revealed. Do not edit seemingly unconnected or irrelevant brief flashes of inspiration, intuition, or imagination that may arise. Make a note of them and record them in your journal for later understanding and integration.

The Self is the wisest teacher on Earth. It knows exactly what is needed at all times. In this respect, it could be called the inner coach. Educate your mind to listen to the inner coach and carry out its orders!

If you feel tense, anxious, or disoriented, it means your personality/local self has taken dominion over the Self. When you feel this way, fully experience the feeling and become a neutral observer. Watch as the feeling dissolves and disappears. Non-resistance is a key to true freedom.

If you wish, develop a simple gesture or practice that returns you to a centered space easily and quickly. One way might be to take a few deep breaths as you remember your true identity. Another way is to place your hand on your heart. As you continue your daily practice, you witness new possibilities and miracles. The results will encourage you to keep up these practices and will serve as sufficient evidence to keep your doubting mind in check.

A. Practicing the Presence—Living in the Now

...what is it that determines the quality of your consciousness?
Your degree of presence. So the only place where true change can occur and where the past can be dissolved is the Now.

Eckhart Tolle

Learning to live in the eternal present, releasing the unreality of past and future is a potent way to awaken the Self. Every day, practice listening impartially to the voice in your head. Be aware of recurring thoughts and patterns. Is there a tendency to worry? Or to judge? Does sadness arise easily? Or never? What about anger? Do you feel "put upon"—a victim of bad luck or unfair circumstances? Do not judge or condemn your thoughts, just notice them.

Be aware of body sensations. Feel where the body is tense and where it is relaxed. What causes this to change for you?

Notice that there are thoughts, feelings, and body sensations and that there is awareness of thoughts, feelings, and body sensations. This awareness is the Self. Notice that the Self is unlimited and free, spacious and clear, unbounded and infinite. It is who you are. It resides in the present moment when the mind is still and the body is relaxed.

~ ~

B. Observing Your Thoughts, Setting Your Intention

Whatever gets your attention gets you! What enters the mind repeatedly, shapes the mind. Learn to be a master of your own attention and to be conscious of your stream of thoughts. Thoughts are energy. They create reality. Think in terms of choices and clarify your dreams and intentions. Let insignificant, unwanted thoughts pass through

Inherent in every intention
and desire is the mechanics
for its fulfillment. . . intention and desire. . .
have infinite organizing power.

Deepak Chopra

without reacting and without judgment. Neutral observation brings true freedom.

When thoughts challenge you, or difficult decisions arise, do not struggle from an anxious state. Still your mind and open to guidance. The way will be revealed.

The mind cannot differentiate between "reality" and imagination empowered by desire. As you think, so you create. Set your intention and bring order to your life by focusing your attention on what you choose. Align your perceptions with your desires. Set aside some time to get in touch with your vision. What does your heart desire? What kind of life do you want to have? What do you believe is possible? Write out the vision of your ideal life and read it each day. Creation is a function of focus, not force. Creative intentions determine your destiny! Life shows up differently when you shift your focus, clarify your intention, believe in all possibilities, align with your passion and surrender to Spirit. Let go and let God. **Attention and intention are partners in co-creating the reality you choose.**

C. Words and Affirmations

Be careful of the words you use in your thoughts and speech. As you speak, so it shall be done. "Try" to do it and you will forever be trying. "Do" it and it shall be done. Do something you "should" and it will feel like a burden. Do something you "choose," and it will feel like a joy. "Can't,"

Watch your thoughts; they become words.
Watch your words; they become action.
Watch your actions; they become habits.
Watch your habits; they become character.
Watch your character; it becomes your destiny.

Frank Outlaw

"don't," "won't," "should," "ought," "but," are words that disempower. If you say, "I can," "I choose," "I have," "I am"—you are and you will!

Your perspective changes your world. For example, do you see yourself as an angry person? Change your perspective to that of awareness, manifesting as a person who sometimes has feelings of anger.

Affirm what you choose to believe. Your beliefs influence your reality. Believe in your potential to be a co-creator with no limitations as the first step to experiencing that this is so! Believe in the possibility of a positive future, and you will act to achieve it.

Believe with all your heart and mind in the world that you choose. Release anxiety and relax into presence. Have faith that the force that is creating the universe is co-creating with you. Approach life with a sense of gratitude and appreciation. You will find that you draw to you the people, resources, and opportunities needed in each moment.

D. Exercise and Diet

Taking walks or practicing some form of physical activity such as yoga, tai chi or aerobics are important ways to keep your body functioning smoothly so that you can stay in a centered state. Balance vigorous physical activity and slower meditative activities. Drink plenty of purified water. Eating healthy alive food, that is appropriate for your personal body needs, supports mental clarity, emotional balance, and physical vitality. Listen to your body and find the balance of exercise, relaxation, diet, and activity that is right for you. The ultimate goal is to keep the body finely tuned to nurture the Co-creative Self.

E. Keeping a Journal

A journal can be a powerful tool for personal growth. In your journal, record your insights and the answers received during inner listening. Take time each day, preferably in the early morning while all is quiet, to access your deeper knowing. Create a space of peace and inner calm. You may wish to make an altar and place objects that are sacred to you upon it. Light a candle. Then pose questions that are relevant to your current situation and write down the guidance that you receive. Create an inner dialogue with the Beloved/Essential Self.

Use your journal to record your journey through this Handbook. Write down your dreams. You might want to keep a note pad or tape recorder nearby to capture your inspired insights during the day or night.

Set aside time each day and each week to honor the spiritual dimension of your life. The Self needs sacred time and space to blossom and take dominion.

F. Call on your Quantum Partner

Jean Houston suggests that each of us has a Quantum Partner or partners who we can call upon to co-create with us and guide us in our lives. Take a few moments in silence to tune into your partner(s). This might be someone who is alive or an important historical figure, like Gandhi, Jesus, or Joan of Arc—or an archetypal energy, like Demeter, Apollo, Isis or Athena. Ask for support and guidance. If you are writing a book, composing music, working on a community project, or focusing on any other creative endeavor, call on your partner(s) for energy and empowerment. Ask for support in being the Essential Self. Dialogue with your Quantum Partner and record any guidance you receive in your journal. This is an ongoing process. Different Quantum Partners may come into your life as circumstances present the need.

G. "Advances" and Retreats

Stepping out of the world to deepen as the Co-creative Self and to connect with nature has been called a "retreat." We prefer to call it an "advance" because these valuable times of renewal empower us to go forward. (For information on Global Family Advances and other gatherings and events, go to www.globalfamily.net.)

If at all possible, arrange a few days to be alone, in silence, in a beautiful place that feels sacred to you. Go to a quiet place where you will not be disturbed or interrupted and use your meditative techniques. If taking a few days seems impossible, give yourself a few hours. You might take your journal but no other stimuli. Leave behind agendas and plans. Eat lightly. Feel your oneness with nature. Allow an attitude of gratitude to fill you. Feel the presence of Spirit as you.

Be sure to share any insights or experiences you have during the week with your Core Group at the next meeting.

You receive warmth by giving warmth.
You hold the co-creative state by sharing the state.
You awaken to knowing your true nature
by absolute faith that you already know.

The leap from local self to co-creator is quantum.
It is precipitated by leaping into the unknown,
in absolute faith that I AM you.

You cannot hold onto the past and be the new
at the same instant in time.
Once you have let go of it, you regain it,
but from the other side of the river of life.

You do not take this leap because all is well.
All is well because you take this leap.

You do not have faith because it produces results.
Results are produced because you have faith,
Because you are willing to be cause, not effect.

Remember who you are and feel blessed by this knowing.
Open your eyes and rejoice in the beauty of
your many expressions.

Barbara Marx Hubbard

Acknowledgments

We are deeply grateful to the following individuals for their contributions to this Circle:

Arjuna Nick Ardagh for **The Heart Meditation** and the processes **Connecting Self to Self** and **Meeting the Beloved**

Tim Clauss for the **Aligning Body, Mind and Spirit** process and for co-creating the **Principles of Inner Listening**

Jean Houston for inspiring the **Speaking as the Self** exercise and for introducing the concept of the **Quantum Partner**

Circle 2

CONNECTING AT THE HEART:
CO-CREATING GROUP RESONANCE

Where two or more are gathered in my name, there I Am.
Jesus Christ

When you love, you should not say, "God is in my heart," but rather,
"I am in the heart of God."
Kahlil Gibran

The attraction of love for love remains irresistible. For it is the function of love to unite all
things unto itself, and to hold all things together by extending wholeness.
The Course in Miracles

It is only with the heart that one can see clearly,
for what is essential is hidden from the eyes.
Antoine de Saint Exupery

The process of co-creation begins by loving as the Essential Self.
It grows through resonance with those who attract us and
blossoms through loving the potential in others.
It matures through the sacred practices of acceptance, non-judgment, trust and compassion.

It releases its mighty power when fusing with others.
Its fruits are the works, the contributions,
the projects we do that evolve each other and the world.
Its source and its fuel is pure consciousness: the Self in each of us.

The idea of loving one another as ourselves is the greatest and most obvious precept on
Earth. We have all heard it through our religions and ethical systems.

"Love your neighbor as yourself."
"Do unto others as you would have them do unto you."

Thousands of books have been written, millions of people give lip service to it.
Why would it work now?

Because there is a new condition on Earth, an evolutionary driver requiring us
to change our behavior if we are to survive.

What was esoteric or impossible in the past is essential now.
The time has come to create a loving world.

In a world where love has been considered soft, weak and ineffectual,
evolution demonstrates that co-creative love is powerful, courageous and
the most effective force in "getting the job done."
In fact ... it IS the job that needs to be done!

~ ~

Circle 2

CONNECTING AT THE HEART: CO-CREATING GROUP RESONANCE

Unconditional love is the radiance of your Spirit shining.
Alexa Young

*Listen to each other from your heart and you shall hear far more
than your ears will ever reveal.*
Barbara Marx Hubbard

We are all born for love. It is the principle of existence, and its only end.
Benjamin Disraeli

As we believe in our hearts, so it is done. When we connect with others in our heart, the universal force of creation works through us to guide us to our perfect place of service. When we align our energies heart to heart, an invisible field of union, oneness, and creativity is born. We call this resonance.

Resonance is the heart of the Core Group Process. It is the way to birth and nurture the culture we choose. It occurs only in a field of love, trust, unconditional acceptance and mutual support and is born and nurtured in "safe spaces." Resonance disappears in the face of judgment, criticism, tension, and animosity. We start with self-love and the unconditional love that is freely given by Spirit. Accepting this love is accepting that one is blessed and worthy of such love. It does not depend on other people; it does not depend on what we do, or on our daily successes and failures. If we judge or condemn ourselves, we are denying the worth of the Creator and the creation of which we are a part.

Resonance comes from intention, attention, telling the truth, and connecting center to center. Practices such as meditation, yoga, prayer, chanting, song, dance, silence, mindful speech, and conscious movement allow us to attune to higher vibrational frequencies. When we are in our centers, experiencing the Essential Self, we are in resonance with all that is—and we attract resonance into our lives.

We learn to cultivate this energy consciously until it becomes a natural way of being. We intensify our practice by connecting heart to heart in Resonant Core Groups, bonded by our passion to release the highest potential in each individual to be the Self.

When the field of resonance is built, we feel lighter. The body seems less dense as we move to a higher energy frequency. Emotional and physical healing occur spontaneously as love opens the cells of the body, releasing the contractions of anxiety and dis-ease. Boundaries between us dissolve. The Co-creative Self rises up and comes forth. It is magnetized into the light of day by the field of love. A vibrating frequency, a harmonic, blends our energies into a common chord. An aura of euphoria permeates us. The heart opens and fills with love and joy.

What would it be like to live in a world that is built on acceptance and love? How would it be to have a world where everyone told the truth with compassion in an environment of trust and integrity, where fear was an archaic concept that had long ago been replaced by the fullness of love for one another's unique potential?

We, as co-creators, know that everyone born upon this Earth is needed. Everyone is a vital part of the whole, including ourselves. Our joy is to accept the magnificence of each part of the creation and to realize the potential in others as in ourselves.

We can begin by living these values and spreading them to others through our example. By our actions, we model the changes we would like to see in the world, and thereby change the world. As we see reality, so we act, and as we act, so we become. By holding the highest image of others and placing our attention on that potential, we empower others to awaken fully and fulfill their deeper destiny.

In our groups, we practice loving our neighbors as ourselves and each other as co-creators. If we love ourselves as creations of the Divine, we can easily love another in the same way. Loving our own gifts, we can appreciate the gifts that others have to offer. Joyfully, we join together for the conscious evolution of ourselves in an accepting world.

When we connect with others at the heart, we take a quantum leap beyond the capacities of individuals alone. Social synergy results, creating a whole greater than the sum of its parts. We experience total alignment. We experience a jump in consciousness, freedom, and creativity. We experience that we are one.

Maintaining group resonance is a delicate act of orchestration requiring sensitivity, trust, and the highest integrity. It cannot be forced, but is an act of both personal and collective will. A successful Core Group is a sacred space that embraces diversity, brings forth individuality, and creates unparalleled possibility for all participants. As such, it is to be honored, nurtured, and graced with the commitment of each member.

PRINCIPLES OF RESONANCE

Attention: Place your attention in your heart; feel yourself and others as part of one larger body.

Attraction: Be aware of your natural affinity for one another.

Connection: Allow the Spirit of Creation to unite your group.

Intention: Put this purpose first, above all else.

Relaxation: Release and trust in the design of creation.

Please note that the exercises in this Circle will take more than one meeting to complete. Remember to take breaks and to move your body each time you meet. Shifts in awareness must be integrated into the body to be lasting.

Suggested Process Sequence

- Open your session with the Visualization that follows—or create your own attunement process.

- Remember to check-in. All members of the group take 1-3 minutes to say how you are feeling and report on any insights or experiences you may have had since the last meeting.

- Read The Co-Creator's Agreements aloud.

- Read the Introduction to the Circle. Take a moment in silence to reflect on this. Then share your inspired insights with the group.

- Select one or more of the Experiential Exercises that follow.

- Take a break! Move around and stretch.

- Select who will fill the key roles at your next meeting.

- Create a closing that will maintain your heart connection. (See the Appendix for suggested closing exercises—or create your own.)

EXPERIENTIAL EXERCISES

GUIDED VISUALIZATION

The facilitator slowly reads this aloud, remembering to pause between phrases.

With soothing music playing in the background, ask people to get comfortable, close their eyes and relax. You may hold hands, if you wish.

Sit with your spine erect . . . Take some deep breaths . . .

(Pause)

With each exhalation, let any tension and thoughts float away with that breath . . .

(Pause)

With each inhalation, imagine the breath being drawn into different parts of your body. First your feet and your legs . . . Then see the breath going to your hands and arms . . .

(Pause)

Keep going until you have brought energy and fresh vitality into each part of your body.

(Pause for 1 - 2 minutes)

Now, let your breath concentrate in the center of your being, in your heart . . . With each breath, feel a warmth growing in your heart center . . . like a little bead of light, glowing like an ember with each breath . . .

(Pause)

As you breathe deeply, that little bead of light grows and sends radiant warmth throughout your body . . . Imagine rays of golden light emanating from your heart to all parts of your body . . .

(Pause)

Each cell of your body responds as if being bathed in sunlight . . . All your cells begin to vibrate at the same frequency . . .

(Pause)

Each cell radiates light back to your heart, like waves crossing the ocean . . . This energy is returned to your heart from all parts of your body . . .

(Pause)

The golden light in your heart grows even brighter as this energy flows back and forth until you feel your whole body beginning to glow . . .

(Pause)

Now, let a thread of this light gently float out of your heart toward the center of the circle . . . When it gets to the center, let the thread collect into a little golden ball as it mingles and dances with the other threads being extended from everyone in the room . . .

(Pause)

Notice how the different energies seem naturally to blend and find their own order for collecting into a larger ball of golden light . . .

(Pause)

From this enormous ball of light, imagine two shafts of light venturing out: one into the Earth and the other toward the stars . . . Notice how the Earth's energy and the radiance from the stars easily flow into our connecting ball of golden energy . . .

(Pause)

And so it is in truth . . . We are all connected to the Source . . . and all connected to one another. . . always . . . in our hearts . . .

(Pause)

As we share with each other, let us keep the awareness of this connection present with us . . . Let us be aware that when another is speaking, it is just another part of our Self which is speaking . . .

(Pause)

Now, slowly, taking whatever time you need, begin to become aware of your body again . . . Notice the floor beneath you and be aware of the others around you . . . Gently move your hands and feet to feel the life force flowing through your body . . .

(Pause)

Let that light from your heart continue to flow to the center . . . Feel your connection to the others in the circle . . . If at any time during this session you want to reconnect with someone, just close your eyes and follow that golden thread over to their heart . . . Let that be our main path of understanding today . . . When you feel ready, open your eyes and return to the room.

Take a few minutes in silence to connect visually with each person in the circle.

Check-In

Personal sharing builds group resonance and can teach us to be better listeners. Using a "talking stick", encourage each member of the group to "check in" and share a personal learning experience that they feel might be valuable to everyone. Being vulnerable and open with one another builds trust and resonance. To create intimacy, you must "see into me."

The facilitator might ask: *"What experience have you had that changed the course of your life?"* You will probably want to set a time limit for each person's sharing. While each person is speaking, listen respectfully to each other. Do not offer advice or discuss what has been said but acknowledge each person by saying "thank you" after they finish speaking.

Discussion: To Open Hearts In A Group

Although there is no one way to create group resonance, the following steps are suggested to begin the process of opening our hearts to others, co-creating love, and maintaining resonance in a group. Read the following aloud and co-create any changes that make them more relevant to your group.

- Acknowledge yourself and others as aspects of Spirit with valuable gifts worthy of love.

- Give yourself and others permission to share the deepest desires, passions, visions, and insights available to unlock the power within.

- Create a safe space void of judgment for people to express their vulnerability, their ups and downs, their strengths and weaknesses—all aspects of their humanity and Spirit—in whatever form of expression is valid and useful to them.

- Connect each member of the group by holding hands, breathing together, and co-creating a shared experience using music, movement, laughter, singing, visualizing, a shared task or simply being together in silence.

- To build trust, allow everyone to communicate his truth often, call for realignment and love, and affirm the purposefulness and value of the group.

- Actively listen to what is being shared and offer compassion and understanding without judgment and resistance. Speak "leanly," avoiding long detailed stories. Differentiate between observation, discernment, and judgment—allowing for perception and comments without labels such as good/bad, right/wrong, should and should not.

- Don't project your own values, opinions, or criticisms onto others when really you are the one needing to make a change.

- Avoid denial and openly share your thoughts and feelings to simply expose and release stored up energy, which may be causing separation. Take full responsibility for owning your truth in the moment.

- Know that you can actively choose to accept someone or something without necessarily agreeing with them or their ideas.

- Drop enabling behaviors. Each member of the group must stand on his own to freely create and give unconditional love and acceptance.

- To re-establish a love space, it is often useful to have people move out of their heads and into their hearts, returning to their feelings and eventually their centers. This can be done by focusing on the heart and taking a few deep breaths together. It may also be helpful to have group members "check in" and speak their truth in the moment.

BUILDING TRUST IN YOUR GROUP

We only open our hearts to others when we feel a sense of trust. Until trust has been established, we ask ourselves:

"Will this person accept me?"
"Is this person going to judge me?"
"Will this person value me?"

For most of us, trust occurs naturally as we get to know each other. The more others open up to us and share their vulnerabilities, the more we open to them. **Creating a safe space of trust and non-judgment is the foundation of building the resonant field.**

You may select one or more of the following exercises for this meeting or for future meetings. Obviously, in all these processes, some common sense is needed and you must make sure that there are sufficient people of the right size to do the process safely. Also, you need to respect the physical limitations of individuals. Read through the entire process before beginning.

Process: The Trust Walk

Pair up with another group member. For the trust walk, one person is blindfolded and the "sighted" person leads the "blind" person on a walk. The guide is responsible for the safety of the other person and should warn him if there are any hazards, such as steps, rocks or steep inclines. This is most fun and effective if done in nature.

After 10 - 15 minutes, reverse roles.

When you have both completed the walk, share your experience with your partner.

If you do more than one trust exercise at this meeting, you may want to wait and share your experience later with the entire group.

Process: Trusting the Circle

In this exercise, the group forms a standing circle around one person in the center. Stand close to the person in the center, but far enough away that he can tilt toward the circle.

Those who are standing in the circle prepare themselves to catch the person in the center by making sure they are standing firmly with legs slightly apart and with hands up and palms facing toward the circle center.

It is clear to me that, given the increasing uncertainties we experience in our daily lives, we can only depend upon Spirit to guide us and the members of our soul family, including our Core Group, to support us as we find our way, grow and evolve. As we move beyond the constraints of finite dogma and external rules, we allow ourselves to open to the infinite possibilities that love, trust and sharing bring.

John H. Zwerver

With eyes closed and arms folded across the chest, the person in the center allows himself to "fall" against the circle. The group members gently push the person back toward the center and another person in the circle. In this way, the person in the center is trusting that the circle will not let him fall.

After a minute or two, someone gives a signal to stop and the group gently secures the person back in the center of the circle.

Repeat the above process until everyone who so chooses has completed the process. Then share your experiences.

Process: The Trust Bridge

Step One

Read through the entire process before you begin. For the safety of each group member, the facilitator provides clear direction to all members of the group and ensures that everyone clearly understands his task and is in place before each participant takes his turn.

Allow at least ten minutes for each participant. This process is best done with as little talking as possible. Silence and focus will enable each member to have the deepest possible experience. A sturdy box, phone book or other object strong enough to hold each person is placed in the center of the room. Be sure the object to stand on is no higher than one foot off the ground. Everyone will have the opportunity to participate. It is important to place some pillows or cushions on the floor where the person who is falling will come to rest once he has been caught and then eased down.

It is also appropriate for anyone to choose not to do the Trust Bridge. If this is someone's choice, it is important for him to share that decision with the group, and feel supported in that choice. It is desirable that the group acknowledges all members during this process, whether they actively participate or not.

Those who choose to do the process will take turns, one after the other. This can be a powerful opportunity to release fears and become a more trusting person. Members may want to reflect on their growing edge in regards to trust. In what area of your life do you want to trust more? Hold this intention for yourself as you are supported by the group in expanding your ability to trust.

As the process begins, the first person stands up on the box with his back to the group and states, *"I choose to do the Trust Bridge to learn I can trust."* The rest of the group will gather in a semicircle right behind the person on the box to form a living cushion. The group will then extend their arms towards the member on the box with their feet braced in a manner which will allow them to catch that person. Two pairs standing across from one another will create a stretcher with their arms to cradle the person once he has been caught. The group remains focused and works as a unit for the safety of each member.

As you stand on the box to do the Trust Bridge, take a few seconds to be silent and get in touch with your feelings. When you are ready to fall, you ask the group, *"Are you ready?"* Those who are preparing to catch will softly answer in unison, *"Ready."* The person who is falling then says his name and *"falling"* (for example, *"Joe falling."*) The group only responds *"Ready"* when at least four of them, two pairs standing across from each other, have locked hands and created a "stretcher" with their arms. The rest of the group will squeeze in close with hands up to cushion the fall.

Those who choose to do the Trust Bridge will gently allow themselves to fall backwards into the arms of the other group members. Those who are catching will initiate their own movement backwards. As each participant falls, the momentum of the person who is falling will be slowed by everyone else's hands moving up to meet him and letting him come to rest cradled in the outstretched arms of the two pairs standing across from each other, about waist high off the ground.

The person who has fallen will allow himself to just relax. The others will gently sway him back and forth, as if rocking a baby to sleep. After one or two minutes, he will be gently lowered to the cushions on the floor.

Step Two

Once the person is lying on the cushions, he will relax and observe his thoughts and emotions. This entire process is done in silence. Postpone the inclination to talk until everyone has experienced the Trust Bridge.

After those of you who are acting as catchers have lowered the person to the cushions, extend your hands toward that person until you are touching or close to touching him. Then, with eyes closed, send that group member energy from your hearts. This can be done by sending love directly to that person, or by first envisioning someone you love and noticing how you feel. Then, take that feeling and imagine it as light circulating through your body. Let this light flow through your hands into the group member on the cushions.

Repeat the above process until everyone who so chooses has experienced it. Remain in silence as the group reconfigures for the next member to engage in the exercise.

For many, this exercise can be a profound healing process. Once all members are complete, take some time to share your experiences with the group.

This would be a good time to take a break or to close your meeting.

GUIDED VISUALIZATION

The facilitator slowly reads this aloud, remembering to pause between phrases. You may want to play soft beautiful music in the background.

Close your eyes, breathe deeply, and relax.

(Pause)

Let your breath reach deep down into the center of the Earth and breathe the fire of life up through your feet into your body . . . Feel this heat—this flame of life . . . With each new breath, feel your connection with the Earth . . .

(Pause)

Now, as you inhale, expand your awareness and draw into yourself the vast universe beyond the Earth . . . Feel the solar system, the magnificent Milky Way, the billions of galaxies filled with more planets than there are grains of sand on Earth . . . Feel your presence at peace with the multitudes of this universe . . . See yourself in total harmony with the universe, moving in and out among the stars and the galaxies as if you are visiting old friends.

(Pause)

Now allow your feeling for the whole creation to fill you with wonder and gratitude . . . Let your unconscious remember what creation felt like—love unfolding and expressing . . . Feel yourself expand . . . Experience the beauty of all of creation, including yourself . . . Imagine a giant mirror . . . See yourself reflected in the light of love as the Creator sees you.

(Pause)

Now gently begin to feel the motivation of love that brought this Universe into creation . . . Feel the presence of the Creator expressing love through you, as you . . . Tangibly feel the Creator's love for you . . . Feel the gentle winds of creation blowing its love of life through you . . . Breathe this love through and around you . . . See the light of love shining on you and all beings . . . Bask in the glow of this love . . . Enjoy its warmth as a child being held securely and wrapped in a soft blanket . . . Feel that you are loved fully and unconditionally.

(Pause)

Filled with this love, let its continuous flow move through you and expand out to others in the world . . . You can carry this feeling of being loved and of loving with you . . . Recreate this feeling at any time by taking a deep breath and experiencing yourself as a growing part of the whole creation.

(Pause)

When you are ready, open your eyes, and look into the eyes of the others present, giving and receiving unconditional love.

Process: Moving from Head to Heart

The following exercise is a useful practice for coming back into center when you are feeling angry, depressed, afraid, or upset. By dropping all resistance to any situation or circumstance, you expand your energy, release stress from the body, and move fully into the present moment. Select a partner and guide one another in this exercise.

Think of a time when you felt off center or contracted and were operating from your local self rather than from the Co-creative Self. Briefly share this situation with your partner.

Now place your hand on your heart and take a few deep breaths. Fully experience whatever feelings are occurring and be aware of any contractions you are sensing in your body. Become a neutral observer to the story that is unfolding. Don't try to fix or change anything that is happening. Simply be present to your experience.

Affirm out loud: I am unlimited awareness.
I am love, peace, and harmony.
I am all that is.
I am pure consciousness, and I am always free.

Notice that by releasing all resistance, the body sensations melt away and a feeling of neutrality, or possibly wellbeing occurs. Be with this experience of expanded awareness and neutral observation, knowing that full acceptance of any circumstance is the key to true freedom.

BUILDING THE RESONANT FIELD OF LOVE

Process: The Love Seat

The purpose of the following exercise is to allow you to practice and experience unconditional love. It increases the resonant field of love in your Core Group.

In this process, each person in turn stands, sits, or lies in the center of a circle formed by the rest of the group. The center is the "love seat." The person in the center then "receives" unconditional love from the other group members. In this way, everyone has the opportunity to express and receive love. By expressing love non-verbally, you can move out of your head and into your heart.

Create a comfortable space with peaceful music playing softly in the background. Soften the lighting, if possible, but make sure there is sufficient light for each person to see the others' eyes clearly. If everyone is seated on the floor, you can move freely, but a circle of chairs will also work. If you use chairs, put a stool in the center so that the person in the center can face each person in the circle in turn with a minimum of disruption. Allow about ten minutes for each person. If your group is large, break into smaller groups of 4 - 5 people.

1. The facilitator explains the process to the group.

2. One person sits in the center of the circle. This person is the "receiver".

3. Everyone closes his eyes. Allow a few minutes for everyone to become centered. Then, with eyes still closed, those in the circle focus their attention on the receiver—sending love to that person. The receiver in the love seat relaxes and becomes like a sponge receiving the love energy from the others.

4. Open your eyes. One person becomes the "giver", looking deeply into the eyes of the receiver, seeing the loving person there. Then, non-verbally, through motions of your arms, touch, or any other non-verbal way, express love to the receiver. If you wish you might touch the receiver and transmit love energy through your hands or simply visualize light surrounding his body. Both the giver and the receiver can stand, move, dance, sit, or whatever feels appropriate. This connection can be potent, even though brief. The other people in the circle continue to send love to both the giver and the receiver. Repeat this process around the circle until every person in the circle has had a chance to be a "giver".

5. Repeat steps 2 through 4 until every person has been a receiver.

Take some time to share your experiences. What was this experience like for you? Was it easier to give or to receive? How might you apply this experience to other areas of your life? Do you think it is easy or difficult to express love non-verbally? What are other ways to express unconditional love within your group?

Process: Acknowledging One Another

Form pairs. Sit across from one another. Look deeply into each other's eyes. After one minute, the facilitator asks that one of the pair speak to the other, saying and completing the phrase: *I see in you . . .*

Repeat the phrase with the different endings that occur to you spontaneously, allowing the love energy to flow. Speak authentically from your heart to the Essential Self of your partner.

After a few minutes, the facilitator asks the partners to switch roles and repeat the process.

When both of you are complete, take some time for sharing.

SHARING AND EXPRESSING YOUR GIFTS

Set aside a celebratory evening to share your gifts and talents with one another. You may want to have a potluck dinner. Does your group have artists, musicians, gardeners, storytellers, cooks, and so forth? These may be latent, unexpressed, or hidden gifts or talents that might not necessarily correspond with your current occupations. Members can bring their art, original stories, music, or a favorite dish of food to share with the group. Encourage the expression of these talents as you continue through the Handbook.

MAKING A COMMITMENT

There is power in making a commitment to your Core Group and to continuing the process through Circle 6. In that Circle, you will be exploring your soul's purpose and deciding whether it's appropriate to proceed together or to differentiate. You might create a commitment ceremony to honor this important step or use the suggested Ceremony of Commitment in Circle 5.

Closing - The Silent Greeting

This process can be used to close this meeting or at the completion of any gathering of family or friends.

Play beautiful music that builds group resonance and opens the heart. (See the resources in Section 4 for suggested music.)

The facilitator instructs the group members to find a partner and to hold hands and look into each other's eyes. He instructs the group: *"You will greet each person as though you were meeting him for the first time AND as though you have known him forever."*

Participants are to remain silent but will send love to one another through their eyes, hands, and hearts. Allow about 30 - 60 seconds for each pair to greet one another before moving on to other people.

Continue until each person has silently greeted every other person in the group.

Note: This greeting works particularly well with groups of people of different nationalities who are unable to communicate with words but know the language of the heart.

Some day, after we have mastered the winds, the waves, the tides,
and gravity, we shall harness the energies of love. Then for the second time
in the history of the world, man will have discovered fire.

Teilhard de Chardin

DAILY PRACTICE
(Exercises to be Done Outside the Group)

Once you've experienced resonance, you won't want to live without it in any area of your life. Patiently and with sensitivity, incorporate the principles and practices in all your relationships. You will positively effect everyone around you.

A. Reflect on the Co-Creator's Agreements on a Regular Basis.

Apply them in all your relationships including those with family, friends, and co-workers. You might select one agreement to concentrate on at a time or each week. Share your experiences with a friend, relative or other members of your Core Group.

B. Initiatory Love

If you encounter someone who is upset (and maybe acting destructively), remember that he is also the Self. Do not react; pro-act. Open up the flow of love from you to that person. Tune into the deeper meaning behind the person's words or actions. Have compassion for his predicament. Be gentle, reach out, and touch him with your eyes.

If you find yourself in a group or family gathering that feels hostile, tense, negative, or unloving, center yourself by taking several deep breaths. Turn off your analytical mind. Tune up your intuitive sensitivity and empathy. Scan for the areas of disturbance. When you sense that someone is feeling upset, empathize with him. Then, consciously radiate love energy.

If you are unable to change the energy from negative to positive simply by shifting it within yourself, overtly share your experience and say that it does not feel good to be in this environment. Ask people how they feel. State your own experience without blaming others. Tell them about the process of truth telling. This often unlocks the negative stranglehold on the group. Note what works and what doesn't work and share your experiences with your Core Group. Remember not to have expectations or to try to control the outcome of your truth telling. You will be practicing loving detachment as you express yourself, while letting others choose their own behavior.

C. Expressing Love

A loving touch penetrates further than "skin deep". Appropriately express your love daily. You can connect just as deeply through a warm handshake or a gentle touch on the shoulder as you can with a bear hug. The key is to feel connected to that person in that moment.

A sincere compliment or loving words can make someone's day. When you are thinking loving thoughts about someone, share them with that person. Nobody ever got too many sincere "strokes". Tell people—your family, significant others, friends, or co-workers—you love them.

In your journal before you retire, you can note the kind and loving things you have done for others during the day. Resolve to be a more loving being each day, inviting the Creator's unconditional love to express through you as your Essential Self.

D. An Attitude of Gratitude

Focus on the positive in each relationship and that which you love will blossom. Set aside a moment at the same time every day, perhaps before you retire or during a silent or spoken "grace" before dinner, to recall what you are grateful for that day.

E. Take Care of Yourself

Nurture your emotions through intimate communication with your friends and family. Practice sharing deeply with those you love. Open up and be vulnerable. Tell your truth with love. Do you feel in resonance with your family, friends, and colleagues? If not, what can you do to bring your relationships into resonance? (See Circle 3 for many exercises and suggestions.)

In the morning, when you are looking in the mirror, say loving words to yourself. You can say, *"The things I love about you are..."* Turn negative self-talk into positive self-talk. Remember that you are the Self manifesting as a unique, beautiful person.

F. Track Your Progress

Write in your journal any insights that you have about your ability to create and maintain resonance and connect at the heart. Make an inventory of your life. What are you doing that shows that you love yourself? What are you doing that is not so loving? Think about the ways you can love yourself more.

Each day, do at least one special loving thing just for you. At the end of the day, record in your journal the things you have done for yourself that reflect your acceptance of the fact that you are worthy of the unconditional love freely given to you …that you are love itself.

To put the world in order, we must first put the nation in order;
To put the nation in order, we must first put the family in order;
To put the family in order, we must first cultivate our personal life.
We must first set our hearts right.

Confucius

Acknowledgments

Special appreciation to Tim Clauss for his assistance in co-creating the information utilized in **To Open Hearts in a Group.**

Circle 3

OVERCOMING
THE ILLUSION OF SEPARATION

One does not become enlightened by imagining figures of light,
but by making the darkness conscious.

Carl Jung

As we surrender our little selves, we gain entry into the larger God/Goddess Self.

Sage Bennett

I tell you one thing. If you want peace of mind, do not find fault with others.
Rather learn to see your own faults. Learn to make the whole world your own.

Sri Sarada Devi

*The fundamental problem facing humanity today is the illusion of separation—separation from each other, from nature, and from our Source/Self.
It is this illusion that causes all criminal behavior, every war and skirmish, the dysfunctional disparity between "haves" and "have nots,"
and the disregard for and destruction of the Earth's environment.
The vast majority of all problems faced by humanity are caused by humanity and stem from the illusion of separation.*

*The essential solution is the experience of union, an inner shift from fear to love, and—most fundamentally—the consciousness that we are one.
This shift can occur "in the twinkling of an eye" or it may be the result of years of deep intention, conscious attention, "due diligence" and practice.*

*When each of us accepts all aspects of our local selves, bringing the darkness into light, we support the Essential Self to take dominion in our lives.
What we do for ourselves, we can do for one another.*

*By forgiving ourselves and others and learning the communication skills that are required for healthy, harmonious relationships, we open to seeing and acknowledging the beauty that is the essence of every person.
We do our part to shift the collective field of consciousness from fear to love.*

~ ~

Circle 3

OVERCOMING THE ILLUSION OF SEPARATION

The highest purpose of communication is communing...becoming one with each other.
Joyce and Barry Vissell

Listen, or thy tongue
will keep thee deaf.
American Indian

Reason sees a holy relationship as what it is: a common state of mind
where both gladly open to correction so that both may happily be healed as one.
A Course in Miracles

What would it be like if everyone in the world was fully encouraged and supported to do and be his best? Think of a world in which everyone is living up to his full potential. This is the world we are helping each other to create.

In a crew of astronauts or an Olympic team, each member's ability is vital to the success of the whole. It is natural for teammates to assist each other to achieve the highest level of individual excellence for the good of all. In the same way, in our Core Groups in a resonant field of love, we can help each other to expand our Co-creative Selves and become fully aligned with the will of the Divine. Like the "imaginal cell" within a caterpillar about to become a butterfly, each of us holds the seeds of our full potential. In an environment of love and safety, these seeds can blossom and grow. Each person's gifts can come forth to serve the whole and build a new cooperative society.

The key to expressing Self is learning to stay centered. Centered means being at cause not effect. It means experiencing difficult situations without reactivity, fear, or defensiveness. When you are centered, you are not experiencing the illusion of separation. You are experiencing connectedness, at-one-ment with all others, even if they are attacking you. You recognize they are in pain, crying out for love. Feeling at one with Source, you are not vulnerable. You extend love rather than react or defend.

The communication skills that follow in this Circle are designed to dispel the illusion of separation and to assist you in expressing your gifts and abilities fully as you experience the joy of union. They can be used with your family and friends, your co-workers and business colleagues, within organizations or in established communities. With knowledge, sensitivity and practice, each of us can support ourselves and others to be our best. From a place of love and partnership, the Essential Self is liberated in each of us—allowing each person to be free, to be abundant, to be great, to be fully empowered.

By reflecting and loving the Self within and in others, we bring it forth. We learn from one another, acknowledging that each of us is a master in our own area of expertise. We become mentors to one another and each is transformed into a "human-butterfly". Collectively, we move to a higher frequency of love and unlimited possibilities for all.

Note: You will need a series of meetings to complete the exercises in Circle 3. The facilitator(s) should read through all the exercises in this Circle before your meetings, as some of them call for special music, art materials and/or recording equipment.

Be sure to take a number of breaks and to dance and move your bodies between processes. You will be shifting a lot of energy as you bring the unconscious aspects of yourself into conscious awareness and darkness into light. Remember to "check in" at the beginning of each session and to select a closing from Section 4 as you complete your meetings. As always, you can create your own "closings," if you prefer.

Suggested Process Sequence

- Open your session with the Visualization that follows—or create your own attunement process.

- Remember to check-in.

- Read The Co-Creator's Agreements aloud.

- Read the Introduction to the Circle. Take a moment in silence to reflect on this. Then share your inspired insights with the group.

- Select one or more of the Experiential Exercises that follow.

- Take a break! Move around and stretch.

- Select who will fill the key roles at your next meeting.

- Create a closing that will maintain your heart connection. (See the Appendix for suggested closing exercises—or create your own.)

EXPERIENTIAL EXERCISES

GUIDED VISUALIZATION

The facilitator slowly reads this aloud, remembering to pause between phrases. You may want to play some soft beautiful music in the background.

Relax . . . Breathe deeply and allow any thoughts or cares to drift away . . . Invite your body to relax fully . . . Create an aura of silence around you . . .

(Pause)

Place your attention in your heart . . . Allow the warmth of the love in your heart to permeate your being . . . Feel the utter peace of that love . . . Allow all distractions and concerns to disappear . . . to be washed away with each breath . . .

(Pause)

Now take a moment to reflect on the values that you hold most dearly . . . Do you treasure honesty . . . beauty . . . generosity . . . love or compassion . . ? Just bring into your awareness all the values that you honor and aspire to uphold in your life. . .

(Pause for 2 - 3 minutes here.)

Now, once again, take a few deep breaths. . . Become aware of your body, seated in this room . . . and when you are ready, open your eyes and come back to this time and place.

(Pause)

Without speaking to others, make a list of the values that came forth in the visualization.

_____	_____	_____	_____
_____	_____	_____	_____
_____	_____	_____	_____
_____	_____	_____	_____

Review your list. Which of these do you live by and which do you aspire to live by?

After you "check in", discuss your values with the group. You may want to make a record of the values you share as a group, as they will be useful when you come to Circle 7: Exploring Our Shared Destiny.

COMMUNICATION SKILLS FOR HARMONIOUS LIVING

As we evolve and integrate our authentic values into our lives, we may trigger unconscious reactions. Fear, blame, shame, judgment, feelings of inadequacy and doubt may come to the surface as the ego resists moving into new ways of being. The emotional body may go through a detoxification process to shed old patterns and assumptions. When we are allowed to fully experience feelings, an alchemy can occur which frees us from the grip of the past.

Overcoming the illusion of separation requires a sense of Self and an awareness of "shadow" aspects of the ego/personality that are underdeveloped or unconscious and sabotage the Self. It also requires a set of skills that facilitate healthy relating. **The information and exercises in this Circle are designed to provide basic training in the communication skills that will allow you to discover and accept many aspects of your local self and move quickly into an experience of deep connection and union with others as the Essential Self.**

PRINCIPLES FOR HEALTHY COMMUNICATION

Discuss the following principles in your group and modify the list in any way that is appropriate for you.

- Truth is the rock upon which good relationships are built. Share your feelings and be honest in your communications.
- Be aware that what you have to say is both honest *and* worth saying. If it does not add value to a conversation or to the relationship, don't say it.
- True communication includes body language and intent, as well as words. Positive intent facilitates the experience of connection or union.
- Timing, safety and receptivity are key to clear communication. Be sensitive to the needs of others before launching into conversation. Don't bring up important issues during rushed or stressful times of the day.
- People long to be heard and seen, received and understood in their communications. Common courtesy, respect and reflective listening are keynotes of conscious communication.
- The mind creates separation; the heart creates connection. If you are feeling judgmental, critical, victimized or separate in any way, try shifting your energy from your mind to your heart. Practice empathy.
- Reply rather than react, if you are able.
- Address only one issue at a time.
- Silence is often the best bridge between hearts. Don't feel you always need to speak to be heard.

- As best you are able, confront your shadow and accept your light. Be aware of your own growing edge, to avoid projecting negative thoughts and feelings on others.

- Stay current in your relationships. Unfinished arguments accumulate. Unspoken feelings can build in the body and create disease. The residue from unsettled questions can create separation in relationships. Do your best to complete your communications.

- Learn to make requests and honor your commitments to foster a sense of connection. Do what you say you will do in a timely manner to build trust in your relationships. If you break an agreement, acknowledge that you have done so and talk about it with the relevant other(s).

- Remember your humor.

Listening to the Wisdom of Your Heart

If you are feeling off center, stressed out, or antagonistic, practice the following to create a feeling of peace and well being:

- Recognize the stressful feeling and take a time out.

- Make a sincere effort to shift your focus away from your analytical mind or disturbed emotions to the area around your heart. Pretend that you are breathing through your heart to help focus your energy in this area. Keep your focus on your heart for at least ten seconds.

- Recall a fun, positive feeling or time you've had in the past and attempt to re-experience it.

- Now, using your common sense and sincerity, ask yourself: *"What would be a more beneficial response to this situation. . . One that will minimize the feeling of stress?"*

- Listen to your heart. What wisdom does it have to offer you? Do what it says now.

Process

Allow at least 20 - 30 minutes for this exercise.

Select a partner. One of you will be "A"; the other is "B." Each of you think of a situation from the recent past in which you felt off center, operating as your local self.

"A" will share with "B," briefly describing the situation, the feeling, and the thoughts that were occurring at that time. He will then go through the steps above, shifting his energy from the mind to the heart.

Reverse roles. When both of you have practiced listening to the wisdom of the heart, share your experiences with one another.

CO-COACHING EACH OTHER TO DO AND BE OUR BEST

There is no criticism or judgment in a Core Group. There is discernment, assistance, and voluntary self-correction. In the practice called co-coaching, we access our own inner coach and ask for coaching from others. All the energy heretofore used to protect ourselves from criticism or to make ourselves right goes into self-evolution. Requesting coaching from a peer stimulates that person to do the same. A positive cycle of self-improvement begins, which leads to self-mastery for a whole group.

Every member of the group receives discernment from each member. It is important to note the difference between discernment and judgment. Judgment is criticism and causes separation. Discernment is coaching and creates connection and expansion.

Co-coaching comes from the genuine desire to bring forth the potential of each member of the group or family. We seek coaching to support full Self realization of each member, as a team. As we coach others, we hold up an imaginary mirror to help them see their own highest image. As we receive this coaching ourselves, we step more fully into the Self—great, liberated, and fully empowered beings.

Co-coaching occurs naturally when we recognize that each person's growth and excellence is as important to us as our own, and that we can better actualize our potential if our teammates are actualizing theirs. When we decide to co-create together, each of us will be empowered to do our best so that we can all experience our success.

TIPS FOR CO-COACHING

In your group, you will want to discuss and review the following tips for co-coaching so that everyone understands what it is and how to be coaches for each other. This practice is useful at work, home, or in your Core Group. Remember, you can say anything to anyone, if you come from your heart, tell your truth, and use "I" messages.

1.   Create an environment that is safe for vulnerability and honesty.

2.   Establish resonance first. Ask for permission before coaching another person.

3. Tune into your Essential Self and the Essential Self of the person you are coaching. Go within often for direction. Begin the co-coaching process by acknowledging the unique gifts, qualities, and potentials of the person who is being coached.

4. Coach from a state of kindness, compassion, love, forgiveness, and non-judgment. If you are feeling anything other than love or compassion, or if you feel judgmental, do not coach others. Center yourself first.

5. If the person you are coaching is being dramatic, caught up in a story or blaming others, coach that person to be objective, truthful, direct, and clear rather than focusing on somebody else's actions.

6. Notice how your coaching is being received. Communicate frequently about the effects of your coaching style. Ask your coaching partner what coaching and learning style is best for him.

7. Be specific and keep it simple. Communicate what you heard and what behavior you observed. Leave out interpretations and advice. Remember that good coaches support their teammates to develop the capacity to interpret their own behavior so that they can take appropriate actions. They do not tell them what to do.

8. Take your time. Listen carefully.

9. If someone asks for your interpretation, share your own personal experiences rather than offering "universal truths". An example might be: "I know that whenever I'm talking a lot, I'm usually fishing for approval". Notice the difference between this statement and a statement like: "All people who talk a lot are insecure".

10. Tell the truth. Do you want to improve? Co-coaching will not be effective if one of you does not want to change. Be honest about your own and others' strengths and weaknesses. Do not coach with a hidden agenda to change someone for selfish reasons. Be open to yourself and others about your intentions.

11. Listen to the words. The words, "I have to . . .", "I need to . . .", "I should . . . ," can be replaced with "I choose to . . .", "I can . . .", "I am . . .".

12. Give feedback to your coach and be open to feedback.

13. Be patient. Co-coaching is an ongoing process to overcome self-imposed limitations that may have been acquired over a lifetime.

14. Remember that every attack is a call for love. Re-establish resonance before continuing in the process.

15. Allow others to coach you. Reveal what you perceive to be the model of how you want to be and what your limitations or roadblocks are and what may be holding you back from being your best.

16. When being coached, listen to the higher meaning of what is being said, rather than just the words or emotions. Reflect on the help you have received.

17. Do not depend on others to keep you "on track". Take responsibility to consult your own inner coach. Notice how you are creating your reality and what you are attracting to yourself. Does it fit with your highest potential? If not, make the needed changes.

A Co-coaching Process:

After you have read the tips and discussed ways you can co-coach each other in your group, form pairs and practice the co-coaching exercise that follows. The timekeeper may allow 30 minutes or so for this exercise. Each person should practice co-coaching the other.

If you prefer, you can do this exercise in triads with one person serving as the process observer. If you do the exercise this way, be sure to switch roles so that each person has a turn to be the speaker, coach, and observer.

Identify a situation that has created a sense of separation between you and another person and ask for coaching from your partner. Briefly share the scenario with your partner. Practice co-coaching using the tips provided above. Give each other feedback on your coaching styles. You might try sharing the same situation with a different partner to appreciate the similarities and differences in coaching styles.

The following example of co-coaching is provided to assist you in this process.

Person A: "May I coach you?" (ask permission)

Person B: "Yes, please."

Person A: "I noticed last night that Mary seemed hurt by your comment about her son Bill. I felt that you had some valuable things to share with Mary. In the future, I invite you to slow down a little when you communicate sensitive issues with others, to make sure that it is the appropriate time and place, so that your communications can be fully received."

Person B: "Thank you for telling me that. I'll reflect on what you've said."

After the co-coaching exercise, discuss the process with the larger group. Were you able to coach another honestly? Were you able to stay in your heart and really serve the other person? How did you receive the coaching?

A useful tip: When you feel separate from another person and feel inclined to blame him, try substituting "the mind" for the personal pronoun. e.g. Instead of saying, "He did this" try saying "the mind did this." The mind can create suffering by blocking the heart and creating the illusion of separation.

Observe your fear as "the fear in the mind," your jealously as "the jealousy in the mind," your anger as "the anger in the mind." Relate *to* fear or jealously or anger instead of *from* fear or jealousy or anger.

~ ~

This would be a good time to take a break. Put on some lively music. Move and shake your bodies. Let go of memories and feelings left over from the co-coaching exercise. Relax and be present in the moment.

CLEARING

When we do not accurately express our truth in the moment, this suppression of thoughts, emotions, or physical acts often accumulates and blocks the free-flow of energy, inhibits results, and eventually can even cause significant physical ailments. Telling the truth or "clearing" in the moment and having it received completes the expression and creates a void or space for the next appropriate truth or possibility in a relationship to appear.

TIPS FOR CLEARING

1. Time must be open-ended and sufficient.

2. Agree that anything anyone says in the process cannot be used against them outside the session; that is, used for historical proof in some future disagreement. (The intention of clearing is to disappear any suppression or limitation, not to hold onto it.)

3. Each person takes a turn to share his truth (thoughts, emotions, physical sensations, and/or spiritual guidance) until he is complete. It is important to use the pronoun "I" in sharing, claiming full responsibility for your truth. Everyone else remains quiet and receives. Listen to the essence, not just the words or emotions of people. Sense what's really wanting to be communicated. No matter what the other person communicates, experience it as his truth in the moment. Know that a person's understanding of the truth varies depending upon his perceptions, experience, and level of consciousness. Remain detached, if possible, and allow for the clearing out of suppressed, accumulated expression.

4. Allow for each person to take his turn and share until complete. (Use the talking piece to support deep listening.)

5. When it appears that the person has finished expressing himself, ask him, "Is there any-

thing you have not been able to express yet and would like to add?" Allow him to clear out any remaining thoughts or feelings.

6. Take note of the one, two, or three bottom-line issues really needing to be addressed, given the interaction. Acknowledge your "soul connection" with each other and agree to continue now or set up time soon when it would be more appropriate for you collectively to seek out win/win solutions.

7. In addressing the selected bottom-line issues, go within to that "place of all-knowing, compassion, and oneness" for a response to move everyone forward on his journey. Co-create solutions and agreements that express everyone's integrity and Self.

8. Acknowledge everyone's willingness and courage to tell the truth and co-create positive, forward moving resolutions.

A Clearing Process:

Read through the instructions before you begin. Then pair up with someone in your group. Select an "A" and a "B". If the situation is laden with emotion, you may wish to invite a third party to witness your interaction, be a neutral observer, and provide for a safe space.

Whether working in pairs or in a triad, you agree to talk about your feelings, to allow the other person to share fully without interrupting and to look for a solution. When the process is complete, if using an observer, he can offer insights and objective comments about the interaction. Be sure to switch roles so that each of you has an opportunity to be "A", "B" and the impartial observer.

"A" goes first. *Very briefly,* tell your partner about a relationship in your life that invites "clearing". (Ask yourself, "Who do I feel separate from?") Then take ten minutes and practice clearing with your partner—as though he were that person.

"B" then has an opportunity to practice clearing, following the directions given above.

When you have both practiced clearing, coach one another. State what you heard and share how you felt as the receiver of this clearing. If there is a witness, that person should provide coaching and share his observations as well, before assuming the role of "A" or "B."

This exercise may release energy that has been blocking your flow of love. You may notice that you no longer feel separate and may not need to clear with your designated person; or, you may feel motivated to share with your person and move beyond separation to the experience of unity.

Process: A Two-Minute Release Exercise

The following process can be used with another or by yourself to shift feelings very quickly and bring yourself back to center.

Select a partner. Read through the following and then take turns guiding one another through the exercise. First, "A" will ask the questions and "B" will respond. Then reverse roles.

Think of a time when you felt upset or off center. . . Identify the feelings and the body sensations that are occurring as you recall this incident. . .

(Pause and wait for responses)

*"**What** are you feeling?"*

(Pause and wait for response)

 *"**Could** you let this go?"* (Are you able to release this feeling now?)

(Pause and wait for response)

 *"**Would** you let this go?"* (Are you willing to move beyond this feeling?)

(Pause and wait for response)

 *"Are you willing to let this go **now**?"*

(Pause and wait for response)

If you are willing, take a deep breath and step fully into witness consciousness . . . Notice that you have feelings and you have a body . . . but you are not your feelings or your body . . . You are the Self, unlimited and free . . . You are Spirit having a human experience.

(Pause)

When both of you are complete, share your experience with the group, and remember that you can use this whenever you feel off center—simply by asking yourself these questions and shifting your awareness from local self to Self.

Process: Sharing "Withholds"

"Withholds" are thoughts, feelings, or judgments that you resist sharing with another person. The withhold can be negative or positive. It is not uncommon to withhold "I love you" from those who matter the most to us. Withholds block the flow of energy and can create a feeling of separation with another person. The following process may be used to release "withholds" and come into the experience of connection with family, friends and colleagues. The ability to remain neutral as an observer facilitates moving quickly into union with another.

Select a partner from the members of your group. One of you is "A"; the other is "B." Take a moment to center yourselves and to move into witness consciousness. Look to see if you have a "withhold" from your partner. If so, take this opportunity to share your truth with him. If there is no "withhold" with this partner, think of another person and pretend that your partner is that person.

Person A says, *"I have a withhold. May I share it with you?"*

Person B says, *"Yes, you may."*

Person A states the "withhold." (For example, "I've never felt attracted to you because you remind me of a teacher I didn't like when I was in grammar school." OR "I really appreciate your sincerity and I've never told you that." It is important to tell your truth, rather than look for the easy way out of this exercise.)

Person B says, *"Thank you for sharing."*

Person A says, *"Thank you for listening."*

Switch roles and repeat the process. When you are both complete, share your experience in the larger circle.

This might be a good time to take another break and to move your body. You may want to eat some fruit or some other light refreshment.

Process: There is No "Other"

Be sure you have at least 45 minutes to complete this exercise. If not, save this for your next meeting and move on to **Practicing Forgiveness**.

Note that this process is conducted in silence. You will be speaking to "the other" in your mind and not out loud.

The facilitator slowly reads this aloud, remembering to pause between phrases. You may want to play soft beautiful music in the background.

Take a few deep breaths and invite your body to relax . . . Be aware of the Earth beneath you . . . Feel your body becoming grounded and centered as you align your energy with the Earth . . . Now bring into your awareness an incident that occurred that contributed to or caused a feeling of separation between you and another person . . . You will be having an imaginary conversation with someone you're wanting to forgive.

(Pause for about 2 minutes.)

See yourself facing that person. Both of you are seated, looking at one another . . . Notice your body sensations and your feelings . . . If you feel any tension or tightness in the body, notice where that is . . .

(Pause)

Now place your awareness on the other person . . . Notice his or her hair, face, and eyes. . . What clothes is this person wearing?. . . What is this person's body posture? Take in all the details you notice about this other person.

(Pause for about 2 minutes.)

Now, in your mind, begin to speak to this person . . . Silently express all of your thoughts and feelings . . . Say everything you need to say . . . Tell this person everything you've avoided saying in the past . . .

(Pause for about 2 minutes.)

After you've expressed everything you needed to express in your imagination, allow the other person to respond and say everything they need to say. . . Listen carefully as they tell their truth. . .

(Pause for about 2 minutes.)

Continue to speak and listen, back and forth, until you experience your body relaxing . . . You speak and then the other person speaks. Pay attention to feelings as they arise and share them with the other.

(Pause for about 2 minutes.)

Now, take a deep breath all the way into your belly and become the other person . . . That's right, shift your awareness and become the other person . . . Take your time to feel what it's like to inhabit this body and feel these feelings . . . Fully become this person, looking back at you.

(Pause for about 2 minutes.)

Taking another deep breath, shift your awareness again and become yourself, looking over at the other person . . . Notice your body sensations and your feelings . . .

(Pause for 1 - 2 minutes.)

With your next deep breath, become the awareness that is observing these two people. You are no longer the person you thought yourself to be, nor are you the other . . . You are the spaciousness in which all meetings occur . . . Relax into this unlimited spaciousness . . . Now feel these two bodies being absorbed into formlessness, like waves falling back into the ocean . . . You are silence and emptiness . . . You are peace and love . . . There is no "other."

(Pause for 1 - 2 minutes.)

Take a few deep breaths and slowly bring your awareness back into the room.

Take a few moments of silence and then share your experience of this guided visualization with one another. Be sure to notice how your relationship with the "other" person unfolds in the coming weeks.

PRACTICING FORGIVENESS

Forgiveness allows us to make peace with our past to be present and current in our lives. The need to forgive arises when our unfulfilled desires give rise to frustration, confusion, resentment and/or anger. In essence, all of these feelings are states of mind. Once this is recognized, there is an opening for forgiveness—remembering that you are not the emotion or the story—but the space in which all this is occurring, the Essential Self. This shift in identity is key to the forgiveness process.

> *Forgiveness is the process
> that puts an end to the business of
> unfinished business.
> It is a giving that
> requires nothing in return.
> It has the potential of letting us take
> birth at last, fully alive.*
>
> Stephen and Ondrea Levine

Note: Forgiveness cannot be forced. You're simply opening your heart with kindness to those qualities in another that you reject in yourself or, perhaps, releasing judgment that you have directed toward yourself. You are forgiving the person, not the action.

A Forgiveness Process

The facilitator guides the members of the group, reading slowly and remembering to pause between phrases.

Take a few deep breaths and focus your energy in your heart.

Think of a time you deeply desired something and that desire was blocked. Briefly describe the scene in writing: _____
_____
_____
_____

Now, gently close your eyes and observe the process that occurred. Remember the feelings that arose—perhaps frustration, resentment, confusion . . . Use your mind to track the process—to observe the play of emotions that occurred . . . Stand back as the Self and allow the drama to unfold . . . Watch your ever-changing states of mind . . . Notice that when there is observation with no identification and no holding, there is anger but no one angry . . . resentment, but no one resentful . . . Forgiveness becomes natural and appropriate.

(Pause)

What is your intention? . . . Your willingness? . . . Do you desire to forgive and move on in your life? . . . Would your ego prefer to hold on to this?

(Pause for 1 - 2 minutes)

Be aware of your body . . . With forgiveness, the body relaxes and feels lighter . . . How does your heart feel? . . . Watch your emotions . . . How do you feel as you observe your feelings? . . . Is there a sense of relief—or a feeling of contraction in your heart?

(Pause)

Take a few deep breaths and shake out your arms and legs . . . Become aware of the others seated in the circle. . . When you are ready, open your eyes.

(Pause)

When you are ready, take a few minutes to write down your insights. Then, turn to a partner and share your experience.

_____
_____
_____
_____

A useful tip: You can also use the Two-Minute Release Exercise if you are needing to forgive someone in the moment.

If it feels appropriate, take a break here. Put on some upbeat music and move your bodies.

*Forgiveness, love and our connection
with the Divine
is the medicine that is healing the
sickness of our time.*

Jeremy Roske

When you return from your break, discuss with your group other exercises, practices, and ceremonies that you have found to be useful in forgiving yourself or another.

"MIRRORING" OR BEING A PURE REFLECTION

Mirroring is a reflective listening technique that allows people to express their feelings, discharge emotion and—on occasion—to complete experiences, so that nothing lingers.

Mirroring consists of:

- Hearing the other person's thoughts and feelings
- Looking or listening for the deeper message beneath the words
- Observing body language
- Recreating the other's experience within yourself
- Stating their words as a question, or, repeating their words exactly as you heard them without adding other thoughts or emotions
- Asking if your listening and interpretation is accurate

Mirroring is about clarifying the other person's communication, not about expressing your own opinions.

A useful expression is: *I heard you say _____. Is that what you said?*

Process: "Mirroring"

Read through the instructions that follow before beginning the exercise. When you feel clear about the instructions, select a partner. One of you will be Partner "A"; the other is "B". The time-keeper should allow about 10 to 15 minutes for each person and alert group members when it is time to switch roles.

Partner "A" thinks of an experience involving another person that provoked an emotion such as fear, sadness, shame, jealousy, anger, shock, rage or hopelessness. (For example, your brother shares a confidentiality that is very sensitive for you with one of his co-workers. You feel betrayed, angry and upset.)

Partner "A" will take two minutes to *briefly* explain his personal incident to Partner "B."

Next, Partner "A" expresses his thoughts and feelings about this experience to "B", as though he were clearing with the person involved with that experience. (In the case of the example given above, "A" would pretend that "B" is his brother. "A" would share his thoughts and feelings, one "piece" at a time. "B" would pretend to be the brother and would mirror "A's" words and feelings back to him.)

Now switch roles. Partner "B" will think of an upsetting experience and *briefly* set the scene for Partner "A". "A" will practice mirroring what he heard back to "B."

When you're done with the exercise, take a few minutes to share and provide feedback to one another. Then share with the entire group. When done correctly, mirroring provides a profound experience of validation by being heard and seen.

Process: Being a Pure Reflection

The following is a different version of a mirroring exercise. In this version, you will form small groups of three or four people. Read through the entire process before you begin to be sure everyone is clear about his role. Within these groups, one person will be the "sender," one the "listener," and the other(s) the "observer(s)."

Those who are senders can take a minute to think of a recent situation which presented or created a problem for them. It should be a situation around which they felt some emotion and one in which they still have some concern. It doesn't have to be a personal or monumental problem, just one which created some emotional energy which is still present. The sender then relates the situation to the listener. The objective for the sender is not to paint himself as good or bad in the situation. Release concerns about being judged. Just relate the situation simply and clearly according to what was true for you.

The focus for those listening is divided into two parts:

1. **The first part of the process is to make sure the listener hears the words accurately.** Do this by paraphrasing what you hear back to the sender: "What I hear you saying is..." Then, state in your own words, or verbatim if you can, what the sender was saying to you. If the sender has a long situation to relate, he should stop at short intervals so the listener can repeat back what has been said up to that point.

   The sender needs to verify that the listener has heard the words correctly before going on with the situation. If the listener has not heard him correctly, the sender needs to repeat the story until the listener can repeat it accurately.

2. **When the sender has finished and is satisfied that the listener has heard the situation accurately, the second part of the listener's job comes into play. The listener centers himself to "sense" or intuit what is behind the words of the sender.**

What feelings does the sender have about the situation which may not have been stated? What other thoughts or emotions does the sender harbor which may be hidden to the sender? The listener then relates what he is sensing about the sender. The sender listens until the listener is through or has asked for confirmation regarding his intuitions. At this point both the sender and the listener can enter into a spontaneous dialogue. This is an excellent way to check for projections on the part of the listener!

Be sure to allow enough time so everyone can experience the process. Unlike usual conversations, **the listener is not there to give feedback or advice.** It's important to adhere to the process by reflecting back what he has heard at both levels.

The role of the observer is also important. The observer makes sure the process is honored. It's easy for both the sender and the listener to get caught up in their own reactions to the situation and each other. Those observing need to remain objective during the process. The observer can stop the conversation if the sender is getting too far ahead of the listener or if the listener is not repeating back the words accurately. The observer watches that the sender verifies the listener's reflections. Once the listener begins relating what he is sensing, the observer can also intuit what he has received. At the end of the entire discussion between the listener and sender, the observer can relate what he has picked up from both participants.

Repeat the process until everyone has had a chance to be the sender, the listener and the observer. Then share your experience with the entire Core Group.

Take a break at this time, if you need one.

Process: A Group Co-coaching

When your group has connected deeply and the feeling of trust and safety is shared by all members, you can coach one another in the larger circle, rather than one on one. **This process requires a great deal of sensitivity, as the person being coached is choosing to be very vulnerable.** You may want to do this process now or save it for another occasion when coaching from the group is more appropriate. **As in any coaching exercise, the purpose of this process is to support group members to release conditioned patterns that create separation with others or block the experience of Self.**

In this process, the person being coached (the "receiver") sits in the middle of the circle and asks for coaching.

- Everyone takes a few minutes to center himself in the Heart Meditation and "tune into" the receiver.

- When it feels right, someone in the circle begins the coaching process. Start with an acknowledgment, speaking from your heart and reflecting what you love and respect about the receiver.

- Next, reflect the person's "growing edge" succinctly, clearly, and compassionately.

- The receiver mirrors what he has heard and thanks the coach.

- The coach confirms or corrects the receiver.

- Another person in the circle begins the process, starting with an acknowledgment.

When you have completed the process, have a group hug. Depending upon the needs in the group, you might repeat this process with another person who has requested coaching; or you might take a break by putting on some lively music and dancing.

TIPS FOR CREATING
CONSCIOUS COMMUNICATION IN GROUPS

Discuss these tips and use them as a foundation from which to co-create guidelines for future discussions in your Core Group. You may want to share them with some of your other groups, if that feels appropriate and helpful.

- Select a facilitator to monitor the process.

- Be mindful of the amount of airtime you are taking to make a point.

- Express thoughts succinctly.

- Raise your hand to be recognized by the facilitator to speak next.

- Use a talking piece if this feels appropriate.

- Acknowledge others' contributions to the discussion.

- Language your comments to be fully heard. Offer your perspective, rather than saying "I agree/disagree."

- Let others finish expressing their thoughts fully before responding.

- Set a stop time for each agenda item and if more time is needed, set a new stop time.

- See different perspectives as opportunities to strengthen relationships in the group.

- Engage in deep listening at the feeling level when others speak.

- Keep an intention to dialogue for better understanding rather than to win a debate.

The Process: Drawing Your Co-creative Self

Your Co-creative Self portrait is the template for yourself as a fully actualized co-creator. The more precisely you can characterize your Self, the better able your coach will be to help you bring these characteristics forth in your life.
In this process, you will express and characterize your Co-creative Self through art.

Before beginning, you will need to have art materials such as pastels and crayons and a large sheet of butcher paper available for each person. Make sure there is adequate space for everyone to draw his creation. You may want to play heartful music in the background. The Self-portrait that you begin in this session can be taken home and completed over a period of weeks, if you wish. If you choose, you could repeat this exercise in a few weeks to see how your creation evolves.

- Select a partner. Sit facing one another and practice the Heart Meditation for a few minutes.

- Slowly, maintaining the Heart Meditation, Partner "B" will lie down on the piece of butcher paper. Partner "A" draws his outline with a pen or crayon. Then change places and Partner "B" draws an outline of "A" on another large piece of butcher paper.

- Using the crayons or pastels available, begin to depict your Co-creative Self. This can be a realistic self-portrait or it might be a depiction of your feelings or scenes that are meaningful, appealing and beautiful to you. Allow about 30 minutes for each of you to work in silence on your portrait.

- When everyone has completed this phase of his portrait, place them in the center of your circle and walk around, silently tuning into each other's work.

- When the portraits have been returned to their creators, you can talk, in turn, about your own creation with the group. Share with each other your sense of your own and each other's art work. Be sensitive and mindful of not projecting your personal issues on the creation of others.

- Choose a partner to be your coach. Your coach mirrors back your beauty to help you see yourself, as depicted in your art work. This co-coaching will magnetize you into acting as the Self more and more frequently.

- Take your Self-portrait home and work on it in future weeks. If you wish, cut out pictures and words from magazines that you feel depict your Co-creative Self and incorporate them into this art work. Be creative and have fun with this. Allow your portrait to be unique and playful or sensitive and contemplative.

THE POWER OF ACKNOWLEDGMENT

We live in a culture that often ignores our essential beauty and focuses instead on our shortcomings. As teachers, parents, and employers we are sometimes short on praise and long on criticism, fostering a sense of shame and a lack of self-love. **The following exercises are designed to support you in shifting your identity from local self to Essential Self and experiencing the magnificence of your being.**

In order for an acknowledgment to "hit the mark" and truly touch the soul, it must be authentic and come from the Self. Flattery is transparent and builds the ego rather than supporting a shift in identity. True acknowledgments are powerful, nurturing and often transformational.

You will probably want to experience one acknowledgment process at this meeting and save others to savor at future sessions. Allow plenty of time to enjoy each of them and feel free to repeat them as appropriate.

As you are about to experience, acknowledgment is a powerful tool in dispelling the illusion of separation.

Process: See and Be Seen

Select a partner. Sit facing one another, holding hands if you wish. Close your eyes, relax, breathe, and center your energy in your heart.

When you're ready, open your eyes and look at your partner Allow yourself to be open—to see and to be seen. See the timeless quality, the essence of your partner. Open your heart fully and allow yourself to give and receive love. Maintain soft eye contact for a few minutes, staying present to your experience, as energy flows between you and your partner. Experience your oneness, consciousness meeting consciousness, love meeting love, Self meeting Self, the Beloved seeing the Beloved.

When complete, take a few minutes to acknowledge your partner and to dialogue about your experience.

Process: The Angel Process

Divide your group into triads. The person receiving the acknowledgment sits on a chair facing forward. The two people who are doing the acknowledging sit on each side facing the sides of the person's face. You may wish to close your eyes to block out visual distractions in the room.

With soft heartfelt music playing in the background, center yourselves and feel your hearts opening to one another. Now, the two people lean forward and begin to whisper their acknowledgments into the ears of the third person. Both speak from their hearts at the same time, reflecting to the receiver all the qualities that they admire in this person. Continue until you have said everything that reflects your knowing and experience about the receiver.

Switch roles until each person in the triad has been acknowledged. Finish the exercise with a group hug.

Process: The Wheel of Love

It is desirabe to record this session for all participants. Each person will need a recording device to have his acknowledgments recorded. Each person in your Core Group will have an opportunity to be acknowledged by every other member of the group in this process, so be sure to leave plenty of time for The Wheel of Love.

A pillow, cushion or chair should be placed in the center of the circle. If all are sitting on chairs, a chair of equal height should be used. Play heartful music in the background. Close your eyes and take a few minutes to open your hearts more fully to one another.

When it feels right, one person sits in the center of the circle, facing someone in the outer circle. Your eyes may be open or closed, as you wish.

Those in the outer circle take a minute to focus on the person in the center. Allow your inner voice to answer the question, *"What do I love/admire/respect about this person?"* When someone in the circle is ready, he shares what he is feeling about the person sitting in the center by saying, *"What I love about you is..."* This sharing may last one or two minutes and is authentic and caring. When the person in the center has received the sharing from the first person, he says "thank you" and turns to the next person who begins to speak.

The person in the center continues to turn to each member in the circle until everyone has shared. Then another person sits in the center of the circle and the process begins again. If you are recording the acknowledgments, be sure to put a new tape in the machine for each person. Complete the exercise with a group hug. You may want to listen to your recording on a regular basis to remember who you are and how others see you.

Note: A special closeness is usually experienced as a result of this process. The group might choose to get together socially for a pot-luck or go on a mini-retreat between sessions to reinforce this growing sense of family.

A Gifting Process

You might begin this process during this session and complete it many weeks later or at your final session.

Write the name of each person in your group on a piece of paper. Fold the paper and place it in a bowl. Pass the bowl around and allow each person to select one name. Do not let anyone else in the group know whose name you have drawn. If you get your own name, you may keep it—or put it back in the bowl and select another name.

For the next number of weeks, "track" this person by observing him very closely. Notice all the qualities and behaviors that you appreciate about this person. Think of a small gift that would be appropriate for your special partner. It might be a poem or something from nature, or perhaps a sacred object that you already own. It is not necessary to buy something for this person, although you may do so if you wish.

At your final session, or anytime it feels appropriate to the group, set aside a meeting to present these gifts and acknowledgments.

One person will begin by lovingly describing the qualities of his partner before revealing the identity of that person. Once he says the person's name, the partner joins him in the middle of the circle and receives his gift. Then the person who has been gifted describes the admirable qualities of the person he's been tracking and calls this person into the circle.

The process is repeated, one set of partners at a time, until each person has been called into the middle of the circle, one by one, and has received his gift. Be sure to allow plenty of time for this exercise. Be creative and sincere in your appreciation while enjoying the playful quality of the process.

DAILY PRACTICE
(Exercises to be Done Outside the Group)

Choosing Your Coaches

You probably have excellent coaches in your Core Group, but you might also want to consider who else may be a significant coach for you. If you were preparing for the Olympics, you would not only get coaching from your high school coaches, you would seek out the best coach—the best model—to help you reach your goals.

Your Core Group is analogous to your high school coaches. You know them well and you know they care about you and are committed to your future. But, ask yourself if someone else also might help you to reach your full potential and be the best you can be. Could you use support at work, at home, or on a special project? Ask yourself, *"Who would be the best model for the way I want to be and who might be the best mirror?"* Think about how you want your coach to be. Do you want a coach who is gentle or strong or some of both?

When you have identified candidates, interview them! Tell them how you would like them to coach you. Find out if they are willing to be your coach. If they are, establish a protocol for working with each other. This is not a full-time job, but it does require a commitment. You want them to care enough to tell you when you are "right on" and when you appear to be "off track". Remember that you are free to change coaches.

When you ask someone to be your coach, they may ask you to be theirs also. So, be ready to support the other person in the same way that you want to be supported.

The Mirror of Judgment

You can use "the mirror of judgment" to release judgments about others by dropping an imaginary mirror in front of the person you might be judging. Your coach can also hold that mirror for you when you are judging someone else. This can be very powerful for both you **and** your coach, because together you will determine whether you or your coach or both of you are being judgmental.

Ask your coach to be as objective a reflection for you as possible. Your coach can tell you precisely what you did or said without interpretation.

Forgiving Yourself and Others

In the first part of this exercise, use your journal and write down the name of every person in your life who you feel you may have hurt or offended in any way, specifying what you perceive you might have done to them.

When you see a man of worth, think about how you may emulate him. When you see one who is unworthy, examine your own character.

Confucius

Before you enter the temple, forgive.

Jesus Christ

Now, close your eyes, and evoke the presence of the first person on your list. Explain to him what you did, ask forgiveness and envision him forgiving you. Repeat this with each person on your list.

When you're finished, write on the bottom of the paper: "I forgive myself for all past transgressions and absolve myself of all feelings of guilt and shame." Then burn the piece of paper or tear it into small pieces and throw it away.

In the second part of this exercise, you'll write down the names and incidents of all people who have ever mistreated, angered or betrayed you in any way. Again, close your eyes, relax, and bring them into your awareness one by one. Have a dialogue with each person and express your desire to forgive and move on in your life. Bless them and affirm their happiness.

Write on the bottom of your paper, "I forgive you and release you." Then burn the paper in a small ceremony. You may want to complete the process by listening or dancing to heartful music or taking a walk. *If you prefer, you could do this exercise with other members of your Core Group at one of your meetings.*

Exploring Trust

Using your journal, reflect on different areas of your life where you might be more trusting. (At work? With your family? In regards to your finances?) Be very specific. Record your insights.

For each item that you have recorded, what is the worst thing that could happen if you let go of control in that area of your life?

How could you benefit from being more trusting in each of these areas of your life?

A Different Kind of Clearing

As you shift, change and evolve on the mental, emotional, and spiritual levels, take time to go through your drawers, closets, and garage, clearing out any accumulated items that are no longer needed in your life. Reflect on your relationships. Are any of them wanting to be released at this time? If so, let go of them in a loving, conscious way. This will keep the energy flowing, anchor your new state of awareness, and open the door for more good things to come your way.

Practicing and Sharing These Skills

Share the Co-coaching, Clearing, Mirroring, and Two-Minute Release tips and exercises with family, friends, and co-workers—if that feels appropriate. With their permission, practice these skills during the week and on an on-going basis. Be sure to practice acknowledgment exercises as well. You don't need a special occasion to tell others how magnificent they are and how important they are to you!

Birthdays, holidays, and graduations are wonderful times to acknowledge friends and family, but "non-occasions" can be potent opportunities for allowing others to shift their identity and tap into Self. Take every opportunity to acknowledge the unique gifts, qualities, and talents of everyone with whom you interact, including yourself.

Practice tuning into the Essential Self of everyone you meet and relate to them from Self to Self. As you become adept at these skills, notice how your relationships become deeper and more intimate and how communication becomes communion in your life.

Be Silent

Set aside a time this week to observe silence. Spend time with someone you love in silence, opening the door for communication from soul to soul/ essence to essence.

Honor Yourself

Honor your body with exercise, rest, play, and a nutritious diet. Feed your emotions with beautiful music, graceful movement, and nurturing relationships. Follow your heart and invite Self to take dominion over your personality and become your eternal coach in every situation and circumstance of your life!

Acknowledgments

We offer special thanks and appreciation to those who have contributed to this chapter:

Tim Clauss for co-creating the **Tips for Co-Coaching** and **Tips for Clearing**

Arjuna Nick Ardagh for the **Sharing Witholds** exercise and providing the inspiration for the guided visualization that follows

Ralph Huber and the Hummingbird Ranch Community for providing **The Tips for Creating Conscious Community in Groups**

Susan Campbell for sharing **A Gifting Process**

Rich Treadgold for the **Mirroring** and **Being a Pure Reflection** processes

Circle 4

ACCESSING OUR COLLECTIVE WISDOM

Intuition is God in man, revealing to him the realities of being,
and just as instinct guides the animal,
so would intuition guide man if he would allow it to do so.
This experience comes in the stillness of the Soul,
when the outer voice is quiet, when the tempest of human strife is abated;
it is a quickening of the inner man to an eternal reality.

Ernest Holmes

Imagination is more important than knowledge.

Albert Einstein

~ ~

At the very heart of the Co-Creative Self resides an intuitive,
loving and comprehensive intelligence. We hear it as our inner voice.
It comes forth in a circle of trust and safety and feels light and all knowing.
It hovers just beneath the surface of our waking consciousness, awaiting an environment
of resonance and love to express itself in the world.

We learn now to speak as this inner voice,
amplifying and giving it substance through the spoken word.
Through speaking directly as our inner voices, the word becomes flesh.
The guidance for our actions is given. The design is revealed.
The deeper plan for our lives unfolds.

We can no longer turn to authorities, seers, priests or oracles for answers.
The oracle is within us. We tap into the universal wisdom which is our birthright.
With practice, it becomes our natural language.

Every cell in our physical body has within its genetic code the plan for
the whole body as well as its specific function within the body.
So we humans may have within our "genius code" the plan for the evolution of the whole
planetary body as well as our specific function or purpose within it.

Our intuitive flashes, hunches, and unitive experiences are moments of expanded reality
when we gain access to what we already know but tend to block out through the narrow
spectrum of daily waking consciousness.

When we join together in resonance with other humans,
we are forming a multi-human cell, whose nucleus brings forth and expands
the unique function of each of us. Through the increased resonance
and requisite variety of a multi-celled organism rather than a single cell,
we gain greater access to universal intelligence.

This intelligence comes forth as our inner voices,
offering inspired insights which can guide our actions.
Brilliant ideas begin to flow effortlessly. Deep insights suddenly explain
unrelated experiences. Hidden truths are magically revealed.
A critical mass of people in resonance
would know the program for planetary evolution
and the plan for birthing a co-creative society!

~ ~

Circle 4

ACCESSING OUR COLLECTIVE WISDOM

Listen to the stillness until it speaks to you.
Look into the darkness until you see the Light.
Lay down your life until you are lifted to higher ground.

Richard Walters

In quietness are all things answered and is every problem quietly resolved.

A Course in Miracles

In the silence is the field of all possibility.

Deepak Chopra

When two or more are gathered in love, there is bonding and the emergence of a resonant field of co-creation. We recognize other as Self. Where there is allowance, trust and surrender to a higher order, a spontaneous unfoldment occurs that is naturally aligned with creation. Attuning to our inner wisdom and following the guidance of the heart, we experience the dynamics of telepathy, synergy and synchronicity. It is critical that we call upon this collective alignment with Spirit to lead us forward during this historic era of planetary transformation.

In every moment a source of unlimited wisdom and inspiration is available to each of us. This source has been called intuitive knowing, our inner voice, clear vision, and "the still small voice of God." It is not bound by time or space. We access it by quieting the chatter of our mind and going within to the "place of stillness." Although this source is always available, many of us do not listen because we are distracted by the information from our senses, our thinking mind, or our egos. Our high stress lives block our intuitive thinking process. In order to creatively respond to the problems that besiege us, we must slow down, relax, and allow our inner wisdom to emerge.

There is a growing sense of freedom and stabilization in the emerging paradigm as we trust and act upon our inner knowing. In order to birth a co-creative culture, we are each called upon to integrate the mind and the heart, the rational and the intuitive, and the masculine and feminine aspects of our selves. Following the ancient truth, "know thyself", we have the potential to unleash our creative genius. The guidelines for evolution are within us. To meet the enormity of the challenges that confront us in this time of planetary crisis, we must invite the well spring of brilliance that lies in our souls to be fully expressed.

"You cannot solve a problem with the same thinking that created it." The forward thinking of Albert Einstein reflects the critical need to evolve to a higher state of consciousness. Our very survival may depend upon our ability to make a transformational leap out of the linear model. Logic will not solve most dilemmas. Reliance on outside authority has undermined our expression as unique creative divine beings. It is now time to direct our attention to our inner authority and to act as though our lives depended upon it. This may, indeed, be true.

Resonant Core Groups provide an environment of safety, trust and love. Surrounded by supportive and caring friends, our inner knowing is invited into full expression. As we open, relax, and listen deeply, the wisdom of our heart is easily accessed. It is the natural expression of our true, whole and integrated selves. Sharing inspired insights with one another stabilizes our confidence in our inner knowing. Over time, there is no experience of separation between mind and heart, inner coach and analytical mind. Mindless chatter ceases to dominate our awareness. Complex issues are resolved effortlessly. Speaking soul to soul, our communications are rich and fulfilling. We are collectively lifted to a higher frequency and stabilized as our Essential Selves.

In the past, we had to retire to mountain tops or hidden sanctuaries to experience a mystical state of being. Now we are making "ordinary" what was once "extraordinary." We can no longer delegate awakening to a few saints or mystics. The time is upon us to consciously evolve a future of unlimited possibilities. As we stand on the threshold of the unknown may we collectively make the choice to trust the heart, honor the mind and allow ourselves to be guided on our evolutionary journey home.

Suggested Process Sequence

- Open your session with the Visualization that follows—or create your own attunement process.

- Remember to check-in. All members of the group take 1-3 minutes to say how you are feeling and report on any insights or experiences you may have had since the last meeting.

- Read The Co-Creator's Agreements aloud.

- Read the Introduction to the Circle. Take a moment in silence to reflect on this. Then share your inspired insights with the group.

- Select one or more of the Experiential Exercises that follow.

- Take a break! Move around and stretch.

- Select who will fill the key roles at your next meeting.

- Create a closing that will maintain your heart connection.

EXPERIENTIAL EXERCISES

GUIDED VISUALIZATION: Meeting Your Teacher

The facilitator slowly reads this aloud, remembering to pause between phrases. You may want to play soft music in the background.

Make yourself as comfortable as possible. . . To relax your body, tighten and release one part of your body at a time, beginning with your feet and ending with your face.

(The facilitator may choose to guide the group through each body part separately. . . tightening and releasing.)

(Pause)

Feel a sense of lightness, comfort, and general relaxation. . . Take a moment to follow your breath, noticing if there are any emotions. . . If there are any feelings, note them and allow them to be present.

(Pause)

In your imagination, go to a beautiful place in nature—a place where it is private and safe, and totally protected—a place of great beauty.

(Pause)

Before you, you notice a clearly defined path. . . You easily find your way along the path, moving toward the sunshine and a meadow ahead.

You notice that you are surrounded by trees, grass, and wildflowers. . . As you move into the meadow, feel the warm sunshine upon you. . . Allow yourself to feel a sense of gratitude for being in such a wonderful place.

(Pause)

Ahead of you, you notice a crystal clear, beautiful lake. . . You feel excited, because, as you make your way to the lake, you know that your teacher or guide is waiting there for you.

(Pause)

As you come to the edge of the lake, you find the perfect place to sit and be comfortable.

(Pause)

Once you are seated, you ask your teacher or guide to come to you. Your teacher may take the form of someone you know—or a historical or mythological figure, or perhaps the form of an animal, or a more etheric energy body.

You sense who your perfect teacher is, and when you invite that guide or teacher to join you, he or she is with you. . . Take a moment to greet one another in an appropriate way.

(Pause for 1 - 2 minutes)

Whenever you are ready, allow whatever question you have to come forth, knowing that your teacher is all wise, can be totally trusted, and loves you unconditionally.

Receive whatever answer is being presented to you.

(Pause for 1 - 2 minutes)

Continue to ask any questions that are necessary so that you will have the clarity you want. Your guide is here to support you totally. And, when you ask, you will receive.

If at any time you feel you are not receiving an answer, be attentive over the next few days. Answers often come from an unexpected source and sometimes when you least expect them.

(Pause)

Continue to be with your teacher for as long as you choose, asking as many questions as are on your mind.

(Pause for 1 - 2 minutes)

Any time you choose to return and be with your guide, you will be able to do so, by returning to the same beautiful spot and asking this being to come to you.

(Pause)

When you are complete, thank your guide in a way that is appropriate for both of you. . . Say goodbye and once again, make your way through the meadow, back to the path, and back to the room where you are now. (You know that this teacher is your Essential Self and that all answers are to be found within.)

Feel the chair or the cushion beneath you. . . Move your body a bit. . . Take whatever time you need to return to the room and open your eyes.

Take time to write a few notes in your journal or in the following space.

_____

_____

_____

_____

_____

_____

Check-In

As you check-in with one another, share any insights which you received during the visualization. Did any feelings arise from reading the context for this Circle? Can you imagine a world where everyone followed the guidance of his heart rather than childhood conditioning or the agreement field of the collective?

INNER VOICE COMMUNICATION

Group Discussion

Discuss the ways that you check into your inner guidance. How do you keep the mental body in check and tune into your inner knowing? How does your ego mimic inner knowing to serve its own ends? Think about examples of how the ego might express itself. How do you know when the analytical mind is speaking? What are the different ways in which you receive information? For some it may be emotions, others may hear messages, while those who are kinesthetic may experience body sensations.

Ponder the difference between discernment and judgment. Discernment comes from an expanded awareness; it is helpful, loving, and promotes evolution. Think of the masters you know or know of who always speak and act from their inner knowing. How have they expressed discernment? How did it differ from judgment? What are the characteristics of their speaking?

Process: Dialoguing in Pairs

A simple way to begin communicating inspired insights is to work with a partner with whom you are comfortable. To prepare for this activity, choose a quiet, comfortable, and private space where you can sit facing one another. One of you will pose a question. The other will intuitively respond from a place of deep knowing. Do not edit your responses or judge them. Just allow them to flow naturally. You will be surprised by the quality of the responses that flow when you listen with your heart.

Have a brief conversation to determine what question(s) you would like to contemplate. For the initial exercise, it may be easier to agree on one or two questions that are meaningful to both of you. You might play soft music in the background or surround yourself with the sounds of nature. Decide who will go first in asking the question(s) and then proceed as a dialogue. First one partner will ask the question and the other will respond. Keep asking the question until you have received all of the insights from your partner. Then, switch roles.

Both partners close your eyes and breathe deeply, feeling a sense of expansion with each breath. You might want to use the Heart Meditation to center yourselves. When each of you feels relaxed and balanced, you may signal the other by saying, "I am ready." Begin the questioning and answering dialogue and continue until you both feel complete. You may want to record your answers or insights in your journal or in this Handbook.

_____
_____
_____
_____
_____

Process: Attuning To Your Body

Begin by playing music that invokes slow quiet movement. The purpose of this exercise is to attune more deeply to your body. The facilitator should read through the directions for this exercise before beginning.

Stand up in the room, giving yourself enough space to move around. The facilitator will guide you through your body, just as you have done in some of the visualizations. Begin with the feet and slowly move up through the legs, hips, abdomen, chest, arms, shoulders, neck and head. Guide the group to move some body parts in isolation from each other and then in concert with each other (hands and feet together, or shoulders and hips, etc.)

When listening to another person, don't just listen with your mind, listen with your whole body. Feel the energy field of your inner body as you listen. That takes attention away from thinking and creates a still space that enables you to truly listen without the mind interfering. You are giving the other person space—space to be. It is the most precious gift you can give.

Eckhart Tolle

After each person is in touch with all parts of his body, the facilitator will invite each person to move intuitively to the music, moving slowly enough so that each movement arises spontaneously. . . as the body wants to move, not as the mind plans the movement.

The facilitator then asks the group members to close their eyes and to move in a way that represents their current feeling state. In this exercise, the feeling state and body expression become one.

At the end of the exercise, the facilitator instructs the group to lie down and fully relax their bodies. *"Allow yourself to be, releasing all thoughts and feelings as best you are able."*

After a few minutes, share your experience in the larger circle.

Process: Group Dialogue of Inspired Insights

The purpose of this practice is to allow you to experience deep inner listening and to provide practice in communicating inspired insights with others. This is a very effective practice to use when clarity is sought by an individual or a group. A question is posed and then the individual or group takes the question into meditation to access their collective wisdom. Resting in stillness you quietly wait for a response. When you receive an insight, you share it gently out loud with the group. Speak only if and when you feel inspired. Do not censor or judge your thoughts. Relax and let the insights flow. One person's speaking tends to inspire another's and activates a co-creative intelligence. Some people hear actual words, some see visual images, and others may have an intuitive feeling about the question. When practiced through time, individuals become aligned with each other and this practice can become the primary means of decision making. **This is a foundational process for building a co-creative culture.**

For the purpose of this exercise, you might choose a question such as:

"What is our purpose together?"
"What shall we do about _____?"   (a particular situation)
"What is our next step as a group?"

If you want to focus on a transpersonal issue, you might ask a question such as: *"What can be done to overcome the feeling of separation between Arabs and Jews in the Middle East or between Protestants and Catholics in northern Ireland?"*

Have a brief discussion to co-create the question that will be addressed.

Next, the facilitator reads the following visualization:

Close your eyes. Take some deep breaths and allow any thoughts to drift away. . .

(Pause)

Visualize a glowing light in your heart, radiating as your Essential Self . . . See this light expanding from your heart to your whole being . . . See this same light in each member of the Core Group . . . See the expansion of light in the other people present.

(Pause)

Slowly move the light glowing in your whole being, connecting to the light of the others in the circle . . . See your light merge with that of all the others . . . Feel yourselves as members of one body within a glowing sphere of light.

Now, the facilitator asks the question which the group has selected and then reads the following:

Let the question remain with you as you continue to expand. . . Release any thoughts about the answer to the question. . . Allow the answer to reveal itself.

When an insight comes, speak as your inner voice. . . Trust what arises. . . Offer it out loud to the circle.

Allow as much time for speaking as the group needs. You may need ten minutes or more initially.

When there is a long period of silence after many have spoken and the process feels complete, the facilitator says:

When you are ready, return to this time and place and gently open your eyes.

You may wish to record insights in your journals or in this Handbook. Then share your feelings and experiences with the group.

_____
_____
_____
_____

Note: The first few times you do this practice, you may find it easier to talk afterwards **about** what you heard, rather than speaking as you heard your inner voice. As you practice communicating your inspired insights aloud, it will become easier to participate directly in the inner voice dialogue.

This might be a good time to take a break or conclude your meeting.

DIFFERENTIATING BETWEEN THE MIND AND THE INNER COACH

You can fine tune your ability to expand beyond your analytical mind and allow pure insight to emerge. Sometimes the mind gets in the way of expressing inner knowing and may mimic it. The mind may believe in limitation and separation and may resist the expansion that means the death of its limiting perceptions. It is fearful, critical, and judgmental. With practice, you can learn the difference between telling "your story" and communicating your insights in the present moment. Observe your daily life and notice when you are in your analytical mind and when your inner coach is speaking.

Discussion

Refer to the following chart to clarify the differences between the mind and the voice of the Self, the Inner Coach. Observe what arises in your thoughts and emotions. Notice if you can hold the analytical mind and inner coach in the same degree of love and acceptance.

There is a tendency as we shift from self-centered to whole-centered consciousness to have judgment toward our analytical mind. This may also manifest as judgment toward others. Discuss how you can support each other to embrace and draw forth both the intuitive and logical aspects of your mind so they are able to work in concert with one another.

Characteristics of
The Voice of Your Inner Coach and The Analytical Mind

The Inner Coach	The Analytical Mind
Intuitive and sensing	Rational and mental
Present	Past/future
Uniting, common purpose	Separating, self-interest
Certainty and peace	Confusion and conflict
Ease and flow	Struggle and effort
Expansive and aware	Tense and self-conscious
Alive and energizing	Tired and draining
Acceptance and surrender	Judgment and resistance
Trust and spontaneity	Fear and hesitation
Creative possibilities	Restrictions and limitations
Patience and divine order	Urgency and concern
Love and presence	Approval and survival
Quiet, calm, gentle voice	Chattering conversational voice

Process

Play a game similar to charades where you enact these different qualities from the perspective of the Inner Coach and the Analytical Mind. There are many creative variations of role playing that are both fun and insightful.

Variation 1: Divide into two groups with one person acting as a facilitator. The facilitator calls out a situation and each group responds from their perspective. For example, the facilitator describes a scenario involving buying a house. Each group acts out buying a house expressing the characteristics of the Inner Coach/Self or Analytical Mind. Or you could enact a difficult interaction in a marriage, or dealing with a rebellious child, or making a financial decision as a Core Group. The possibilities are endless! Exaggerate the characteristics so the behavior is clearly experienced. Laughing at ourselves and the dysfunctionality that can arise out of the mind, is both healthy and revealing.

Variation 2: Instead of dividing into two groups, have two individuals step forward and enact how they would respond to a situation (like those described above) if resting as the Inner Coach/ Self, or contracted in the limited mind. Take turns so that everyone plays both parts. (Inner Coach and Mind).

Variation 3: Any way you might invent. Be creative and enjoy.

DAILY PRACTICE
Exercises to be Done Outside the Group

The natural way of being for the co-creator is to make the communication of inspired insights a normal part of daily interactions so that they can be used effectively in the world. Whenever possible, encourage people to check their inner guidance. You can share your knowledge of ways to get centered even in the most dissonant situation. Often, just telling people to stop, be quiet for a few minutes with their eyes closed, and do some deep breathing will help people to quiet their minds enough so that new insights can come through. When you have the opportunity, you can give people permission to SLOW DOWN when making decisions and encourage them to get in touch with their inner coach.

Recording Your Inner Voice Communication

Journaling

The power for each of us comes through our own inspired insights as we experience the process. No one can give them to us or do it for us. What others can do is motivate us and "touch" our soul-knowing.

For me, the most powerful personal practice has been consistent journaling—the act of writing down in the meditative state the inner promptings. It is a sort of translation of a soul-energy knowing into language. Every message is personal but is often appropriate to share with others because soul-energy knowing is universal in nature.

Bob McLellan

As the inner voice becomes experienced expressing images, ideas, words, or feelings, you might record these in writing in your journal. Do not judge or edit your thoughts. Let them be. They may surprise you! They are arising from the source of your being, moving you forward in the direction of your deepest choice. Be sensitive throughout the day to your inspired insights. They often appear and disappear fleetingly as do dreams. Capture them in writing.

Audio Recording

Audio recording is a very beneficial way to capture your inspired insights. Your entire mind "sits up and takes notice" when it hears your own voice speaking as the inner voice. Listening to your inner voice seems to activate deep cellular memories, reminding us of that part of our mind that we may have forgotten as the intellect developed. We gain access to inspired insights and deeper wisdom from the vast intelligence of which we are all a part. The rational, critical intellect quiets down and listens, enchanted by the wisdom within. This wisdom is not irrational; it seems super-rational, more intelligent than the intellect alone. The intellect learns to honor this deep wisdom, using its powers to execute, rather than trying to lead by "figuring-it-out".

In a quiet, private place—perhaps as you are lying down to go to sleep—listen to your recorded insights. If you are able to do so, play soft music while listening to your words. Baroque music with a largo tempo is especially helpful for relaxing your mind and enabling your inspired insights to reconnect deeply with you. Listen for the timbre of the inner voice. It is resonant, rich, and relaxing.

An insightful practice to assist you in discerning between the mind/ego and the Self is to do a writing exercise. You begin by speaking as the mind about the Self and the relationship between the two. Then you switch perspectives and write from the Self about your relationship with the mind. Observe without judgment what is revealed. Be sure to share your insights with your Core Group at your next meeting.

Acknowledgments

Special thanks to Marion Culhane for creating the visualization, **Meeting Your Teacher.**

Circle 5

HONORING THE SACRED:
CEREMONY, RITUAL AND CELEBRATION

Through rituals we open up to Divine Grace.
Consequently rituals are a powerful means of communicating with
and creating alliance with the Divine in all creation.

Tiziana de Rovere

When your life is filled with the desire to see the holiness in everyday life,
something magical happens: ordinary life becomes extraordinary,
and the very process of life begins to nourish your soul!

Rabbi Harold Kushner

Ritual and ceremony empower our deepest passions.
They open us to a pattern that serves evolutionary processes
and connects us to our feminine nature.
Rites of Passage help us meet the unknown and move
from one stage of life to the next.

Music, silence, symbol, and myth
are used to bring forth sacred time and space
to anchor a new level of consciousness,
and to evoke archetypal energies.

When we bring our aspirations to life through symbolic expression,
we evoke the power of creation.
This is a realm for artistry, imagination, and genius.

Through ceremony and ritual, we can experience
ecstasy and union with the Divine.
We live our lives as an act of worship and
remember who we are!

Celebration is our offering of gratitude
for all that we joyfully receive!

~ ~

Circle 5

HONORING THE SACRED: CEREMONY, RITUAL AND CELEBRATION

Ritual is one of the symbolic languages by which we are able to instruct and communicate with the inner realms or magical reality...a link is formed with the collective unconscious, the world, or perhaps universal consciousness.

Marian Green

Life must be lived as play, playing certain games, singing and dancing.

Plato

A deep hunger for meaningful ritual and ceremony pervades our society today. Many live in the experience of disconnection from the holiness of Earth and the deep feminine, that which embraces, supports, nurtures and heals. The rituals from the traditions that we grew up with often do not feed our souls and enrich our lives. We feel the loss of not having relevant rites of passage to mark the transitional points in our lives.

This Circle invites us to access our intuition and imagination to co-create meaningful rituals, ceremonies, rites of passage and celebrations. We draw upon the richness of our past and the wisdom of our ancestors to weave with the knowing of our heart. Honoring the sacred, we deepen our sense of interconnectedness.

The essence of the Circles of Co-creation is alignment in relationships—with each other, with nature, and with the indwelling Spirit. Ceremonies and rituals honor all life as a sacrament, as we once again bring meaning to simple tasks. From our daily activities such as eating, gardening and parenting—to the precious moments of attunement to the Earth, we discover the good, the miraculous, the holiness in all our relations. We join as community and rejoice as a collective voice.

Honoring the cycles of the moon and the turn of the seasons brings us into deeper alignment with the natural order. Ceremonies kindle a sense of remembrance of ancient times, connecting us to our roots. We are drawn into the experience of the feminine aspect of our being. An attitude of gratitude transforms each experience into a blessing. Our interconnectedness with all life is affirmed and celebrated.

Note: Unlike many of the other Circles in this Handbook, the ceremonies and celebrations described in this Circle are meant to be used as the occasion arises and not as a

series of exercises to be experienced one after the other. They can also be modified to suit other occasions.

CHARACTERISTICS OF SACRED CEREMONIES

Sacredness: In rituals, we are making life sacred. To do this, we bring our full attention and sense of the sacred to the ritual. If rituals lose their sacred quality, they become routine and lose their significance.

Symbology: Words, movement, and physical symbols are transpersonal and archetypal. The ordinary becomes heightened and is rendered potent and meaningful.

CREATING SACRED SPACE

It is important to give attention to the physical environment where a ceremony will occur. A beautiful and harmonious space that honors each of the senses will serve to set the environment apart from the ordinary. Candles, flowers, aromatherapy, incense, special lighting, music, bells, gongs, and items of beauty all enhance the experience of sacredness. Awareness of the temperature of the environment, as well as avoidance of possible distractions, are important elements contributing—or taking away from—the effectiveness of a ceremony. Unplug the phone and ask family members to honor your privacy.

On occasion it may be appropriate to create an altar which commemorates a specific situation, individual or time of year. This can be built by the one who is hosting the gathering or co-created by your group. You might ask each person to bring an item that is relevant to the theme to contribute to the altar. This could include a treasure found in nature, a statue, a ceremonial object, picture, or perhaps an item that symbolizes your present feeling nature.

The physical location of a sacred space may be indoors or outside. Many people find that ceremony enacted outside in a grove of trees, a garden, or by a body of water, carries special meaning because it enhances our connection to nature. Earth altars, medicine wheels, labyrinths, and specially designed gardens can be created outside for use over an extended period of time.

ELEMENTS OF A CEREMONY

For a ceremony to be authentic and engaging, it is important to trust your inner knowing and guidance. The various processes may stir up emotional responses. Attune to those participating and be sensitive to their needs. For many people, participation in ceremony and ritual brings them into unknown territory. Be allowing and gracious, creating a welcoming comfortable feeling for all who are involved.

In facilitating ceremony, you are dealing with alchemy and magic. It is like being a great cook. Look at the recipe, use your imagination, and then let it unfold. The amount of planning necessary depends somewhat on the complexity of the ceremony (for example, an elaborate wedding compared to a new moon ceremony). It is wise to think through details, estimate the length of time for each aspect of the ceremony and consider individuals needs for comfort, both physical and emotional.

The following elements of a ceremony are given as suggestions. Any or all of these processes may be appropriate at any given time. Remember to be flexible and attuned to the natural unfoldment of the moment. Most importantly, create a safe, sacred space and bring focus, openness and presence to the ceremony.

1.   Purification Rites

Purification rites are usually included at the beginning of a ceremony as people are arriving. They provide for a transition between the world of the ordinary and the sacred. Water, herbs, incense, fire, light and sound assist us in harmonizing with the Divine.

In the Native American tradition the burning of sage and sweet grass is used to cleanse the space and provide an opportunity for those present to release thoughts and emotions which do not serve them. Cleansing with water (simple washing of hands with scented water) or washing one another (hands or feet) is a sensitive way of honoring one another. Blessings may also be shared by anointing one another with oil.

2.   Invocation

What do you wish to invoke into your presence? What beings do you call upon for guidance and blessings? How can the other dimensions assist you in that which you wish to bring into manifestation? In the ceremonies of many indigenous people, the guardians of the directions, the spirit of the elements, and the ancestors are invoked at the beginning of any sacred activity. A circle is cast and sacred space is consecrated.

Other individuals might feel a connection with specific masters, saints, prophets, holy beings, goddesses, spiritual and religious teachers and may wish to invoke their presence by saying their names. There is a process referred to as "coning" where you invite in beings from the invisible realm to work in co-creation with you on any earthly activity. For example, you might call upon Athena to assist you in writing a book or the spirit of the Earth to keep you attuned to the wisdom of nature.

3.   Attunement

The process of attuning brings you into alignment with each another, grounds you in the present moment, and allows for full engagement in the circle. Attunement can take the form of silence, chanting, conscious movement, guided visualization or focused meditation.

The purpose of an attunement is to support group members to release tension, be present as the Essential Self, still the mind, and align in resonance with the others in your circle and with nature. The attunement may be brought to completion with a simple statement, a chant, or the quiet ringing of a bell.

4.   Stating Your Intention

What is the intention for the gathering? To whom do you dedicate this ceremony? To focus your attention with clarity of purpose will magnetize the intended result. When you collectively are aligned with the intention of a ceremony, there is a showering of support from the invisible realms. Stating a clear intention is akin to shooting an arrow into the sky. Once released, the results are surrendered and the universe handles the details.

---

*When we pray in the correct fashion, we are not
asking God to do something.
God is inspiring us to act in his place to enact
his will on the Earth.
As divine emissaries, we create
the physical domain.
Every thought, every expectation—all of what
we visualize happening in the future—is a
Prayer, and tends to create that very future.
But no thought or desire or fear
Is as strong as a vision that is in
alignment with the divine.*

James Redfield

---

5. Prayer or Blessing

We have the opportunity to extend blessings in every aspect of daily life, be it driving the car, smelling a flower, standing in line at the bank, paying the grocery clerk, dealing with a business partner or bathing our children. Whenever we hold the consciousness of extending a blessing we are opening to receive a blessing as well.

When we pray we speak to God; meditation is God speaking to us. Prayer connects us with the unified field, and as we gather and focus our hearts together in prayer, we have the potential to shift the collective consciousness.

6.   Song, Dance, Theater

The expressive arts have always been at the heart of any ritual. They provide an effective way to bond the group, release tension, unlock creative energies and open individuals to their inner muse. Participation in these activities draws forth untapped potential. Exploration of the mythic realm can set a context to better understand your personal story. Song, dance and theater always enliven any ceremony and create active engagement for those present. Music also plays an important role in creating the atmosphere for any ceremony. Take time to carefully select music to accompany various aspects of the ritual or celebration.

7.   Closing

Just as you open any ceremony with an invocation and attunement, it is important to consciously close the circle. This can be a brief prayer or benediction that releases the circle and an expression of gratitude for what has been shared. You might want to hold hands and affirm your connection. The closing reflects the intimacy of your time together.

EXPERIENTIAL EXERCISES

GUIDED VISUALIZATION

The following guided meditation incorporates invocation, attunement, and blessings into one process. As with any suggested process, please feel free to improvise. This exercise is best done in a circle holding hands.

The facilitator slowly reads this aloud, remembering to pause between phrases. You may want to play soft beautiful music in the background.

The facilitator informs the group that there will be an opportunity during the process for all those present to invoke into the circle any being or energetic that is benevolent and with whom they feel a specific connection. Spiritual teachers, archetypes, guides or aspects of nature, when consciously acknowledged, are empowered into the process of co-creation. Examples include: Christ, Buddha, a master, saint or prophet, a mythological goddess, invisible kingdoms and so on. Encourage individuals to speak freely into the circle.

Please hold hands and close your eyes. . . Become aware of your breath gently moving in and out. . . With each exhalation allow the tension in your body to be released, as though it were flowing out from you and down a river into a great sea.

(Pause)

As you breathe in, experience the life giving force—that which sustains you, the breath of life that comes as a gift to you in each moment.

(Pause)

Breathing in and breathing out. . . Being filled and letting go.

(Pause)

Feel your feet firmly planted on the Earth. . . As you breathe in, feel the energy rising up from the core. . . Draw the fire from the core of the Earth right up into your heart and allow it to move through your body.

(Pause)

With each breath, connect with the sacred web of creation. . . the exquisite diversity of species and kingdoms. . . mineral, plant, animal, birds and those that swim in the sea, the myriad forms of life all feeding off one another, interconnected and interdependent. Experience yourself as integral to this incredible dance of life.

(Pause)

And now extend your consciousness out into space. . . Open with each breath to the vastness of sky. . . beyond the beyond. . . to the sun, moon, stars, planets. . . expanding beyond our universe. . . with each breath relaxing, letting go, opening, expanding.

(Pause)

And now from this experience of connection with all that is, invoke the presence of beings with which you feel most connected. Softly speak their names into the circle.

(Pause and allow enough time for the invocation so that each person has an opportunity to speak.)

Now gently bring your attention back to the circle. . . Feel the hand on either side of you. Acknowledge the billions of years of evolution that has shaped that hand. . . Going into the cells of the body, experience the fluidity of creation. . . as vibration. . . constantly changing, ever emerging.

(Pause)

Tune into the circle. . . Feel gratitude for all that has brought each of us to this moment in time . . . the continuity and perfection of our life experience, the grace that allows us to be together.

(Pause)

Expand from this circle to family and friends around the world. . . Extend blessings and invite them into your heart. . . Feel your connection with beings everywhere. . . Experience the incredible web of light that invisibly surrounds the planet, uniting us as one family. . . Our circle is part of the intricate web of dedicated souls who are consciously engaged in the evolutionary dance.

(Pause)

Feel the blessing of being alive at this auspicious time of transformation and rebirth. . .

When you are ready slowly open your eyes. . . Look into the eyes of each person in the circle. Silently affirm your love and connection.

SAMPLES OF CEREMONIES

Many practices of the Core Group—blessings, attunements, council, songs—are aspects of ritual and ceremony that serve to deepen our connection with one another and to the divinity that we are. Holding a ceremonial space can enhance many situations.

The effectiveness of the Core Group lies in its ability to be sensitive to the needs of the moment and to create a safe, nurturing environment. As situations spontaneously arise, the agenda for a meeting may need to be altered to address a specific individual or group need.

Without ritualization, life can easily become a series of seemingly disjointed events, unrelated to any larger context. We need to enact rituals that highlight our initiations and transitions, honoring the changes, letting us know what is required at each stage, and how to develop in relationship to those requirements.

Carole Kammen and Jodi Gold

There was a Core Group in Boulder, Colorado that had been meeting for about six months. The group was drawn together by resonance, but did not have a particular agenda or purpose to achieve. What spontaneously arose during this short period of time included: a blessing way for a new baby; a ceremony for a departed family member; enacting the "Blue Bowl Ceremony"; celebration of the winter solstice; a house blessing; a healing ritual; co-creating several entrepreneurial ventures; a differentiation ceremony for a couple and deep personal sharings.

It is important to honor the diverse traditions and religious and spiritual paths within your Core Group. Create an environment where everyone feels safe and free to express. Invite each person to share what is sacred to him. There is infinite possibility to what can be co-created within your group as you deepen with one another and honor the sacredness of life.

Listed below are suggestions to spark your imagination.

Honoring the Cycles of Nature

Deep attunement to the cycles of nature, the new and full moon, equinoxes and solstices, planetary alignments, lunar and solar eclipses, are foundational to any tribal culture. We have much to learn from our indigenous brothers and sisters who are living close to the Earth and are guided by the wisdom inherent in nature.

There is a wide diversity of key ceremonial times during the year. Times of potent astrological configurations invite you to align with celestial energies and open to the beneficial aspects of unseen forces. These can be opportunities for spiritual expansion and deeper connection to the Self.

Discuss in your Core Group how you would like to relate to the various cusp points listed below as well as other auspicious times in the year ahead. You may wish to reference an astrological calendar or research planetary alignments that are forthcoming. Do any of these times feel important to you? How would you like to honor the cycles of nature? As you look into the months ahead, do you feel inspired to gather at these times and create ceremony together?

Listed below are a sampling of various cusp points and relevant themes for you to consider.

New moon

The focus of the new moon is on the feminine aspect of our nature. It is an opportune time to plant the seeds of new ideas, initiate a project, or open for inspiration and guidance. The healing energy of the new moon makes it an especially good time for women to gather and share deeply with one another.

Full moon

The full moon represents the energy of fruition and completion. Each moon cycle has a unique energetic depending upon the astrological configurations. Take the time to celebrate accomplishments and affirm intentions with drumming, songs, and dance.

Equinox and Solstices

The equinoxes and solstices usher in a new season. They beacon us to give thanks for the blessings that have come before and envision what we want to manifest as we enter a new cycle.

For the **Spring Equinox** the focus is on what is bursting forth with new life. There is a feeling of expectancy, inviting the planting of seeds and the initiation of new projects. What has been gestating through the winter is ready to be born.

The **Summer Solstice** is a time to celebrate as community and express gratitude for the fullness of life. Music, song and dance enliven a Solstice celebration, while thoughtful prayer honors our connection to all of creation.

The **Autumn Equinox** celebrates the abundance of the summer's harvest and invites us to journey within as the weather shifts and the light begins to fade. As the leaves fall from the trees, we may also reflect on what aspects of the personality are ready to shift and fall away. What no longer serves our evolutionary journey?

The **Winter Solstice** is the darkest time of the year and commemorates the shortest day. It coincides with all major traditions as a time of renewed hope and faith when light emerges from the darkness. We experience the potency of the great mystery and are drawn to stillness. It is a time to build energy at the core of our being and to affirm the divinity that lies within.

Ceremony of Commitment

After your Core Group has met for several weeks it is beneficial to anchor each person's commitment through ritual. This type of ceremony can also be utilized when starting any new endeavor, be it a project, an entrepreneurial venture or creating a one-time event. You may want to do it in conjunction with the Ceremony of Manifestation.

As described in Section 2, before making a commitment, members of the Core Group will want to engage in a courtship period, an exploration of relationship like the traditional engagement before marriage. This honors the sacred nature of your relationship with one another and gives all members of your Co-creative Core a period of time to bond deeply with one another.

Secure your commitments to yourself, to your work, or to the world. In your Core Group, create a "Rings of Fire" ceremony. Play "Chariots of Fire" or other inspiring music in the background. Be witnesses for each other as you each light a candle from a central flame and state your commitment. When fire is used in ceremonies, the flame continues to "burn" within you after the event. In future meetings you may wish to have a single candle burning, reminding the group of the bond that has been established as well as the Spirit that lives in your midst.

Ceremony of Manifestation

Initiate each new co-creative project with a ceremony to anchor your connection to the success of the project. The ceremony may be more elaborate at the beginning of the project. Then an abbreviated version may be repeated for about ten minutes at the beginning of each day or work session. Rotate the role of the facilitator. Don't forget to plan periodic progress ceremonies and honor the means as well as the end. The following is an example of a project manifestation ceremony:

Gather in a sacred circle. Place an object representing your completed project in the center of your circle. Read your mission or vision statement aloud. Then close your eyes and breathe deeply until relaxed. Envision your project complete and successful. Speak aloud what you see, hear, smell, and feel. When silence indicates that all who want to speak have done so, the facilitator asks everyone to gently open his eyes, make eye contact with one another and experience the interconnectedness of the group.

Take a few minutes to communicate anything about the project that is crucial for everyone present to hear. Ask for any support you may need to accomplish your tasks. And then begin!

Ceremony of Empowerment

Use this ceremony when a member of your Core Group has stepped forward to focalize an event or an activity on behalf of the team. This might be a community event, such as Earth Day, a special project, or an on-going task. This person needs your collective support, encouragement, and vote of confidence. The Ceremony of Empowerment acknowledges that the entire Core Group trusts, respects, and aligns behind this person and the project. You could also use this ceremony when a member of the Core has taken on a leadership role at work or as part of a community or church organization and requests the support of his Co-creative Core to move into this new role.

Begin this ceremony by creating sacred space: move all personal belongings to another room, dim the lights, and light a few candles. Ask this leader to be seated in the middle of your group. Everyone else takes his place in the circle. Take a few minutes to attune and build the resonant field of love. You may want to hold your hands up, facing the person in the middle of the circle, to send love and energy his way.

The first person who feels guided to speak acknowledges the leader, reminds him of his strengths, and affirms that he is there to fully support this person. As each person gives his blessing, the leader listens and takes in their words of encouragement.

You may want to complete this ceremony with a group hug and a celebration!

Mistake Ritual

We have heard about a company that rings a loud bell in celebration every time someone discovers they have made a mistake! This company knows that to make progress, one has to make mistakes—and learn from them! Incorporate this into your own repertoire. You or your group may think of other ways to honor the progress made through mistakes.

Ceremony of Differentiation

Make separations as sacred as unions. Whether leaving a job or a Core Group or leaving a relationship, recognize the value of what was. One phase has ended but each person is going onward to the next level of growth. Now, there is a new relationship, rather than no relationship. The old way was to separate with animosity. The new way is to differentiate with love.

Create a sacred space that holds within it a positive symbol of the time together, as well as a symbol of the time to come. Create a ceremony that acknowledges the meaning that the relationship had when both parties had a common purpose. Then, acknowledge the differentiation, the natural changes that have created the new relationship. Express your present feelings of love or respect for one another. Ask for support in your next steps without the other. Commit to continuing to support each other in a new way.

The Give-away Ceremony

The Give-away Ceremony is a rich experience of the joy of gifting and the magic that can occur as you gift that which has meaning for you.

Each member of your group brings an item which is special and offers it to the circle. Gifts can be wrapped or not and offered to the circle in a variety of ways. You may each bring your gift to the center and speak to the meaning that it has for you, or gifts may be offered anonymously. A person comes forward to receive a gift when they feel called. This process is very revealing as to how we each give and receive. Notice what feelings arise as you release an item that you may be attached to or when someone else chooses a gift that you had your eye on. Be creative and attune to doing this process in a way that best serves your group. Take time to journal any insights at the completion of the ceremony.

Note: The Give-away Ceremony is a poignant way to come to closure as a Core Group. Perhaps your group has done a retreat weekend together or you are completing the experiences of *The Co-Creator's Handbook*. You also may choose to include the process as part of your holiday festivities.

Healing Ceremony

If the person needing healing is present, have him come into the center of the circle. He may want to sit or lie down. Each person can gently put his hands on the individual receiving the healing. You may want to proceed in silence or have a facilitator lead a group process (guided visualization). It is important to envision the person in radiant health, whole and complete. If the individual is not present, the group can hold him collectively in their consciousness and send positive prayers for healing.

House or Land Blessing

It's very beneficial to come together and bless a new home or consecrate a piece of land.

Ask those participating to bring an elemental offering. This could be a cutting from a plant, a tree sapling, or a rock or soil from their garden that creates a weaving of nature between homes. You may want to include a purification ritual (with water or sage) to clear away any negativity that might be present from prior occupants. All present can offer a prayer for the well being of the home and all who live there. Intentions are empowered as they are held by those gathered. The celebration is further enhanced by song and dance! It's a joyous time!

Rites of Passage

Initiation rites taken at the right time burn off what is no longer relevant,
opening our eyes to new possibilities
of our own uniqueness.

Carl Jung

Our initiations and life passages are often difficult, but they lead us to new potential,
new birth and new possibilities;
through them we learn to take on life's challenges with grace.
Through the initiatory process, accompanied by recognition, rites and rituals,
we move ever closer to the mastery of the art of living.

Carole Kammen and Jodi Gold

Rites of Passage illuminate the next stage of our lives and orient us to the sacred nature of our transitions. We feel the companionship of a supportive community as we walk into the unknown. Rituals help us to embrace change, to let go of the past and open to the Great Mystery.

Questions to consider as you create a Rite of Passage

- What is the significance of this passage?

- What is to be honored and what released?

- How can the individual experience full empowerment to walk forward in strength and clarity?

- How does the community consciously witness and participate in this transition?

- What words, music, movements, and physical objects are symbolic of the passage and enhance the ritual?

Common elements of a Rite of Passage

- Recapitulation and honoring of the past: walking the circle of our life in gratitude for all the lessons.

- Acknowledgement circle: reflections from the community that honor the individual's qualities and good deeds.

- Reflections from the elders: all those who have walked the path before us sharing the wisdom they have gleaned.

- Stating of intention, dreams, and aspirations as one moves into the next phase of his life.

Passages most commonly celebrated in our society include birth, baptism, Bar and Bat Mitzvah, confirmation, graduation, marriage, and death.

A. Blessing Way for an Incoming Soul

This ceremony invokes prayers of protection for the baby, empowers the mother as she prepares to give birth, and brings blessings to the family. Those attending the blessing way may participate by:

- Bringing flowers to adorn the mother to be

- Co-creating a medicine bag, each person bringing a small item that symbolically represents a blessing for the baby (something from nature or a little treasure)

- Nurturing the mother-to-be by washing her feet, massaging her, anointing her with oil

- Candle lighting ceremony with prayers for the birth. If possible, these candles can be re-lit at the time of the birth itself, bringing the blessings of the group to this powerful moment of passage and initiation.

B.   Adolescence to Adulthood

A young person may be supported in this transition in an afternoon event, or a process that builds through many months. The ritual for a young woman may occur at the time of her menses or in anticipation of her first moon cycle. A young person may experience his rite of passage in the wilderness, perhaps on a vision quest, challenging the youth to meet his fears and find a place of inner strength.

C.   Parenthood into Elderhood

This rite of passage is particularly relevant for a woman. It may coincide with becoming a grandmother or reflect the transition out of active mothering into a new phase of creative expression. For most women this ceremony would occur sometime in their 50's. It is an acknowledgement of becoming a "crone" or woman of wisdom.

The ritual may include a recapitulation of one's life by walking in a spiral, acknowledging significant moments and lessons learned along the way. The woman is invited to give voice to that which she wishes to lovingly leave behind. The circle of women then witnesses what she is passionate about, and collectively holds with her a vision for the future. As she stands in the center of the spiral, she is acknowledged. Her life is honored as a continuity of experience in an ever-evolving upward spiral.

D.   Life Changes

Some major life transitions—such as career change, divorce, health crisis or loss of a loved one—come unexpectedly and are often experienced in isolation. These difficult times are often accompanied by confusion, emotional distress, and fear of the unknown. It can be very transformative for an individual to experience the support of a loving community at such times. We feel companionship in our passage and can draw upon insights and reflections from our Core Group. Enactment of all the elements of a rite of passage empowers someone to access his own inner strength and wisdom and meet the future with intention and courage.

As the community witnesses a rite of passage, we step forward and meet each new challenge with greater strength, clarity and empowerment.

CELEBRATIONS

Joy, play, and delight (which means "of light") live within us as part of our essential natures. Cultures around the world have formalized celebration into birthdays, holidays, and special occasions or passages like promotions, weddings and graduations. The core of celebration is giving and receiving love—expressing the language of the heart in any

> *Everyday is my best day. This is my life.*
> *I'm not going to have this moment again.*
>
> Bernie Siegel, MD

way that gives rise to joy, nurtures the soul, and energizes the physical body. In celebrating, we automatically release our minds, become present to the moment, let go and touch the Earth; we discover the extraordinary within the ordinary.

The following exercises are provided as resources to lift your spirits. Just as you will want to integrate ceremonies and rituals into your Core Group practices, be sure to incorporate celebrations as well! Your group members will, undoubtedly, know many additional games and ways to celebrate. Be spontaneous and acknowledge all of your victories, large and small, in a celebratory manner!

COOPERATIVE GAMES

Name Games

The following games are helpful when you are meeting new people and trying to remember names.

> *There are at least two kinds of games.*
> *One would be called finite, the other infinite.*
> *A finite game is played for the purpose of winning,*
> *an infinite game for the purpose*
> *of continuing the play.*
>
> James P. Carse

Sounds and Gestures

(No supplies needed.)
In this game you begin by standing in a circle. The person who goes first says, shouts, or whispers his name and makes a gesture to accompany it. Everyone else in the circle mimics his sound and motion. Then it's the next person's turn to say his name and make a different movement. This goes on until each person has had a turn. Be sure to have fun with this and use a movement that everyone can duplicate. (No fair doing cartwheels or splits!)

Mimicking You

(No supplies needed.)
In this version of the name game, you will also say a name and use a motion, but not your own this time. The first person to begin sings, shouts, whispers, or says the name of another person in the circle and makes an accompanying gesture. The group mimics this as in the above exercise. The one whose name has just been mimicked chooses another person in the circle and so it continues until all who are participating have had their names said with an accompanying gesture. If this is a new group that's meeting for the first time, before starting, you may want to go around the circle and have each person say his name. Be playful, creative, and original.

Crazy Ball

(Supplies needed: 4-5 balls of varying sizes or soft objects that are easy to throw and catch across a circle. Tennis balls work well. This game works best when the ball is continually thrown to someone across the circle, rather than to someone who is standing close by.)
Children have a great time playing this game as long as they are old enough to throw and catch a ball on their own. The group forms a circle and you go around the circle with everyone saying his first name. Then the leader begins and throws one ball to someone in the circle across from him and shouts that person's name. The ball continues to be thrown around the circle in this way, back and forth, with everyone included. After the ball has made it around the circle a few times, a second ball is added, and then a third and fourth until one is either catching or receiving a ball all the time. It is a very effective way to learn the names of everyone in the circle and great fun for groups of ten or more.

Silence

(No supplies needed, unless you do the second version of the game.)
Another way to bond the group is by standing in a straight line and organizing according to one's first name (get in alphabetical order), size (shortest to tallest) or age. Sounds easy? The catch is that you have to do it without speaking and for the variation which deals with size, you are blindfolded as well. Another fun challenge to add to this game is to pretend that you are on a tight rope or narrow bridge. (You can use a railroad tie, 1" X 6" board, or a long narrow cloth). The object is to get in order without stepping off the beam, and being silent and perhaps blindfolded as well! Have fun!

Moving Together

Catch the Dragon's Tail

(Supplies needed: a handkerchief.)

Members of your group line up with your arms around the waist of the person in front of you. The last person in line has a handkerchief in his pocket. The player at the head of the line tries to grab the handkerchief. Participants in the middle of the line must follow the movements of the person in front of them. No one can break the line. Rotate the players and repeat the game, if you wish.

Mirror Dancing

(Supplies needed: lively music.)
Select a partner. Face one another and hold your hands up, about one inch apart. Begin to dance with one another. First one partner will lead and the other will follow. Then reverse roles. Go back and forth, taking turns leading and following. Have fun with this. See if you are able to co-create the dance and lose sense of who is leading and who is following.

Bumper Cars

(No supplies needed.)
Find a partner of about the same height. Both face the same direction, one in front of the other. The person in front closes his eyes, bends his elbows, and places his arms chest high in front of him. These are his bumpers and he is the car! The driver in back drives the car by the steering wheel (shoulders) deftly through traffic with no collisions. If you have uneven numbers, a group of three can invent a vehicle. After a few minutes, reverse places and the driver becomes the car. This (and the following game) might be fun alternatives to the trust processes provided in Circle 2: Connecting at the Heart.

Running Blind

(No supplies are required, but you do need at least 5 players. You may want to do this outside on a flat surface.)
Form two lines facing each other, about six feet apart. Everyone in the lines stands with his arms outstretched to guide the runner if he goes astray. The blind runner stands with eyes closed. When the facilitator says "Ready," he runs through the two lines. Two people at the end of the lines are prepared to bring the runner to a halt by patting his arms, shoulders, and hips. Continue until each person has had a chance to run blind through the two lines. If you're feeling adventurous, you might even run backwards through the two lines.

Blanket Volleyball

(Supplies needed: a ball and a blanket.)
Members of your group will hold the edges of the blanket. Place a ball in the center of the blanket and begin to toss it in the air. See how high you can toss the ball and still catch it in the middle of the blanket. A variation on this game is to provide a sheet with a small hole in the middle (just big enough for the ball), and see if you can get the ball through the hole in

the middle of the sheet. Either of these games is good for groups of all ages and sizes!   Even a five-year old can enjoy and contribute to the game!

Ball in the Circle

(Supplies needed: a ball of any size.)
Everyone sits on the ground with their feet almost touching in the middle of the circle. Use your hands to balance yourselves. Now place a ball in the middle of the circle. Keeping your heels on the ground, pass the ball around the circle—using only your feet or bodies. If you wish, pass more than one ball at a time!

Friendly Musical Chairs

(Supplies needed: lively music and chairs.)
Remember the old game of musical chairs? For one to win, many had to lose. In this version, you'll still remove a chair each time the music stops, but if someone can't find a chair, he can sit on the lap of someone on a chair! Lots of touching, hugging, and fun with this one!

Straw and Pretzel Relay

(Supplies needed: straws, a container of pretzels, an empty container.)
Divide your group in half and form two lines. Each person receives a straw. One member of each group holds a container of small pretzels, while a person at the end holds an empty container. Participants pass the pretzels down the line on their straws. Hands should be behind your backs.

Beach Ball Balance

(Supplies needed: one beach ball.)
Members of your group will divide into pairs of similar height. Place the beach ball between the heads of one pair. This pair needs to pass the ball to another pair without touching the ball with their hands. You can vary this game by using your backs, chests, or legs instead of your heads.

Easy and Fun Games

Raising the Energy

(No supplies needed.)
Form a circle and hold hands. One person begins by squeezing the hand of the person on his

right. Continue to pass the hand squeeze around the circle as quickly as you are able. Then see if you can maintain two energy pulses going in opposite directions. This means that one person will receive energy from both directions at once and will squeeze back with both hands. Now do this with your eyes closed. After about ten seconds, send two more energy pulses around the circle.

The Monster Game

(No supplies needed.)
Stand in a circle. The facilitator makes a grotesque face. When everyone has had a chance to see it, the person on his right mimics him. Then both face the center of the circle so that everyone can see how successful his attempt is. Now the second person makes a funny face and the person on his right impersonates him. Continue around the circle until everyone has had a chance to be a monster.

Knots

(No supplies needed. A fun game for six to twenty people.)
Form a tight circle with your hands in the middle. Close your eyes, mix up your hands, and when the facilitator gives a signal, take two hands. If someone takes the hands of the person next to him or both hands of the same person, let go and reconnect with others. Now you're in a knot. Arrange yourselves in a circle without letting go. You may need to go over and under people to do this. You don't need to maintain a tight grip, but you must maintain hand contact.

The Lap Game

(No supplies needed. Ideal for a group of ten to fifty people.)
This game connects people and gives them the experience of our interdependence. Everyone stands in a circle facing his neighbor's back. Next, everyone puts his hands on his neighbor's waist, being careful to be not too close and not too far away. When the facilitator says "Ready," everybody sits, making sure their knees are together, guided by the person behind him. Now you have a seated circle. In a minute, the facilitator says, "Ready," and everyone stands up.

Planet Toss

(Supplies needed: one egg for each two people who are playing the game. Do this one outside.)
Everyone finds a partner. Stand facing each other in two straight lines. To begin with, you are standing about two feet apart. Each couple is given an egg that represents our fragile planet. The game begins as each couple tosses the egg back and forth one time. Then each person takes one step back and tosses again. This continues until the couple decides that they

have gone far enough and don't want to break their egg. The object is to be slow and sensitive as you are dealing with the fate of the planet! The winning couple are those who have gone the furthest apart without breaking their egg. Another good activity to do with children. . . outside!

Songs and Music

The list of group songs and rounds is endless. The following are provided to spark your imagination. These also make excellent closings for your meetings or gatherings. Don't forget to dance and move your bodies as you sing-along!

Row, Row, Row Your Boat   (A children's "round" with meaning!)
It's a Small World (Do this one to the Bunny Hop, if you wish!) (Two kicks to the right; two kicks to the left; one hop forward; one hop backward; three hops forward. Repeat.)
Heart to Heart
Imagine
The Rose
It's in Every One of Us
He's Got the Whole World in His Hands
Let There be Peace on Earth

Making Music Together

Drumming; playing with spoons, pots and pans; and stomping rhythmically is a fun way to celebrate. This is guaranteed to lift the energy of the group—and no special talent is required!

If you have musicians in the group, your celebrations will be enhanced by their talents. You may want to set aside one or many evenings to share a potluck dinner and party together.

Share Your Talent

A planned or spontaneous talent show is a great way to celebrate. Tell jokes, share humorous true stories, team up with others to do skits or create dance routines, sing duets.   Don't be afraid to make a fool of yourself. This, too, is cause for celebration!

At the heart of play is love and a deep sense of wonder and mutual discovery.
Play is about balance, mystery, belonging, inclusion, trust,
sacredness, fearlessness, touch reciprocity, kindness,
openness and joy. It is about awareness, joining, blending,
following and contributing of energy.

Joel and Michelle Levey

DAILY PRACTICE
Exercises to be Done Outside the Group

Morning Ritual

Start each day in a sacred way with your own morning ritual that energizes you and connects you with life. Some examples are: communing with nature by taking a walk; lighting a candle on your altar and saying prayers; meditating and being still; writing in your journal or recording insights on tape; performing ancient movements like t'ai chi, chi gong, or yoga.

Every morning we have twenty-four new hours to live.

Thich Nhat Hanh

Look in the mirror and smile at yourself. Give thanks for the beautiful being who is looking back at you. Invite sacredness into your day and set a clear intention that will carry you along with ease.

Evening Ritual

Many traditions also follow an evening ritual either at the time of sunset or before going to bed. Taking the time to pause when the day has come to completion encourages an expression of gratitude for all that you really cherish in your life. It is an opportune time to review the day's experiences, to give thanks and to note, from a place of non-judgment, what arose (be it feelings, responses, reactions, gestures). Let this be a time to appreciate what contributions you made—whether a smile or a grand plan. Where would you like to correct course (make some small shift) to bring yourself into greater balance?

It's also important in the evening to unwind from the activities of the day. Breathe in the wonder of life and relax. Meditation, prayer, yoga, singing, slow dancing and journaling are all useful ways to come into balance before going off to sleep.

Blessing Your Food

Before each meal, take a moment to be grateful for that which provides you with nourishment and to acknowledge the life processes that brought food to your table. When you are with others at mealtimes, join in appreciation for the food prepared with love, for the insights gained that day, and especially for that very moment in which you are together.

In The Home

Family life is deeply enriched by incorporating ceremony and ritual into activities in the home. This might include simple gestures such as giving each other foot rubs, taking a daily walk, or reading together at night. Create a night of the week when all members of the family are requested to be at home and share in an evening of games, massage, or storytelling. Take turns with various family members making dinner and create family favorites.

Creation of nature tables which honor the cycles of nature are delightful for young ones. Begin with a beautiful colored cloth that represents the turning of the season. Then add treasures collected from nature and items that symbolically represent the theme of the time. A ceremony can be created in the evening by lighting a candle, inviting a child to share a special moment of the day, and perhaps add a new treasure to the nature table. Saying prayers for loved ones and those in need actively engages a child in the practice of extending blessings.

The traditions and ceremonies created around holidays stay with children throughout their lives. Together, as a family, co-create ceremonies that are relevant, heartful, and engaging. They may indeed be passed down from generation to generation!

> *Observe the wonders as they occur around you. Don't claim them. Feel the artistry moving through and be silent.*
>
> Rumi

In the Workplace

If you are unsure how those individuals that you work with may respond to ritual and ceremony, begin with what feels comfortable. In some offices, you can expect a "surprise" birthday cake on your birthday. There may be a company routine for welcoming and saying goodbye to employees. Many companies celebrate individual and group successes with rewards, trips, and parties. Participate in these events and be a leader in expanding them into more meaningful activities. Allow work-related celebrations to deepen your relationships with one another and the Spirit of Co-Creation.

ADDITIONAL PRAYERS AND BLESSINGS

Sioux Prayer

Grandfather Great Spirit
All over the world the faces of the living ones are alike.
With tenderness they have come up out of the ground. Look upon your children
that they may face the winds and walk the good road to the Day of Quiet.
Grandfather Great Spirit fill us with the Light.
Give us the strength to understand, and the eyes to see.
Teach us to walk the soft Earth as relatives to all that live.

Blessing

On awakening, bless this day, for it is already full of unseen good, which your blessing will call forth; for to bless it is to acknowledge the unlimited good that is embodied in the texture of the universe and which awaits each and all.

On passing people in the street, on the bus, in places of work and play, bless them. The peace of your blessing will accompany them on their way, and its gentle fragrance will be as a light on their path.

On meeting and talking with people, bless them in their health, their work, their relationship with God, themselves and others. Bless them in every conceivable way, for such blessings not only sow seeds of healing, but one day will spring forth flowers of joy in the waste places of your life.

As you walk, bless the city in which you live, its government and its teachers, its nurses, its children and its bankers, its priests and its prostitutes. The moment anyone expresses the least aggression or unkindness to you, respond with a blessing. Bless them totally, sincerely and joyfully, for such blessings are a shield which protects them from the ignorance of their misdeeds, and distracts the arrow that was aimed at you.

To bless means to wish, unconditionally and totally, unrestricted good for others and events from the deepest wellspring of the innermost chamber of your heart: it means to hallow, to hold in reverence, to behold with utter awe, that which is always a gift from the Creator.

Pierre Praverands of Geneva

Acknowledgments

We'd like to acknowledge Lila Tressemer and Anastasia Nutt for their wise womanspirit and creative input which inspired a number of the processes in this Circle.

Thanks also to Susan Hopkins, author of "Hearing Everyone's Voice," for sharing a number of cooperative games with us.

Circle 6

DISCOVERING OUR SOUL'S PURPOSE

Whatever you are born with is God's gift to you.
What you become, is your gift to God.

Anonymous

Your mission is the most important gift you will ever receive in your life. It has only one requirement: that you follow the inner voice of your soul.

Naomi Stephan, Ph.D.

The Great Spirit, our spiritual guides, the Earth itself, and our own innermost essences are beckoning to each of us to bring into the world a project or central life's work that will contribute to humanity and the Earth as well as enabling us to express our own uniqueness.

Greg Bogart, Ph.D.

Our soul's purpose is the innate calling,
the code of genius that must be expressed
for each of us to feel whole and fulfilled.

It is that which Spirit created us to do and be.

Our soul's purpose pulses in us with the fierce power that drives
the green shoots up through the frozen soil in the spring.
We are driven to grow by the force of creation.

We have known in the secret depths of our hearts the desire to be more, to fully actualize
ourselves, but for most of us, the time has not been right.
We have not been called forth fully.
The social forms to empower our full creative potential have been missing.
Thus, we've often kept ourselves in limited jobs, doing repetitive tasks,
and struggling to survive.

Now, we have entered a new cycle.
Evolutionary crises and opportunities are activating large numbers of us to
extend our lives from the immediate concerns of self-maintenance
and reproduction to the evolution of ourselves
and the development of a conscious, sustainable community.

We are at the threshold of the greatest release of human creativity
the world has ever known.

~ ~

Circle 6

DISCOVERING OUR SOUL'S PURPOSE

Each of us has a unique calling, a purpose that drives us to full self-expression, a vocation of destiny. This urge to manifest our creativity is as powerful as the drive for self-preservation and self-reproduction. It is the motivation for self evolution.

Barbara Marx Hubbard

Let the beauty of what you love, be what you do.

Rumi

Finding the right work is like discovering your own soul in the world.
Thomas Moore

The world is a symphonic whole. Every person contributes his or her own unique melody to the great song of the Cosmos, conducted by Divine Wisdom.

Hildegard of Bingen

The poets express it so well, yet defining one's life purpose can be, for many of us, a challenging task. What we do know is that our soul is constantly beckoning us to follow our bliss to bring us home to the fulfillment of our true nature. Our life purpose is always in alignment with our highest values and serves to integrate all aspects of our being. It expresses itself in sacred service, moving us toward full and passionate participation in life. True purpose fosters self awareness, trust and self esteem—and honors the Self, while serving the whole. Our purpose may gradually reveal itself over a period of years or may come as a powerful and sudden revelation. In either case, it is what gives value, deep meaning, and authenticity to our lives.

In our culture, it is often a challenge to follow our soul's guidance. We are encouraged to "earn a living" rather than abide by the longing of the heart for joy and full self expression. To be true to our calling we may need to overcome a wide range of admonitions and "shoulds" and move beyond the narrow confines of our comfort level. This will mean learning to tolerate some tension and ambiguity as we begin to clarify our deeper reason for being. As we allow the powerful call of the soul to move us, it may be necessary to drop the need for approval, to resist the expectation to conform to someone else's standards and to overcome the fear of change and the unknown. Often the discovery of our soul's purpose is preceded by a life crisis and a great humbling of the ego.

In following our purpose, some of us may be motivated to excel at something we are doing already. Others may seek new work or creative expression. Still others may reach out and pioneer new social functions or create innovative enterprises.

We recognize that, at this stage of evolution, many of us are pursuing a job or vocation that pays the bills, while we "moonlight" at that which is our soul's purpose. As pioneers traversing into a new paradigm, we may be waiting for right timing to give our gifts in the world and to be appropriately compensated for that.

To fully express our purpose, it is often necessary to collaborate with others whose creativity is also being called forth and to join that with our own. Core Groups are a perfect environment for the emergence of our soul's purpose. Resonance, unconditional love, and inspired insights unlock each person's potential. Deep interactions stimulate creativity and support the ongoing processes of self-discovery and self-actualization.

Wherever we are actualizing ourselves and empowering others in our life purposes, we are on the front lines of evolutionary change. We are embodying the knowing that each of us is an emissary of the sacred, here to play our role in this divine dance called life. We are manifesting as Self and opening the way for others to follow their hearts and fulfill their destiny.

The whole of creation is standing on tiptoe to see the wonderful sight of the sons and daughters of God coming into their own.

Paul's Letter to the Romans Ch. 8

Suggested Process Sequence

• Open your session with the Visualization that follows—or create your own attunement process.

• Remember to check-in.

• Read The Co-Creator's Agreements aloud.

• Read the Introduction to the Circle. Take a moment in silence to reflect on this. Then share your inspired insights with the group.

• Select one or more of the Experiential Exercises that follow.

• Take a break! Move around and stretch.

• Select who will fill the key roles at your next meeting.

• Create a closing that will maintain your heart connection.

EXPERIENTIAL EXERCISES

Note: There are a number of powerful, co-creative exercises in this Circle. It will take several meetings to complete all of the exercises. Be sure to take breaks whenever needed and to add a closing to the end of each meeting. The facilitator should read through this chapter before each meeting, as you may need art materials and/or an audio recorder for some of the exercises.

TIPS FOR IDENTIFYING YOUR SOUL'S PURPOSE

Briefly attune and check-in with one another before discussing the following. Co-create the tips by changing these and/or adding others that are in keeping with your deeper knowing or experience.

How do you know you are on the "right track"—pursuing your true purpose in life?

You will know when:

- your work feels like play and is aligned with your deepest values
- you can't "not do" what you are doing, it flows from your being
- you have a feeling of "fit" and authenticity
- your outer world reflects your inner experience and knowing
- you feel energized and fulfilled, guided by Spirit in expressing your creativity
- those with whom you are co-creating call forth the best in you
- your obstacles are minimal
- your life flows with synchronicities
- your part supports the well being of the whole

GUIDED VISUALIZATION

Before beginning the visualization, make sure to have your journal and pen handy to write down any insights you receive during this process. Have a large piece of paper available to write down the soul's purpose of each member of your group.

The facilitator slowly reads this aloud, remembering to pause between phrases. You may want to play soft, beautiful music in the background.

Close your eyes, relax and invite your mind to be still . . . Feel at peace as you connect with the Earth through your breath . . . Continue to breathe in and out through your heart . . . Feel your energy expanding and merging with all kingdoms of this planet . . . Breathe deeply as a being who is one with all.

(Pause)

Now, think of a time when you felt totally fulfilled . . . when your life was meaningful and you were giving your best . . . What were you doing?

(Pause for 1 - 2 minutes here.)

Have you ever felt totally successful . . . What were you doing?

(Pause for 1 - 2 minutes here.)

Now take a few moments to reflect on your gifts and talents? . . . Where do you experience mastery in your life? . . . What do you do effortlessly and naturally? . . . What are your greatest strengths?

(Pause for 1 - 2 minutes here.)

Where do your interests lie? . . . What are your passions in life? . . . What are your heart's yearnings?

(Pause for 1 - 2 minutes here.)

What forms of creative expression bring you joy?

(Pause for 1 - 2 minutes here.)

If money were no object, what would you be doing?

(Pause for about 1 minute.)

If you had one year to live, what would you do? . . . Who would you choose to be with? . . .

(Pause for 1 - 2 minutes here.)

Take a few deep breaths and become aware of your body seated in this room . . . If you are feeling any sensations in your body, notice where you are feeling them . . .

(Pause)

When you are ready, open your eyes and anchor whatever insights you have had by recording them in this book or in your journal. Stay in your center in silence.

Write down any messages or images you received in the visualization. As you reflect on the process, see if you can begin to formulate your soul's purpose and record it here.

_____
_____
_____
_____
_____
_____

Next, take about 10 - 15 minutes to write down your answers to the following questions.

When I think about my soul's purpose, I feel:
_____
_____
_____

The primary strengths I have to accomplish my purpose in life are:
_____
_____
_____
_____
_____

The external blocks that seem to be in my path are:
_____
_____
_____
_____
_____

The self-imposed, limiting beliefs that seem to be in my path are:
_____
_____
_____
_____
_____

I can begin to overcome these blocks by:
_____
_____
_____
_____

Others in the group can support me in overcoming these blocks by:

_____

_____

_____

_____

Share with the whole group what you have discovered. Then reflect on the following:

There is a vitality, a life force, an energy, a quickening, that is translated through you into action, and because there is only one of you in all time, this expression is unique. And if you block it, it will never exist through any other medium and will be lost.

Martha Graham

If you think you're too small to have an impact, try going to bed with a mosquito.

Anita Roddick

~ ~

This might be a good time to take a short break.

Releasing Blocks And Limiting Beliefs

Freedom lies beyond belief; however, it is our thoughts and beliefs that create our daily lives. Mastery is achieved through aligned intention, focus and action— all founded on supportive beliefs. If you want to achieve mastery in any area of your life, release your fears and limiting beliefs.

Marion Culhane

Often, the blocks that we face in life are self-imposed limiting beliefs or points of view that emerge from past conditioning. For example, you may have had a bad experience in childhood asking a parent for your allowance and project from that episode that it's unsafe to discuss money or to express your needs or wishes with someone you love. This "posture" in consciousness can control feelings and behavior, unless or until it is brought into full awareness and you consciously choose to operate from a different mindset.

Process

The following exercise is designed to release limiting beliefs and points of view that block you from fulfilling your soul's destiny. Allow at least one hour for this exercise and read through the instructions before beginning.

Note: Although this process is designed to release limiting beliefs regarding your life's purpose, it can be adapted to release any point of view.

Select a partner. One is "A"; the other is "B." Make sure there is some distance between you and other pairs in your group to maintain a sense of privacy. "A" may want to lie on the floor for this process, if this is more comfortable.

1. "A" briefly describes any points of view or beliefs that seem to be limiting him in fulfilling his life's purpose. "B" listens carefully, **writes down "A's" limiting beliefs,** and supports "A" to express any blocks he is feeling or sensing.

2. "B" encourages "A" to fully experience the blocks and asks "A," "What are you feeling now?" "Where do you feel a contraction in your body?" In bringing the attention to the body, "B" directs "A" to drop the story and just feel the contraction in the body.

3. Next, "B" suggests to "A," "See if you can feel the energetic contraction beneath the body sensations." (This might be seen as a "contraction in consciousness" . . . a form of resistance, clinging or indifference. For example, the energy of fear feels different from the energy of repressed anger. Although subtle, it can be felt.)

4. "B" guides "A" through a brief relaxation exercise and then asks "A" to find a number from 1 to 10 to represent the intensity of the contraction. Next, "B" directs "A" to consciously exaggerate the energetic contraction—to make it as intense as possible. "B" might say, "Turn up the volume completely," or "Let yourself fully become this energy."

5. "B" asks "A" to build up the energetic contraction until it's a 10 or it cannot be exaggerated any further. This may take a few minutes.

6. "B" now directs "A" to relax completely as Self—that which is aware of the energy. "Just let go and relax as pure awareness." (If all resistance to this block has been turned into amplification, the block will disappear.)

7. "B" asks "A," "What body sensations are you feeling now?" (If the block has disappeared, "A" will say, "I feel nothing" or "I feel warmth" or something similar to this.) If "A" still feels a contraction in the body, "B" repeats Steps 2 to 6 until "A" reports that no contraction remains in the body.

8. "B" completes the process by asking "A," "What happens when you hear the statement, "_____"? (**"B" repeats back "A's" key phrase/limiting beliefs from Step 1.**) You will know that the block has been cleared when the phrase has no charge and is seen as a meaningless thought-form. "A" may even smile or laugh upon hearing the phrase!

9. In the final step, "B" invites "A" to speak about his soul's purpose with clarity and honesty.

10. When "A" has finished, take a few minutes to center yourselves in the Heart Meditation and allow "A" to write down any insights in a journal or in this Handbook. Then reverse roles and "A" guides "B" through Steps 1 - 9.

11. When both of you have completed the process, acknowledge one another and allow "B" to write down his insights.

_____

_____

_____

_____

_____

_____

_____

_____

_____

_____

_____

_____

Calling on Your Clearness Committee

In his excellent book "Callings," Gregg Levoy mentions Quaker "clearness committees," which assist members to gain clarity about important issues in their lives. In the following exercise, your Core Group will serve this function. **You might reserve one full meeting for this exercise, if many members need support in discovering their true destiny.**

A Process to Discover Your Soul's Purpose

Read through the instructions before beginning this process. **You may find it helpful to record this process.**

Any member of your circle who needs to gain clarity regarding his soul's calling can be the "focus person" in this exercise. He may sit in the middle of the circle. He begins by explaining concisely what he needs from the group.

Observe ten minutes of silence together, shifting your attention from the personal to the transpersonal Self, with all members asking for guidance for the person in the center of the circle. In response to what the "focus person" has indicated he wants from the group, other members ask questions only and refrain from making any editorial comments.

The questions might include:

- *What do you feel passionate about?*
- *What brings you joy?*
- *How do you love to serve?*
- *Where and how do you excel?*

Do not censor or judge your questions. All questions that arise in response to this member's request are valid. Do not give advice, try to solve problems, or tell stories. Know that the answer will come from Spirit through the person seeking clarity.

As the focus person, respond as you wish to the questions being posed. It may be helpful to reflect on some of the questions and write your answers in your journal later. Be patient with your own evolution. Your heart must be ready and events may need to unfold before you are able to find your true place of service and creative expression.

Allow each person who chooses to do so to take a turn being the focus person in the circle.

Where your gifts and your joy meet the needs of the world, there lies your purpose.
Dick Leider

Love and kindness strengthen every soul in his or her purpose.
James Redfield

GUIDED VISUALIZATION: Taking a Mythic Journey

This exercise could be used at the beginning of your second or third meeting of Circle 6. It allows you to review your life as a hero's or heroine's journey. In this guided visualization, the treasure you seek is your soul's purpose. The obstacles you have faced are the initiations, tests, and heroic struggles you have endured.

Select a partner. You will take turns reading the following to one another and writing your partner's response in this book or in their journal. Make sure you are far enough away from other members of your group to maintain a sense of privacy. If you feel comfortable doing so, it helps to lie down for this exercise. You will need at least 40 minutes for this exercise, allowing 20 minutes for each person.

Decide who will go first. The other partner will read the following and write in his partner's handbook.

Gently close your eyes and allow the floor to support your body . . . Follow your breath, as you relax deeply, letting go of all thoughts . . . releasing any tension you may be feeling . . .

(Pause)

Continue to breathe deeply, and envision a cloud of pink light enveloping and protecting your body . . .

(Pause)

Let go and feel the warmth and safety of your surroundings, as you relax even more fully into Self...

(Pause)

Now look down upon your body and see yourself lying in this room . . . You are about to take a journey in your mind . . . a hero's journey . . .

(Pause)

Begin with your childhood . . . and see yourself as a young maiden or knight . . . playing and enjoying yourself in nature . . .

(Pause)

What is your mythic name? . . . Who are your allies? . . . What obstacles, if any, do you face?

_____

_____

_____

_____

(Pause for 1 - 2 minutes here.)

Now see this hero as a young person, a teenager. . . Who are your teachers and guides? . . . Who are your allies? . . . What struggles do you face at this phase of your journey?

_____

_____

_____

_____

(Pause for 1 - 2 minutes here.)

And now envision this hero/heroine as an adult . . . What archetypes have you played out in this life? . . . the battle between good and evil? . . . death and resurrection? . . . betrayal and forgiveness?

_____

_____

_____

_____

(Pause for 1 - 2 minutes here.)

What is the theme of your present search or challenge? . . . Are you letting go? . . . Are you waking up? . . . Are you finding your calling? . . . or giving your gifts? . . .

_____

_____

_____

_____

(Pause for 1 - 2 minutes here.)

Who are your allies today? . . . What obstacles face you from within and without? . . . Have you lost a treasure you are seeking to find? . . .

_____

_____

_____

_____

(Pause for 1 - 2 minutes here.)

How have you changed in the past year? . . . What is being born in you? . . . What, if anything, is wanting to die? . . .

_____

_____

_____

_____

(Pause for 1 - 2 minutes here.)

Are you being asked to reset the course of your life? . . . If so, are you willing to do so?

_____

_____

_____

_____

Take a few deep breaths and become aware of your body lying in this room . . . Feel the presence of the other people in this room . . .

(Pause)

When you're ready, gently open your eyes and take a few minutes to reflect on your insights and experience before reversing roles with your partner.

_____

_____

_____

_____
_____
_____
_____

When both of you have completed this exercise, share your insights with the rest of the Group.

Enlivening a Memory of Service

Select a partner and read through these instructions before beginning the exercise. One of you will be "A"; the other is "B."

- "A" will begin by closing your eyes, centering yourself and recalling a time when you were of service to another or others. Recall all the details of the experience: the sounds, smells, the other people and circumstances. In particular, be aware of your feelings and any body sensations you are experiencing as you recall this time. Share all the details of this experience with "B."

- "B" instructs "A" to exaggerate these feelings and body sensations through the breath: expanding the feelings of service on the in-breath and breathing out good will and love for humanity and the Earth on the out-breath.

- Next, "B" requests "A" to take all of these feelings into his heart and to rest as the source of all giving and service. Allow at least three to five minutes for "A" to rest as peace and love.

- Now, trade roles and "A" will guide "B" in the process. When you are both done, make a few notes and share your experience with one another.

_____
_____
_____
_____

Then share with your entire Core Group.

This might be a good time to take a break and move your bodies.

GUIDED VISUALIZATION: Experiencing Your Future Self

Make sure you have approximately 30 - 40 minutes to complete this process. If not, save it for your next meeting.

The facilitator slowly reads this aloud, remembering to pause between phrases. Play soft, beautiful music in the background. **Stand up during this exercise.** Make sure you have enough room to move when asked to step forward.

Take a few deep breaths and begin to breathe in and out of your heart . . . Let go of any thoughts or plans and bring your awareness into this moment . . .

(Pause)

Focus on your soul's purpose . . . Don't worry if it feels rather vague or incomplete . . . just ask yourself, "What am I here to do?" . . . Allow the answer to reveal itself effortlessly . . .

(Pause)

Now see yourself expressing your true purpose . . . and project this out to one year from today . . . What opportunities are presenting themselves to you? . . . What options lay ahead for you? . . . What decisions are you making one year from today? . . .

(Pause for 1 - 2 minutes here.)

Be aware of your body . . . Are you experiencing any changes in your body? . . . Any changes in your relationships?. . . Now take a step forward and step fully into this Self that is expressing your soul's purpose one year from now.

(Pause for 1 - 2 minutes here.)

In your mind's eye, begin to live from this place . . . As you call your future Self forward, what are you doing? . . . How are you being? . . . Sense any changes in your body, mind and Spirit.

(Pause for 1 - 2 minutes here.)

Now take a step and move forward to five years from today . . . Feel that life . . . Notice how deeply different you are . . . How are you in the world? . . . What are you doing? . . .

(Pause for 1 - 2 minutes here.)

Notice how the world has changed . . . Step fully forward into your future Self and be aware of your body and your feelings . . . Where are you living? . . . How are you living?

(Pause for 1 - 2 minutes here.)

Now, in your mind's eye, turn around from the future and face yourself today . . . Open your heart to the beautiful person you see before you . . . Send a blessing to yourself . . . Honor that person . . . Send courage and empowerment to yourself . . . Affirm that all is well and unfolding in its perfection . . . Feel yourself deepened, ennobled, and empowered.

(Pause for 1 - 2 minutes here.)

The facilitator changes the music to something uplifting. (Like "Chariots of Fire.")

Once again, become aware of your body standing in this room . . . With your eyes still closed, begin to move . . . Feel the presence of others in the circle . . . Gently begin swaying to the music . . . In your mind's eye, see yourself fulfilling your life's purpose and connecting with your perfect partners . . . Allow yourself to feel the joy and exhilaration of experiencing your sacred service . . .

(Pause for 1 - 2 minutes here.)

When you are ready, join hands with others and rejoice in this feeling of expansion and possibility.

Your group might finish this process with the Ceremony of Divine Destiny in which each of you acknowledges your life purpose and the people and projects that will support you to fulfill it. Anyone who is unclear about his purpose can ask for guidance and affirm that he is in the process of discovering his true destiny.

Take a short break before beginning the following ceremony.

Ceremony of Divine Destiny

On a large piece of paper draw a "Wheel of Co-creation" divided into eight sectors. In the middle of the wheel, draw a small circle and label this Spirit, Source or God. Name each sector as follows, or select labels that work for your group. You may want to color and decorate each segment of the Wheel.

Once you have completed the Wheel, place it in the middle of your circle. Place a lighted candle in the middle of the Wheel. Dim the lights, if this is appropriate. Sit in silence and reflect on the Wheel and on your soul's purpose.

When you feel moved to do so, go to the Wheel and share the gift of your soul's purpose in the appropriate sector. Say a few words about your purpose and why you've selected this place on the Wheel. Mention any people who you feel might share your divine destiny. If you wish, you may place a piece of personal jewelry or something else that has meaning for you on this sector.

Each person, in turn, moves to the Wheel and places his gift there. Remain silent until each person has had a turn to speak and to give his gifts. Close the ceremony with a song, prayer or a blessing.

When you feel complete, take a few minutes to discuss the relationships that have been revealed in this ceremony. Acknowledge and celebrate each unique path and how your paths connect in a larger pattern.*

Sharing to Clarify Your Soul's Purpose

At your next meeting or in the coming weeks,
help each other to get clearer about your chosen work through co-coaching, inspired insights and shared insights. You might ask: *"With whom do I need to connect now?"* or *"What is my next step?"* This process, if done in depth, could be the focus of an entire session.

Your life's journey has an outer purpose and an inner purpose. The outer purpose is to arrive at your goal or destination, to accomplish what you set out to do, to achieve this or that, which, of course implies future. The outer purpose belongs to the horizontal dimension of space and time; the inner purpose concerns a deepening of your Being in the vertical dimension of the timeless Now.

Eckhart Tolle

What do you plan to do with your one wild and precious life?

Mary Oliver

---

* Note: The Wheel of Co-creation has evolved to include twelve sectors.
        Visit www.evolve.org for the latest version of the Wheel. See Synergy Center.

FORMING AND RE-FORMING YOUR CORE GROUP: THE PROCESS OF DIFFERENTIATION

Now that you have a sense of WHAT you want to express, the next question is WHO are your natural partners? As attracted as you may be to the people in your Core Group, they may not all be your vocational partners.

If your life purpose is not fulfilled in a particular Core Group, it is wise for you to create a new one that is more empowering. Remember that we are in the process of building a new social body with a number of parts that is almost infinite. Know that no one will be left out. It is better to separate now and form a new Core Group than to be unable to express your gifts and to feel unappreciated. Your lack of enthusiasm can affect the effectiveness of the group.

This process of re-formation is called "differentiation." Nature differentiates according to specific functions. Each atom, cell, human, and Core Group has its own unique properties and gifts to give to the planetary body. Dysfunction occurs when cells are not in their appropriate places. In the same way, your differentiation will help you to find the right teammates who share your life purpose so that you can be fully supported, actualized, and successful in your right and freely-chosen functions.

This is a time for some Cores to re-form to come into right relationship with your true co-creative partners. If you wish, you can complete the entire Handbook with your original Core Group, or you can differentiate into other Core Groups based upon your life purposes.

Your group might want to review and discuss the following:

TIPS FOR DIFFERENTIATION

1. Create an "engagement" period to allow for experimentation before committing to a specific Core Group or project. This is like dating: you may need to try out different relationships until you find the one that fits.

2. Be patient, non-judgmental, and compassionate during this process. Trust that each person will find his perfect place.

3. Make sure that you and everyone else involved feels totally safe in telling your truth if people, the situation, or actions are not working. Find solutions that work for everyone including re-formation of groups, if necessary. Communicate fully with one another.

4. Respect the domain and function of each person and group. Do not consider one to be better than another.

5. You must have an affinity for each member of your Core and a respect for your differences. If personal conflicts arise and persist after co-coaching, it may be appropriate to separate and re-form the group(s).

6. Over-inclusion because of personal considerations can affect the resonance in your group. As you move into Circle 7, make sure each of you is aligned with and actualized by the shared purpose. Make sure that the size of your group supports its functions.

You may also want to re-evaluate the meeting format of your Core Group. Perhaps another structure than the one you have now would function better as your work together evolves. For example, if you've been meeting weekly, you may find it more effective to meet for one full day every other week.

As you evolve, your purpose evolves. What you are drawn to today may be fully satisfying this month but not feel accurate next month. Yet what you do today may be essential to building the skills and the personal strength to do tomorrow's work. **This choosing and re-choosing is an ongoing process that will evolve naturally and organically.**

If you do create a new group, be sure to practice at least one exercise from each of the first three Circles of Co-creation throughout your "courtship" period. Become "engaged" long enough to find out if your new group is the right Core for each of you to fulfill your destiny. Deep bonding creates an essential foundation for effective, sustainable work in the world.

Use the Ceremony of Differentiation (See Circle 5), if you feel it is time to re-form into different groups. Acknowledge your deep soul connection to one another as you step from this group into another group. **Differentiation does not imply separation. It is simply a movement into right relationship based on your shared destiny. If done consciously with full communication it is natural and fulfilling for all group members.**

Discuss with your Core Group how you want to proceed from here. You may want to do an inspired insights exercise, asking for guidance in making this decision.

DAILY PRACTICE
Exercises to be Done Outside the Group

A Rite of Passage

For millennia, native people have discovered their soul's purpose by going on a "vision quest" and asking for guidance. You may want to seek your true mission by taking a few days alone in nature. The key elements to this rite of passage are:

- to prepare by setting your intention and asking for clarity and protection
- to separate yourself from your community and your accustomed role
- to place yourself in a situation of uncertainty and physical deprivation
- to listen and follow your guidance

You may want to go on an organized vision quest with an experienced guide, or you may prefer to retreat by yourself. You might go camping or stay in a cabin in nature for several days. You will want to be alone. Take a journal with you to record your dreams, insights, and revelations—but spend most of your time in silent prayer, meditation and contemplation. Eat lightly or fast, if you choose, and drink lots of pure water. If you listen within, the answers will come. (" Ask and you shall receive." " Knock and the door will be opened unto you.")

Embracing Your Soul's Journey

If you are still not clear about your soul's purpose, write or audio record your life story. Look for recurring themes: high points, fulfilling moments, experiences that felt expansive and exhilarating. Assess yourself; describe your personal qualities. Describe your ideal self. What qualities do you want to enhance? Acknowledge the perfection of all aspects of your soul's journey, including the struggles, difficulties, and challenges. Be aware that your purpose might also reveal itself as "being" rather than "doing."

> *Our ultimate destiny is to re-connect with*
> *our essential Being and express*
> *from our extraordinary, divine reality in*
> *the ordinary physical world,*
> *moment by moment.*
>
> Russell E. DiCarlo

Next, have an inner dialogue about your true purpose. Use the questions that follow to stir your soul. You may want to call on your Quantum Partner for assistance. This exercise is similar to the mythic journey you did with the group; however, in this exercise you are focusing on your spiritual/psychological/physical journey—rather than on your mythic journey.

Ask the following questions and write down or record your answers:

- *What do I want to do?*
- *What "business" am I in? What is it that I'm about?*
- *What are my gifts?*
- *What am I really good at?*
- *What gives me great satisfaction?*
- *What do I feel really passionate about?*
- *What are my most beloved pursuits?*
- *Have I ever done anything that felt like I was making a contribution? What was it?*
- *When have I felt totally successful and joyful? What was I doing?*
- *When have I been able to sustain a high level of performance with a high level of per-*

sonal energy? What are the characteristics of these times: the work, the people, the physical environment, the results?

- *If I could wave a magic wand and all the conditions were right (family, education, time, money), what would I be doing with my life?*

- *What limiting beliefs or fears are blocking me from discovering and fulfilling my true purpose?*

Relax and do not force the answers, but set an intention to receive clarity and guidance regarding your soul's purpose in the coming weeks. Repeat this practice; keep asking the questions and recording the answers. Listen to the clues and follow the signals. Read your journal or listen to your recordings and you will begin to catch the thread of your true destiny.

Consciously pay attention to your thoughts, feelings, and emotions. Are you trying "too hard"? This is a clue that you may be looking for outer rewards. Notice when an outer intention is guiding your actions instead of just letting your life flow by itself. Transform the outer intentions to inner intentions. Are you acting out of "shoulds" or what someone else wants you to do or are you actually honoring the Self? Are you following your bliss? Check with your inner coach—the Self—or your Quantum Partner often to get the answers to these questions.

Your Ideal Epitaph

This week, or when the timing is right for you, write your "ideal epitaph." That is, reflect and write down how you want to be remembered at the end of your life. What qualities of being do you value the most? What projects or activities would you like to have acknowledged? How do you want to be seen by those you love and admire the most? Dream your dreams and write them down. This is the first step in bringing your vision into reality.

Many of the so-called larger-than-life people differ from the rest of us chiefly in this respect:
It is not that they are actually larger in mind and soul or more brilliant.
Rather they are profoundly present to the stuff of their lives, to what is happening within themselves as well as without. They use and enjoy their senses more, inhabit with keen awareness their bodies as well as their minds, explore the world of imagery and imagination....engage in projects that reinvent the world, are serious about life but laugh at themselves, and seek to empower others as they would be empowered. Quite simply, they are cooking on more burners. And when at last they lay dying, they can say,
'Life has been an eminently satisfactory experience.'

Jean Houston

Ask for a Guiding Dream

Pay particular attention to your dreams in the next few weeks. Before you go to sleep, ask yourself, "What is my deepest soul's purpose?" Ask for clues and specific guidance regarding the best next step for you. Have paper and pen ready to record any dreams or insights you may have immediately upon awakening—even if they occur at 4 a.m.!

Ask what the dream is telling you. Ask how aspects of the dream relate to your life and your unfolding destiny. Be aware of the relationship between your dreams and the circumstances of your life. What is your soul revealing that your heart and mind should note? The dream that won't go away has a message from your soul that must be heard! Dreams can reveal how we really feel about something and can help us refine our direction and bring clarity to our decisions.

Create a Dream Board

What would your life look like if you were fully living your destiny? Create a "Treasure Map" or "Dream Board," using a piece of poster board. Cut pictures and inspiring words from magazines and paste them onto your board, creating the picture and design of the life you wish to live. Place this where you can see it every day.

Listen to the Needs of Your Body

Your body can be an excellent barometer of your unfulfilled dreams. If appropriate, try asking your body what remedies it needs. Ask your body if something is missing in your life. A body pain, extreme tension, or contraction can reflect a longing in your soul, which is calling to be brought into balance, alignment, and expression.

Creating Space for Your True Mission

To prepare for your soul's purpose, take an inventory of your life. What do you need to let go of to make space for your mission to unfold? What inauthentic activities do you need to release? What internalized teachings, beliefs, and expectations must be liberated to make way for your individual calling? Reflect on these questions and act on your answers.

The following is a useful ritual to release that which no longer serves you. It can be very powerful when done as a group or you may wish to do it privately at home or in a special place in nature.

Create a sacred space by lighting a candle, burning incense, etc. Write down what is wanting to be released on a piece of paper and either burn the paper or tear the paper into small pieces and bury them in the Earth. Clarity, focus, and intention will support you in letting go of that which you want to release at this time.

Evolving Your Work Situation

Often it is more evolutionary to stay where you are and transform your current relationships or organizations than it is to leave. As well as exploring alternatives outside of your current job, you can be creative where you are now. You can seek out others in your work place who may have similar desires. For example, if you are a manager, you can instill co-creative principles in your staff, which ultimately would positively affect all their relationships.

Wherever you are actualizing yourself and empowering others, you are on the front lines of evolution. Ask your Core Group members to help you get ideas about how to evolve and transform your current work situation. Clarify that you are staying in your current job out of freedom and love, not out of fear.

Coaches, Family, Friends, Mentors

As you explore your life purpose, consult with those who love and know you well. Choose people who will give you loving encouragement rather than negative advice. Seek out supportive, like-minded people. Nurture and protect your new "baby ideas" until they are ready to stand on their own. Emerging ideas and inspirations are delicate and require tender loving care.

When you have a clear idea of your true purpose, look for exemplary models through whom you can learn. Ask for their advice and coaching. Apprentice with them, if appropriate. Deepen your knowledge. Become a student again.

Trying it Out

We all actualize our life purposes in different ways. For some of us it is one clear grand task. Others may pursue several activities or projects that weave a web of their true purpose. Value each experience and observe your life flowing as creative expression.

Remember that sacred service is not ranked. One purpose is not better than another. All are needed to build a co-creative culture! Some may choose to lovingly nurture children. Others may be called to start new entrepreneurial endeavors or actualize themselves in an international arena. Meanwhile, some individuals are manifesting their purpose in small groups at their current places of employment.

Once you discover your purpose, see how many ways you can try it out. Is there a way to get an internship or volunteer part time? Can you take a relevant course at a local school? Are there any organizations in which people are doing this type of work? Do they have meetings you can attend or journals you can read? (Your local library and the Internet has lists of all associations.) When you have received confirmation of your calling, throw yourself into developing and deepening your skills.

Reach out. Be inventive. Be daring. Others need you as much as you need them. Network with family and friends. Write a letter about yourself and the type of people you would like to work with. Publish it in a relevant journal or community newspaper. Identify the people you admire, find out their addresses from the library, publishers, or the Internet. Write to them about your ideas; get their ideas. As you go within and talk with others, you will find clarity about your true calling. The world is waiting for your gifts!

> *When you are inspired by some great purpose, some extraordinary project,*
> *all your thoughts break their bonds; your mind transcends limitations;*
> *your consciousness expands in every direction;*
> *and you find yourself in a great new and wonderful world.*
> *Dormant forces, faculties and talents become alive*
> *and you discover yourself to be a greater person*
> *by far than you ever dreamed yourself to be.*
>
> Patanjali

Be sure to discuss your homework with your Core Group at your next meeting.

Acknowledgments

We are deeply grateful to the following individuals and organizations for their contribution to the following exercises in this chapter:

Arjuna Nick Ardagh for the process to **Release Blocks and Limiting Beliefs** and the exercise called **Enlivening a Memory of Service**

Jean Houston for providing the essence of the process **Experiencing Your Future Self**

Barbara Marx Hubbard for the **Ceremony of Divine Destiny**

The Foundation for Conscious Evolution for the **Wheel of Co-creation Diagram**

Circle 7

EXPLORING OUR SHARED DESTINY

When people come together out of genuine Self interest,
willing to share their strengths and to create a shared vision, magic happens,
synchronicities abound and doors open.
Life naturally evolves out of the chaotic and disorderly,
to a higher level of organization.

James Redfield

...the real leadership that matters is actually the leadership of groups. The day
of the "individual" hero-leader is past...We don't need better heroes now, we need groups
of people who can lead—groups of people who can walk ahead.

Peter Senge

~ ~

*The magnetic energy of the Universe that has been forming whole systems for billions
of years, attracting atom to atom, molecule to molecule, and cell to cell,
now joins human to human, creating the nucleus of a new social unity.*

*The seeds of our individual potentials grow to full stature in the resonant field. We fulfill
our soul's purpose by joining our genius with the genius of others.*

*This "fusion of genius" unlocks a force as powerful as nuclear fusion: human creativity.
We experience the binding force of universal evolution activating our systems.*

*The creation that results can be as different and unpredictable from its source
as a child is from his or her parents.*

*We take a quantum leap beyond the capacities of the individuals alone. Social synergy
results, creating a whole greater than the sum of its parts.
We experience a jump in consciousness, freedom and creativity.*

*The path to self-actualization in this new cycle of life is co-creation.
Through synergy we can create what is beyond anything we could do alone.
We are liberated to align with others for the betterment of all.*

~ ~

Circle 7

EXPLORING OUR SHARED DESTINY

---

*The race advances only as all of us surge upward toward the
common goal of enlightenment and perfection.
Therefore, if we would advance rapidly ourselves,
we must make the effort to see that others of like interest
are also given every tool for self-advancement.*

Ruth Montgomery

*Love alone is capable of uniting human beings in such a way as to complete and fulfill
them, for it alone takes them and joins them by what is deepest in themselves.*

Teilhard de Chardin

*It is essential to determine with absolute clarity,
shared understanding, and deep conviction the purpose of the community.
From that, all else must flow.
It is what will bind the group together as worthy of pursuit.*

Dee Hock

Having explored and identified our unique soul's purpose, we join with others to fulfill our shared destiny. Through these connections, we experience how our unique purpose fits into the larger whole…how each of us is a cell in the planetary body.

In this Circle we move to the cutting edge of social change, co-creating a new structure that reflects synergy and cooperation. We shift from the dominator model of hierarchy and bureaucracy to non-coercive alignment in the partnership model. We link with our peers to create a fully functioning whole system. We move from the Resonant Core Group into the Co-Creative Core Group—from deep alignment into full expression, from personal growth to social action.

The Circles of Co-Creation provide a model for social action to spring from inner knowing, love and Source. Usually spiritual groups work on the inner plane and activists work on the social problems of the world. This sourcing of social action from within brings these activities together and is a key to non-violent planetary transformation!

The dominant culture currently prevents natural synergy by utilizing social structures which accentuate separation, create forced ranking and suppress empathy and creativity. Co-creative Core Groups model self-governance by attunement to the universal pattern within each person and through cooperation with others and with the Earth.

In a "shared channel of self actualization", all members of the Core can express their unique talents. If anyone feels unexpressed, the dissonance will greatly diminish the effectiveness of the team. This is a critical cross-over point from inner to outer work and may be a delicate moment in the life of the Core Group. Many have broken up at this point, losing their resonance in the effort to become operative and effective in the world. The critical mind and anxiety may enter in and destroy resonance.

In this process it is important that the analytical intellect becomes subservient to compassion, intuition, and deeper knowing. It is best to hold shared purpose in abeyance until a profound impetus for common action emerges from the group. This may provoke impatience in some members of the group, but it is wise to practice the slow process of bonding and aligning before embarking on taking action.

The successful Co-creative Core Group models each part of a loving body doing what it does best, effortlessly and joyfully, with little or no external direction. Guidance comes from within the individual. Everyone knows what to do, moment by moment. If management and coordination are needed, it is gentle and empowering. Needs are met; discord is cleared quickly. In an environment of synergy, creativity and love, projects are completed harmoniously and each participant feels energized and fulfilled.

The first step in discovering shared destiny is to identify the shared vision and purpose that embodies the deeper callings and chosen functions of each group member. When we join out of the desire to express our highest creativity, the force of creation moves through us—bringing our ideas into alignment and our dreams into reality. Our passion is the fuel that fulfills the vision. This is the essence of co-creation.

In the following exercises, we will "heart-storm" a variety of ideas to identify the joint actions that will express our shared purpose and empower us to live our unique potential. We will create a Success Statement, succinctly stating our shared vision, mission, passion, and action—as a guide that will support us to do our part in co-creating a better world.

Once we have completed all of these processes, the natural next step is to make a commitment to action. This flows easily after having established a common purpose and determined the joint actions we want to take to empower our creative expression. Making a commitment to action is what allows our heart to finally say "yes" to our soul's purpose. Commitment is also the glue that binds us to our teammates and to the fulfillment of our shared destiny.

Suggested Process Sequence

- Open your session with the Visualization that follows—or create your own attunement process.

- Remember to check-in.

- Read The Co-Creator's Agreements aloud.

- Read the Introduction to the Circle. Take a moment in silence to reflect on this. Then share your inspired insights with the group.

- Select one or more of the Experiential Exercises that follow.

- Take a break! Move around and stretch.

- Complete any "old" business from your last meeting.

- Tend to any new business.

- Select who will fill the key roles at your next meeting.

- Create a closing that will maintain your heart connection.

EXPERIENTIAL EXERCISES

GUIDED VISUALIZATION

The facilitator slowly reads this aloud, remembering to pause between phrases. You may want to play soft beautiful music in the background.

Close your eyes and begin to physically and mentally prepare for this time of contemplation . . . Take some deep breaths . . . Adjust your body and settle back into your chair . . . Relax any muscles that are tense and feel your heart opening more fully . . .

(Pause)

Feel a sense of gratitude for the circumstances of your life and for this time when you have the freedom to enjoy just being your true Self . . . Feel your energy expanding and merging with all the people in this circle and all the kingdoms of this planet . . .

(Pause for 1 - 2 minutes here.)

Now, envision yourself on a path in nature. A pool of water appears in front of you . . . It is deep and clear . . . Enjoy the sights, smells, and sounds around this beautiful pool . . .

(Pause)

You understand that if you look into the pool you will see something of great significance to you . . . As you focus on the pool, forms slowly take shape . . . First, you see the image of Canadian geese in flight—in a perfect "V" formation . . . Notice how perfectly aligned they are with one another . . . flowing effortlessly through space . . .

(Pause for 1 - 2 minutes here.)

Now, you see a hive full of bees . . . Notice how they work as a team . . . focusing on the task of making honey, working in total cooperation with one another . . .

(Pause for 1 minute here.)

Next, you see a gorgeous red rose . . . each petal embracing the surrounding petals . . . each petal surrendering its beauty to the perfection and magnificence of the whole . . .

(Pause for 1 minute here.)

Allow yourself to be in awe of the natural order and unity that exists in the universe as you sense the wonder of all this harmony and balance . . .

(Pause)

Now, gaze again into the water of the pool . . . In the depths of the blue water you see people all over the world cooperating with Mother Earth and with the kingdoms of this planet . . . You see yourself aligning your unique gifts and talents with your teammates, co-creating with others in complete harmony . . . Notice how deeply satisfied you feel . . .

(Pause)

Allow yourself to feel a sense of freedom, knowing that by following your soul's purpose you join in synergy with others in this harmonious universe . . . You feel revitalized and energized, ready to take on your present tasks . . . You know that your purpose, although it may not be completely clear, is unfolding in its perfection . . . All is well and you relax into this knowing.

(Pause)

Now, experience the Essential Self of each of the people gathered with you in this circle . . . Focus your attention on each one, acknowledging their light, their love, and their unique gifts . . . See your light now joining with the lights of all the others in this room, creating a great glowing ball of light.

(Pause for 2 - 3 minutes here.)

Now, see the lights of all the people in your community, in your nation, and in the world . . . Sense all of humanity awakening to their true natures . . . Feel the connection of all these lights as they join into one great light enveloping the Earth . . . Humanity is being born as one coordinated body of light . . . Every function is evolving as a part of this whole . . . Relax and rejoice in this fulfillment . . .

(Pause for 2 - 3 minutes here.)

Now, let the image of the pool fade and become aware again of your surroundings . . . Sense your presence in this room . . . Slowly move your hands and feet . . . When you are ready, open your eyes and take in the beauty of each person in the circle.

As you "Check In" at the beginning of this meeting, share your experience of the guided visualization with the rest of the group.

Process: A Mandala of Connections

In your journal or on a clean piece of paper, draw three concentric circles. Your finished art piece will resemble a dartboard.

- In the center circle, write down the names of people you feel most connected to . . . those who share similar values, are walking a similar path, or are connected to your heart—emotionally, spiritually and/or vocationally. They may include people in your Core Group but are not confined to that circle of friends.

- In the middle concentric circle, write the names of others who are supportive, but not as intimately connected to you at the soul level.

- In the outer ring, add the names of teachers, mentors, role-models and any people who have ever guided the way for you. They can be living or dead, human or mythic, imaginary or historically correct—but in some way they have touched your life in a meaningful way.

- Notice if you have any insights or revelations while doing this exercise. Be aware of your feelings and body sensations as you bring these people into your awareness. Is there anyone you need to connect with at this time?

- Ask yourself: "What can I learn from this about myself? Do I have a shared destiny with some of these people? Who? What is the nature of our shared destiny?"

- Finally, share your mandala, insights, and feelings with the rest of your Core Group.

Process: Your Soul's Crest

*When we seek for connection, we restore
the world to wholeness.
Our seemingly separate lives become
meaningful as we discover
how truly necessary we are to each other.*
Margaret Wheatley

Have drawing materials available for this exercise, which will take 30 - 45 minutes. You may want to play inspiring music softly in the background.

Working individually, list at least eight of your core values. (For example: honesty, loyalty, service, etc.)

_____

_____

_____

_____

Now write down eight action verbs. (e.g. change, awaken, motivate, realize, play, etc.)

_____

_____

_____

_____

Next, write a sentence that combines at least two of your values and one or two of your action verbs. Begin with the phrase "My soul's purpose is to" (e.g. My soul's purpose is to awaken and empower others to fulfill their divine destinies and realize their dreams.)

_____

_____

_____

Using the art materials that are available, draw a "crest" of your soul's purpose. You may use the outline of a "shield" or a circle or square . . . any shape that appeals to you. You may want to divide it into four quadrants, representing the spiritual, emotional, mental, and physical aspects of your being. You might prefer to divide it in thirds to represent body, mind and spirit. Be imaginative and creative.

Share your crests with one another. Do any of them resemble one another? At the end of this Circle, you will create a group crest that represents your shared values and destiny!

This might be a good time to take a break.

DEFINING SHARED PURPOSE

Discuss the following ideas and principles. If you wish, co-create any others that reflect your understanding and experience and add them to the list.

- Shared Purpose is never manufactured or artificially imposed, rather it emerges from the vocations and collective visions of its members. Just notice what is real for each of you. Ask yourself, "What do I feel aligned with at the level of my soul?" "What is worth doing?" "What project has true value for me?"

- To have members support a purpose, the purpose must support them! In order to sustain interest and commitment, the shared purpose must result in some personal rewards for each group member, i.e. meeting new people, personal growth, self-actualization, satisfaction from contributing, acquiring new skills, compensation, etc.

- Be sure the joint project or group focus draws forth the creativity of ALL of its members. Each person must be authentic to his soul's purpose.

- Manifestation comes from forces that are totally aligned and integrated. Therefore, the group focus must be sustainable and the vision held by all.

- Shared Purpose is a serious commitment to action and requires the loyalty of each group member to fulfill his agreements to the project or vision. There is a morality in co-creation to care for and nurture the work. Promising to do projects with people and then not following through will not work. This can destroy trust in a group and sabotage your joint project.

- The value of partnership and teamwork without competition must be understood. The gifts of all members are necessary to actualize shared destiny.

- Know that the process of creating shared purpose may be a transformational end in itself. It is not necessary to force an intended result. Follow your guidance and allow the project to flow.

COMMITTING TO A SHARED PURPOSE
THROUGH JOINT ACTION

Dolphins confer just beneath the surface before taking group action. Underwater researchers say each pod member chirps some input.

L.M. Boyd

A functional team is one in which the participants are energized and empowered. It consists of the right people in the right place at the right time doing what they enjoy and fulfilling their unique callings.

The right people for a team are those who have a natural affinity for one another; trust one another's intentions, integrity, and competence; are aligned with the purpose; have the skills needed; want to participate and are willing to take action. In other words, they are able to see the vision, are clear about its mission, feel passionate about the project and are able to achieve its intended results. In addition, they are committed to living the principles of the Co-Creator's Agreements.

When people do what they enjoy, they are enthusiastic and inspired and are able to accomplish remarkable results effortlessly!

Whether you are considering a one-time community project, enhancing your existing work situation, or starting a new business—you will need to identify your shared vision, mission, passion and action to achieve your purpose. These components or steps comprise a Success Statement and are one of the main practices of this Circle.

Be sure to allow ample time. Depending on the complexity of your project, you may need several half-day meetings or one-day sessions to complete all the processes in this Circle. Do not rush these steps. Read the entire set of processes through before planning your meetings and choose the appropriate meeting formats for your situation.

Clarity and honesty are important at this stage. A Success Statement must emerge from the life purposes and collective visions of every member of your group.

Aligning With Each Other

Select a quiet time and place and plan to spend at least four hours with your possible co-creators. Before beginning, be sure that you have materials to record your insights and proceedings. You might want to tape record the entire session to transcribe it later or you might appoint a scribe. Also, you will want to have your own journals and pens handy to keep track of personal insights. Use a flip chart or large sheets of paper and marker pens to record ideas shared with the group.

DEFINING YOUR VISION

Vision is the expression of Spirit on the material plane. It is an expanded perception of what is possible to bring forth in the human experience. A true vision statement inspires and uplifts. It touches your soul and expands your awareness.

The Process

1. The facilitator might re-read the visualization given at the beginning of this Circle or you can silently center yourselves with the Heart Meditation.

2. When you are feeling aligned and centered, the facilitator asks the question: *"What is your vision for yourself and for this group?"*

3. Spend at least ten minutes in silence or until all of you feel you have completed the process, listening carefully to your inner voice and being aware of any images that come to you.

4. As you get insights or images, write them in this book or in your journal. Begin your entries with the words:

My vision for myself is

_____

_____

_____

My vision for this group is

_____

_____

_____

5. When all of you have completed this process, share your insights with each other. Do you feel expanded by these statements? Remember, a true vision statement inspires and uplifts and is universal in scope.

If you prefer, you can use an inspired insights process to discover the group vision. In this case, when the facilitator asks, *"What is your vision for this group?"* you would answer out loud as you feel moved to respond. Remember to begin with an attunement and to record this process or have one member of your group write down the insights.

This might be a good time to take a break and move your bodies.

CLARIFYING YOUR MISSION

Your mission defines what you intend to accomplish with regard to the vision. It activates and aligns the purpose of each member of your group, putting your individual callings into practice. From your mission you derive your goals and objectives and a detailed action plan. A mission statement combines rational thinking and intuitive knowing and provides focused, specific and clear information. For example, the mission of Global Family is to provide a non-profit educational vehicle that empowers people to actualize their life purpose and join with others to build a co-creative culture.

The Process

Read through the instructions before you begin.

1. Make sure you feel centered, peaceful and relaxed by taking a few minutes to create the resonant field of love. You might listen to a piece of beautiful music, create a guided visualization, or be with one another in silence for a few minutes.

2. The facilitator asks the following questions, allowing time for you to respond to each one and write the answers here or in your journal:

What is the mission of this group? What project is calling us as a group?

_____

_____

_____

_____

What are the gifts you bring to this group?

_____

_____

_____

_____

How does the mission of the group relate to your passion, gifts, and to your life purpose?

_____

_____

_____

_____

3. Now, the facilitator says, *"While still in a meditative state, allow any questions that you have about the group mission to surface. Ask your questions out loud as they come to you. Respond verbally to the questions from a place of deep knowing and experience."*

4. When everyone has had an opportunity to express themselves, the facilitator will invite the group to gently open their eyes.

Now share what you have discovered from these questions and answers.

WRITING AND REFINING YOUR SUCCESS STATEMENT: VISION, MISSION, PASSION, AND ACTION

The Process

1. Establish or re-establish a centered state.

2. In your journal or below, write your one sentence version of the various elements of the group's Success Statement:

The vision of this group is:

_____

_____

_____

The mission of this group is:

_____

_____

_____

The passion of this group is:

_____

_____

_____

3. When everyone is finished, one of you can act as the scribe to write all the statements on a flip chart or a large sheet of paper.

4. Together, discuss the words you have chosen. Ask each other the following questions and create the one statement that most precisely reflects your shared purpose:

   • Which words are most accurate for you?
   • Which words best convey the essence of your shared purpose?
   • What does each substantive word mean to each of you?

   This is not a time for compromise! Every substantive word should be deeply meaningful for each of you and the meaning should be the same! Remember, vision inspires;

mission informs; and passion ignites the will, warms the heart, and moves the mission and vision forward. Allow your words to support the purpose of each statement.

5. When you have completed this portion of your Success Statement, ask these questions: Do you love what it says? Does your vision statement uplift you? Is your mission statement clear and informative? Does your passion statement motivate you?

6. Give yourself time to reflect on the elements of your Success Statement. If you have sufficient time, take a break so that each of you can spend some time in solitude and reflection. You might take a long walk in nature or go to a quiet, private place to meditate before resuming your meeting. If it is appropriate, you might schedule your next meeting, do your closing ceremony, and "call it a day".

7. When you come back together, do a centering process, and read your Statement aloud as a way to align your group. Let the essence of its words reach deeply into your hearts and minds. Share any insights you have about it with each other and, if you all agree, make any modifications. Begin your future gatherings with this procedure. (You will complete your Success Statement at your next session, when you add your action statement to your vision, mission, and passion statements.)

IDENTIFYING THE ACTIONS TO FULFILL THE MISSION

At this point, most of you probably already have one or more notions about how to accomplish your shared purpose. Use those ideas to launch a creative "heartstorming" session. Heartstorming—tuning into the intelligence of your heart—in addition to "brainstorming", allows you to release valuable ideas that might be judged by the mind as unworthy, inefficient, impossible or extravagant.

You will need more than two people to do this process. If your group is small, ask other friends or colleagues who may have an interest to join you. Sometimes it is valuable to ask someone completely unfamiliar with what you are doing to participate in your heartstorming session. You will find that they bring interesting perspectives that you may not have considered.

Prepare for your session by having a flip chart, blackboard, or large sheets of paper and markers and a scribe to capture all the ideas for everyone to see during the session. Seeing ideas written down stimulates the creativity of others. You also may want to record the session so you can refer to it later.

You want your facilitator to continually encourage all ideas to flow, and discourage any judgments about the ideas during the session. This is not the time for discussion and critical analysis.

The Process

1. Begin the session with a centering process or visualization to turn the process over to the Co-creative Self.

2. The facilitator poses the question:

   What are all the ways we can think of—no matter how seemingly crazy or unrealistic—to achieve our mission? What are our ideas regarding our possible actions?

3. Let the ideas flow. The scribe writes them all down and numbers all the ideas for everyone to see. The pace will be fast—idea followed by idea.

4. You will know your heartstorming session is over when no new ideas are flowing.

When that happens, it might be a good time to take a break. If so, take a few minutes to center yourselves again after your break. Then continue the process.

5. Look at your list of possible actions.

6. Heartstorm a list of the most important criteria for the joint actions you will choose to undertake. Once again, the scribe writes them all down. Examples of criteria might be: most likely to be accomplished within a reasonable time frame; most enjoyable; least effort for the greatest results; serves the largest audience (customers and/or constituents); adds the most value; greatest potential for generating (the most/enough) revenue.

7. Now, each of you copies this list of most important criteria for joint actions onto a sheet of paper, leaving a margin on the right hand side of the page.

8. Look at both the action ideas and the most important criteria for action lists. Then, in the margin beside each criterion on your list, write down the number(s) of the action ideas that you feel best meet that criterion.

9. Discuss your responses with the rest of the group. Identify the ideas that best match your criteria for successful joint action.

10. Remember to balance your analytical mind analysis with your intuitive inner knowing. To do this, use a centering or breathing process to quiet the mind and release tension in the body.

11. When you have completed this exercise, align by restating your Success Statement. Then, have the facilitator read the ideas for action. For each one, ask the following question:

Is this idea for action likely to fulfill our mission and is it aligned with our shared purpose?

From a quiet, centered state, communicate your intuitive inspired insights as they arise. Once you have completed this round, for each action idea, ask the following question:

What obstacle(s) might impede or hinder us from achieving our joint action?

Communicate your intuitive inspired insights as they arise. Have the scribe note any perceived obstacles or challenges.

Again, allow time for solitude to reflect on the results of these processes. Before taking a break or doing your closing ceremony to end the gathering, affirm that each of you will consider—both logically and intuitively—the best actions to take to fulfill your mission and to express your true calling.

At your next gathering or after your break, do both logical and intuitive processes with just the top action(s). Agree on your course of action.

Idea-Generating Processes

There are many techniques besides "heartstorming" for bringing forth creative ideas. One of these is "mindmapping" in which ideas generated by the group are connected with lines to other ideas. The use of colored markers can help to stimulate creativity. Doing your "heartstorming" in an unusual place, time, or situation or using drama or other arts is another way to help you disconnect from the part of your mind that says, "This is the way it is done because that is how we have always done it". Your group may find or develop other techniques to unlock your creative potential. Whatever techniques you may use, remember to stay centered and connected to your inner guidance.

WRITING YOUR ACTION STATEMENT

After selecting your joint action, write a statement that accurately reflects your chosen action. Use the same procedure you used for writing your mission statement.

An action statement is concrete and clear. It reflects the specific actions you will take to achieve your mission and fulfill your vision. (See the Success Statement for Global Family provided as an example below.)

Action Plan

Depending upon the scope of your action, your next step can be either relatively fast and simple or time consuming and complex. For a one-time community or work project, draft an action plan that lists, step-by-step, what actions need to be taken and what resources are needed to accomplish your goal. A clear action plan contains steps that are time-limited and measurable. For each action or resource, list who is responsible, when the action will begin and end, and describe the action and any criteria or standards for its accomplishment.

Flow with the essence of your shared purpose and do not allow a concern for doing it "right" get in the way. Let it evolve. Be flexible, release expectations, and learn from each experience. If your plan includes starting a business, see circle 9 for additional information.

The following **Success Statement for Global Family** is provided as a model to support you in creating your own Statement.

Vision: The experience of unconditional love and unity for all of humanity.

Mission: To provide a non-profit educational vehicle that empowers people to actualize their life purposes and join with others to build a co-creative culture.

Passion: Reuniting our human family.

Action: Provide and promote activities that enable people to experience their deeper connection with one another, the Earth and their Spirit

Foster the formation of Core Groups to build the resonant field of love around the world.

Model and share the principles and practices of co-creation

Create and distribute educational materials

Provide trainings in the Circles of Co-Creation

Support the development of Hummingbird Ranch as a living laboratory for the evolution of consciousness

Network with other groups and organizations for mutual empowerment

Communicate about global events that link humanity in consciousness

Facilitate international conferences

Foster the awareness that we are one

Model unity and love

TIPS FOR SUCCESSFULLY ACTUALIZING SHARED PURPOSE

Read through the following tips; then discuss and modify them to reflect your knowing and experience.

- Using the power of synergy, the group accesses inner knowing and translates the life purpose of each member into a collective plan of action.

- Each person sources the plan or project, bringing it forth from the depth of his being. People are not helping out one key leader, but rather fulfilling their unique purposes together. Partnership and cooperation prevails with the goal of overall group empowerment.

- Each member takes full responsibility for his part as well as for the whole. It is important to recognize the interdependence of members in the group rather than to operate from dependent, independent, or enabling behaviors.

- Individuals live as their word, clearly communicating their promises and keeping their agreements. If you break your word or make a mistake, you self correct. If someone else makes a mistake, you correct them with discernment and no condemnation.

- Positive and negative feedback are given easily with no one protected from knowing the truth. Self-governance emerges naturally within the group.

- The authority of knowing prevails. This means that the one who knows best leads during the activity when his knowledge is of prime importance. This requires group trust and empowerment. In situations where there is no particular authority needed, collective guidance prevails.

- Alignment takes the place of regimentation. If individuals are centered and actualizing their soul's purpose, they will naturally align with others doing the same. Alignment is experienced as deep, spontaneous agreement, reinforcement, trust, encouragement and love. It makes work a joy and transforms the workplace from an arena of struggle and effort into an oasis of creativity and cooperation.

- Natural leadership is given to those who intuitively know how to empower others for the good of the whole. People who are natural synergistic leaders may not have been able to succeed in manipulative or competitive settings. Every group should be alert to those who have a gift of focalizing, facilitating, and bringing the best out in everyone.

- Everyone aims at win/win solutions. There can be no real win if someone has lost. We are members of one body and each of us is touched by the experiences of others.

- Any competition is transformed into community through shared purpose. All roles are equally important in function to fully manifest the group vision.

- Once action begins, the group needs some sense of order. It is helpful to select a coordinator or coordinators to maintain focus, track results, and serve as a communications link between members of the group. This management is guided by the policies of the whole, yet is given authority to direct the parts as needed.

- Communication is key to maintaining a resonant field of trust and cooperation. Keep members of the group informed about any progress as well as setbacks. Re-create resonance and alignment as necessary.

- Refer to your Success Statement often and affirm it in your meditations and meetings. Also, visualize the successful completion of your plan of action.

- Clear out any fears, resistances, and limiting beliefs which may defeat your purpose and sabotage your results.

- For your Co-creative Core to succeed, you will need vision, resonance, systems or structures and implementation, (the spiritual, emotional, mental and physical components of a whole system.)

- Your Core Group must include at least those members who together can perform all of these functions.

- Group members are committed to practicing all the Circles of Co-Creation as they are acting out their purpose in the world, especially the practices of resonance, inspired insights, and co-coaching. The process and the end results become one in a co-creative culture. We are the change we want to see in the world. By modeling that change ourselves, we do in fact change the world.

_____
_____
_____
_____
_____
_____

A man of knowledge lives by acting, not by thinking about acting,
nor by thinking about what he will think when he has finished acting.
A man of knowledge chooses a path with heart and follows it.
Carlos Castenada

THE EIGHT ENERGY COMPONENTS OF A SUCCESSFUL TEAM: THE HUMAN ENERGY HOLOGRAM

Amayea Rae, creator of the Human Energy Hologram, has found that there are eight energy functions that need to be represented in a team or organization for it to be truly successful. Individual team members may have strengths in more than one area, but each function must be represented by someone. These functions are as follows:

1. **Creators** are natural entrepreneurs with the ability to initiate, to originate, to generate something from nothing. They embody the ethereal energy of PURPOSE. They are able to recognize and honor the inherent value in people and things, the essence of their being. Creators support a group in aligning with higher truth.

2. **Directors** are keepers of the VISION. They are able to see the full potential of people and things. Directors are able to generate and sustain a field of dreams. They have the ethereal energy ability to create the space for things to happen and help people to expand their perception of possibilities.

3. **Connectors** are heart people who generate a nurturing emotional environment where everyone feels cared about and accepted. They are good at recognizing and acknowledging individual contributions. Connectors are conscious of PROCESS and ensure that everyone gets heard.

4. **Promoters** are in touch with their PASSION. They are emotionally strong and are able to generate the enthusiasm necessary to move ideas into action, They provide the fuel required to move the vehicle. Promoters naturally share what is happening in the group and its potential benefits with others.

5. **Instructors** have strong conceptual energy. They are able to define a MISSION, to come up with a description of the job. They are good at gathering and disseminating information, developing goals and objectives and creating strategies and action plans.

6. **Transactors** have the conceptual ability to recognize potential human and material resources and to connect them. This makes them natural peacemakers. They are able to create and maintain tracking systems that provide current information for the group about the STATUS of things.

7. **Producers** embody the energy of ACTION. They get things moving and take the steps required to bring things into material form. Producers are good at implementing goals and producing physically measurable, tangible results.

8. **Completors** have an innate commitment to SERVICE, getting the job done in a way that produces joy and satisfaction for everyone concerned. They naturally provide quality assurance and satisfaction.

The Process: Mapping Your Team

In this exercise you will be creating an intuitive map of your personal energy strengths and a composite map of the team strengths, using the Hologram as a model. Allow at least 60 - 80 minutes to complete your maps, discuss the strengths and weaknesses of your team as a whole system, and do the Web of Connections exercise. You will need different colored marking pens (one for each member of your Core Group) and a large piece of paper to map your team. **Read through the instructions that follow before you begin.**

- The first step is for each team member to read the eight energy descriptions and rank each one on a scale of 1 to 10 based on how well they feel it describes them. The totals for each strength should then be ranked from one to eight (for the eight energy components) with the highest number receiving a 1 and the lowest an 8. If someone has two tied numbers, they need to make a choice as to which is slightly higher. Each number is placed in the appropriate space on their Personal Energy Map. Fill in your part of the Team Energy Chart now. Pass it around and have everyone else do the same, to give you a complete picture of the whole team.

- Each person on the team should select a different symbol, such as a circle, triangle, square, heart, star or hexagon within which he can place a number.

- Using a large piece of paper with the 8 components of the wheel drawn on it, have each person indicate their top three strengths by drawing their symbol in the appropriate place with a 1, 2, or 3 in it. If you have colored felt pens, having people use different colors as well as symbols makes it more fun. The name of the person and their symbol should be put at the bottom to provide a reference key. This creates a visual snapshot of the strengths of the team. A blank page is provided here for participants to make a personal copy of your Personal Energy Map and Team Energy Profile for yourself, if you wish.

- You can create a numerical snapshot of the team strengths as follows: Since a first place strength would have a greater numerical value than a third place strength, give each #1 three points, #2 two points and #3 one point and add them up, putting the total in the hub of the wheel.

Team Energy Chart

TEAM ——————————————— DATE ——————————

TEAM MEMBERS

ETHEREAL / BEING	**(1)** **CREATION**								
	(2) **DIRECTION**								
EMOTIONAL / FEELING	**(3)** **CONNECTION**								
	(4) **PROMOTION**								
CONCEPTUAL / KNOWING	**(5)** **INSTRUCTION**								
	(6) **TRANSACTION**								
MATERIAL / DOING	**(7)** **PRODUCTION**								
	(8) **COMPLETION**								

Your Personal Energy Map

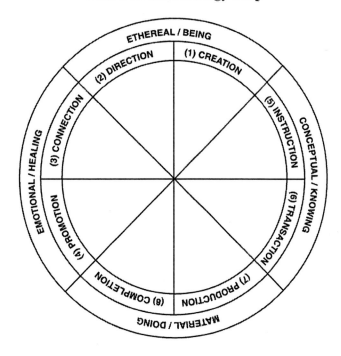

Your Team Energy Profile
Use this Hologram to map your team.

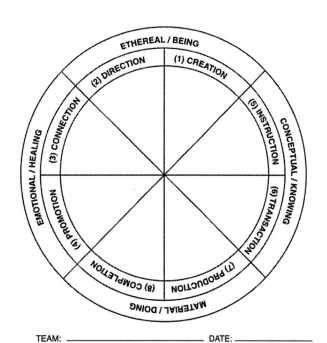

TEAM: _____   DATE: _____

SYMBOL	TEAM MEMBERS	SYMBOL	TEAM MEMBERS

What's Missing?

Now that you have "mapped" your team, determine if it is whole and complete. Which functions are represented on your team? Which are missing? (For example, is your team missing a promoter or a completor?) To fulfill your mission, you will need a team that can carry out all eight functions.

If you are missing one or more functions, state your intention to attract the right people who share your purpose and will round out your team. Trust the principle of attraction and know that your fully expressed passion attracts the resources you need.

Weaving a Web of Connections

The purpose of this exercise is to move your energy from the mental to the physical plane and to demonstrate your connection to every other member of your team. **You will need a ball of yarn for this process.**

Stand in a circle facing one another. One member of your group will take the ball of yarn and, holding on to one end of the yarn, will throw the ball across the circle to another member of your group. As he tosses the ball, he'll call out his primary function—for example, *"Instructor"* or *"Producer."* The person who catches the ball of yarn will hold on to a piece of it and throw it to another member of the group, calling out one of his functions. Continue this across and around the circle until each person has received the ball of yarn many times, identified all of his functions, one by one, and you have created a web of connections within your group. Continue throwing the ball until every function that is represented in your group has been identified, acknowledged, and celebrated!

Drawing Your Group Crest

Allow at least 45 - 60 minutes for this process.

Use art materials and the information you have learned about one another to draw a group crest of your shared purpose. Just as you did with your personal "Soul's Crest," you may use the outline of a "shield" or a circle, square or heart…or any other shape that appeals to all of you. You may divide it into different sections which represent each of your unique gifts—or design it in any way that depicts your collective values, talents, and energies. If you wish, play soft music in the background as you create your crest.

When you have completed your Group Crest, take some time to discuss and admire your creation. You may want to hang it in a place of honor at future meetings.

Reviewing the Co-Creator's Agreements

If your group has not reviewed the Co-Creator's Agreements recently, do that now. Are there any changes you wish to make at this time? These guiding principles are foundational to the actions you will be taking to fulfill your shared destiny.

Acknowledge Your Commitment

When you are clear about your shared purpose and satisfied with the roles each of you will play in the joint action(s), you **will be** committed. So, rather than feeling the need to "make" a commitment, simply notice if you are indeed committed! Your dedication to the team and the joint actions will be firm as long as they continue to fulfill the shared purpose and they empower your personal expression.

There are only two options regarding commitment; you're either in or you're out. There's no such thing in life as in-between.

Pat Riley

Love is the key. Notice if you feel passion for the mission, the actions you chose, and the co-creators with whom you intend to actualize your purpose. If you are not fully committed, clarify what is uncomfortable for you. "Making" a commitment at this point will only overshadow whatever needs to be addressed for you to be truly committed.

This is the time to acknowledge your commitment. Your group can create a ceremony to celebrate your commitment to your shared purpose or refer to the Commitment Ceremony in Circle 5.

Until one is committed, there is hesitancy, the chance to draw back, always ineffectiveness.
Concerning all acts of initiative (and creation), there is one elementary truth,
the ignorance of which kills countless ideas and splendid plans:
the moment one definitely commits oneself, then Providence moves too.
All sorts of things occur to help one that would never otherwise have occurred.
A whole stream of events issues from the decision, raising in one's favor all manner
of unforeseen incidents and meetings and material assistance,
which no man could have dreamed would have come his way.
I have learned a deep respect for one of Goethe's couplets:
"Whatever you can do, or dream you can, begin it.
Boldness has genius, power and magic in it!"
W.H. Murray

A decision is made with the brain. A commitment is made with the heart.
Therefore, a commitment is much deeper and more binding than a decision.
Nido Qubein

Maintaining Resonance

When you are "turned on" and you join with others who are turned on, everything speeds up due to the increased synergy from the group. There is a tendency for people to get over-excited. Some may become impatient and want to jump ahead of the others. Others get confused and fall behind. When this happens, there is a tendency for dissonance to build. If it does, it is important to slow down, center, check with your inner guidance and use the practices of Circles 2 and 3 to resolve any differences and bring the group back into resonance. If it feels appropriate, you may want to do the following exercise now or at your next meeting.

Honoring Diversity Process

It takes all kinds to make a team! As you have seen in the Human Energy Hologram, it requires at least eight energies and functions to manifest your shared destiny. To appreciate one another's unique gifts and styles and to honor the diversity of your group, use this exercise to identify the balance of masculine and feminine energy on your team.

- Stand up and envision an imaginary circle in the middle of the room. Surrounding this inner circle, envision two more imaginary concentric circles.

- The facilitator invites all people who feel most comfortable "relaxing in their being" to move to the inner circle.

- Next, the facilitator invites those people who are most comfortable "acting in the world" to move to the imaginary outer circle.

- Those who are comfortable either "being" or "doing" move to the middle imaginary circle.

- Now, look around and see who is standing where. Notice who shares your circle and who is standing in the other circles.

- Take a moment to appreciate your differences and to acknowledge one another for providing the balance that is necessary for your team to be whole and complete!

- Put on some lively music and celebrate your diversity!

Creating a Group Treasure Map or Dream Board

At a separate meeting, you may want to create a "Treasure Map" that depicts your desired shared destiny.

Each person could bring words, pictures from magazines and photos that symbolize their unique purpose. Together, you could create a collage that depicts your shared purpose. Be sure to place yourselves in the picture! Show your destiny in its ideal, as already existing. Include affirmations, if you wish. (An example might be, "All of us are following our bliss, for the highest good of humanity.") Be creative and have fun with this. Like your Group Crest, you may want to hang this in a conspicuous place at future meetings.

DAILY PRACTICE
Exercises to be Done Outside the Group

Attunements

Between gatherings, you can continue to consciously align with each other. One way to do this is to repeat your Success Statement aloud each day. Say it as a declaration. You might also do other individual ceremonies or rituals to acknowledge your connection with your teammates in your chosen actions.

Assess Yourself

This week do a self assessment:

- How are you spending your time?
- What is getting your attention?
- What are your personal intentions?
- What are your priorities?

Be honest about your commitments because when you say "Yes!" and begin to act, unseen forces align with you to bring your vision into reality!

Journaling

Pay attention to your dreams and any other forms of guidance you may receive this week. Write down all creative thoughts and ideas that apply to your shared destiny. Include your intentions, intuitions and insights and share these with your Core Group at your next meeting.

Acknowledgments

We are most grateful to the following individuals for their contributions to the exercises and/or information in this Circle:

Tim Clauss for providing the inspiration for the **Mandala of Connections** process and for co-creating the material for **What is Shared Purpose?** and **The Tips for Successfully Actualizing Shared Purpose**

Amayea Rae for her insights about functional teams, the design of **Success Statements** and the information and graphics for the **Human Energy Hologram**

Lauri Beth Jones for inspiring the **Soul's Crest Process**

Circle 8

ATTUNING TO THE DESIGN
OF CREATION

The whole idea of compassion is based on a keen awareness of the interdependence of all living beings, which are all part of one another and all involved in one another.

Thomas Merton

Today, something is happening to the whole structure of human consciousness. A fresh kind of life is starting. Driven by the forces of love, the fragments of the world are seeking each other, so that the world may come into being.

Teilhard de Chardin

~ ~

Michelangelo released the magnificent figures he saw encased in stone;
he did not make them. So it is with all co-creation.
Decisions among them.
Decisions are "tapping into the universal design"
to notice how the pattern unfolds in the great tapestry of life.
Decision-making thus becomes "releasing the decision"
by discovering the natural design of creation,
the tao of creative action.

We join together and allow a fuller understanding
of the greater picture to emerge.
We move by inspiration rather than obligation
and discover what most naturally wants to occur with ease and grace.
All are empowered as we collectively co-evolve the inherent design.

Synthesis of personal freedom and union with others leads to transformation,
unlocking the next stage of human potential.
True self-governance arises by our attunement
to the universal pattern which lives within each of us,
expressed as our unique purpose
and released through whole systems decision-making.

~ ~

Circle 8

ATTUNING TO
THE DESIGN OF CREATION

Everything we do—our discipline, effort, meditation, livelihood,
and every single thing from the moment we're born until the moment we die—
we can use to help us to realize our unity and our completeness with all things.

Ane Pema Chodron

All this systems thinking stuff has no meaning without understanding
that we're part of something larger than ourselves.
We've depleted the earth and we're fragmenting our spirit.
We live under a massive illusion of separation from one another,
from nature, from the universe, from everything.
It's the great liability we have inherited from the Industrial Revolution
back through Reformation.
The human species is profoundly out of balance.
If our work has an impact, it will bring us back into the natural order of things.

Peter Senge

As our current institutions no longer meet the needs of our evolving humanity nor feed the hunger of our souls, we seek to explore new possibilities. We choose to create new forms of governance which reflect the experience of ourselves as an integral expression of the universal pattern of creation. Self-governance emerges as we stabilize as our Essential Selves and speak our truth. We are inwardly called to birth whole systems and to co-create innovative forms and structures which express our values and fulfill the destiny of each member of our human family.

In this Circle we explore what it means to operate from a whole systems perspective and to practice self-governance. As we attune to the design of creation, we naturally desire to make optimum choices which honor our interconnectedness with all life. We evolve beyond Robert's Rules of Order and parliamentary procedure, as well as consensus decision making into synergistic cooperative democracy. Revelation joins with thinking to support us in governing ourselves as one living organism.

As we shift from self centered to whole centered consciousness, we make decisions which honor both the masculine and feminine aspects of our being. We come to the circle as equals and all voices are heard and respected. As we move beyond control and manipulation, we open to trust what "naturally wants to happen" in a self-organizing universe. Taking the complete picture into account, we release to guidance through the process of inspired insights.

We are going through an unprecedented planetary transformation in which there are no authorities who can give us the answers. Learning to listen to our inner knowing at this moment of evolutionary change is as vital as learning to read and write. We will not find the answers out there, but must develop the inner tools to create innovative solutions to the vast challenges that confront us. Our ultimate goal is for the authority within to prevail and guide us through our transformation from separated individuals to united members of one global family.

Suggested Process Sequence

- Open your session with the Visualization that follows—or create your own attunement process.

- Remember to check-in.

- Read The Co-Creator's Agreements aloud.

- Read the Introduction to the Circle. Take a moment in silence to reflect on this. Then share your inspired insights with the group.

- Select one or more of the Experiential Exercises that follow.

- Take a break! Move around and stretch.

- Complete any "old" business from your last meeting.

- Tend to any new business.

- Select who will fill the key roles at your next meeting.

- Create a closing that will maintain your heart connection.

GUIDED VISUALIZATION

Before beginning the visualization, create a quiet undisturbed environment and invite each person to sit comfortably.

The facilitator slowly reads this aloud, remembering to pause between phrases. You may want to play soft, beautiful music in the background.

Close your eyes and begin focusing on your breath. As you breathe in, feel your body filling with life energy. . . Relax and let go. . . With each breath allow your body to open more fully. Feel from the inside out.

(Pause)

Rest your feet upon the Earth with a delicate embrace. . . Allow the edges of your body to soften . . .Continue to hear or feel your breath. . . chest rising and falling. . . Body relaxing fully. . .

(Pause)

Experience the miracle of life with each breath . . . Feel from your heart and extend the gift of life back to the trees and the plants. . . Breathe in. . .feel radiant regenerative energy filling every cell. . . Observe the flow as it moves through your body, charged with electro-magnetic energy.

(Pause)

Place your awareness on your cells dancing with life. . . Attune to the deep knowing that lives within you, gathered through 15 billion years of evolution. . . Experience the incomprehensible wisdom living in your genes that knows the universal pattern of creation.

(Pause)

Recognize the exquisite design inherent in the great tapestry of life. . . Allow your awareness to move through various forms of nature. . . Imagine the delicate pattern of the snowflake. . . the veins of a maple leaf in the fall. . . the intricate design of a seashell.

(Pause)

Tune into the co-creative intelligence that dances through every atom and particle of light. . . Experience the force that unites molecule to molecule and cell to cell. . . Feel this force breathing through you. . . Know this as the presence of love.

(Pause)

Expand your awareness to the outer reaches of space. . . Listen for the farthest sound. . . See waves of light moving in every direction. . . Feel your interconnectedness with all of creation . . . Remember that you have come to Earth at this time to fulfill a unique destiny as a member of the collective body of humanity. . . Feel the presence of that which embraces all that is. . . Experience yourself in this grand dance of creation.

(Pause)

Gradually bring your awareness back to the friends who surround you in the circle. . .

Focusing on your heart, breathe in gratitude. . . As you exhale, extend an imagined gesture outward, offering your unique gifts back to the circle and to all life. . . Feel the bond which unites you as a Core Group. . . Acknowledge the shared purpose which is your expression into the world.

(Pause)

When you are ready, open your eyes and look around the circle. . . Gaze into the eyes of each other and recognize the Self.

Take time to write in your journal or in the space below any insights that came during the visualization.

_____

_____

_____

_____

_____

Check-ins

Re-read together the introductory material for the chapter. As you check in, share what you are feeling as you shift from an old to a new way of being and the challenges that you experience as you move between paradigms. How can you support each other through this transformational time?

WHOLE SYSTEMS DECISION-MAKING

Qualities of Whole Systems Decisions

The inherent qualities of whole systems decisions include:

- Resting in a deep knowing that for every challenge there is at least one solution
- Realizing that there is no need to convert, fix, or change anyone
- Aligning in a collective agreement field of shared resonance
- Honoring all perspectives by practicing deep listening
- Releasing preconceived notions, acknowledging that we are not in charge
- Allowing decisions to emerge that are congruent with our inner knowing
- Being actively engaged in the process and taking full responsibility and ownership for the decision

Decisions become a spiritual practice. Our greatest responsibility is to align with our destiny, tuning into the higher pattern of creation and bringing it into manifestation. We are united in our commitment to take action that serves the well being of the whole for future generations to come.

Whole systems decision-making is a practice through which we apprentice our awareness, in a group context, to the aspect of the Divine which choreographs the dance of life. It is an advanced spiritual practice of attunement in the Divine Activity. Among other things, we complete our learning of how choice and effect operate by recognizing the consequences of our choices as they ripple in both directions—into our inner world and our outer world.

When we reach this condition of attunement with the self-organizing dance, we meet in a place where choice and no choice converge. It is place of synthesis unity where the aware-ness of right relation and right timing is so clear that we would consider no other choice than being in optimal relationship with all.

Rich Ruster

Process

Create a picture or chart that reflects the flow of energy in decision making in the current par-adigm as it shows up in most businesses, government, etc. (Think "top down".) Then draw a picture or chart that embodies the qualities of whole systems decision-making provided above. Now discuss what would need to shift either within you or in regards to a particular situation in order to make whole systems decisions.

PRINCIPLES OF WHOLE SYSTEMS DECISION-MAKING

Take time in your group to read and talk about the following twelve principles of whole sys-tems decision-making. Share examples of how you have used or could use these principles when making decisions or working with issues. Make any changes to these principles so that they are aligned with your knowing and experience. Remember that, like other evolutionary processes, whole systems decision-making is not a linear process. Instead, it involves princi-ples to be practiced in concert with one another.

Principle 1: Honor body, mind and spirit.

The value of what is often called the linear, left-side of the brain or masculine way of pro-cessing information is greatly enhanced when used in concert with our artistic, intuitive, more feminine way of knowing. Learning to honor and draw upon both aspects of our mind cre-ates a "whole brain approach" to accessing clarity. It is expansion from linear to holograph-ic thinking.

Your cognitive mind helps you to collect, categorize, classify, analyze, and synthesize data. You can use research skills to scan indexes and electronic databases, interview key people, and track down information relevant to your decision. If you need data and do not know how to find it or use it, find the people whose passion is data collection and synthesis.

Connect with your intuition using the process of "heartstorming". Always listen to your inner wisdom and communicate your inspired insights. Trust your "gut feelings" even when, and especially when, all others on your team may be feeling differently. You may be the clearest at that particular moment and have valuable insights to share.

Just as you want to honor both aspects of the mind, it is also important to tune into what the body is expressing. Be cautious of the messages being transmitted from your body, which sometimes can be expressed through tenseness, pain, or discomfort. Our bodies are inherently wise and often hold the necessary information to make a whole systems decision.

Principle 2: Observe what is naturally occurring.

In a self-organizing system, decisions are revealed by observing what is naturally occurring. Carefully pay attention to where energy is moving and then articulate the process. Release the need to control and predict by trusting life's ability to self-organize. Through this recognition, you can identify new forms and structures that are in alignment with a higher consciousness.

Often a decision has already been "released" and the answer is patently obvious. You simply may not have noticed what has happened naturally and organically. The next time you ask "What should we do?" first look to see what is already happening. You may experience a "blinding flash of the obvious."

Principle 3: Work synergistically with nature.

Align powerfully with your intention; nature will provide the energy to guide you in your actions. You will experience alignment as deep spontaneous agreement, reinforcement, trust, encouragement and love. Call upon the "spirit of co-creation" to move through the aligned "field" you have created. Invite nature's potent ingredient of synergy to help you discover the decisions that you already know within.

Principle 4: Focus on internal values.

The internal process and the path you take to achieve your goals should be consistent. Are you currently modeling the result you want? Are your values embodied in your actions? Plant the seeds in the present moment that are fully aligned with your goals and objectives.

Be accountable to your internal process. Learn to self govern from the inside out and to take dominion over the local self.

Principle 5: Relax and have fun, allow decisions to be revealed with ease.

Have you ever had a word "on the tip of your tongue"? Have you noticed that the harder you try to remember it, the more difficult it is? Finally, you let it go and move on to something else. In a flash the word appears! By relaxing, you "released" the word.

So much brilliance emerges when you are taking a walk, having a shower, or awaken in the middle of the night. The state of resonance is a relaxed state. From this state you can release what you already know. Often when you think it is time to buckle down and get to work, it is when you most need to lighten up! You will discover that many decisions reveal themselves when you think you are taking a break!

Principle 6: Those who know, lead.

Leadership is a reflection of the consciousness and connection of the group and mirrors the highest purpose to which the group aspires. Leadership naturally flows from member to member as the focus of the group changes. In order for true growth to occur, the leadership must be open and flexible. Each individual, through his inner guidance, offers his unique talents and insights in response to the needs of the moment. Therefore, the leadership rotates as the individual with the greatest knowing steps forward to lead.

Principle 7: Co-creative power is empowerment.

In dominator models of social organization, power was understood as taking and holding on to complete control. To maintain "status" or to prevent being left out, people felt that they had to do things which were not their natural gifts.

In contrast, in whole systems decision-making, you discover who has the best knowledge for each activity and then you empower each other to do what you do best. In a co-creative society, power is what you each exhibit when you are in your element—when it is clear you know what to do. You "give away your power" when you do not step forward with your unique gifts and do not share what you know at the appropriate time.

Principle 8: Co-creative structures help to release the decision.

The old forms of domination and submission were characterized by force, coercion, and fear. It is no wonder that the old form of deciding was conducted in organizations that had "divisions" (cut off from others) and "departments" (boxed in). By accentuating separation and suppressing empathy and creativity, these structures prevented natural synergy.

In whole systems decision-making, each part contributes its precise function freely as a cell within a living body. Each person is honored and respected for his unique gifts. Moving beyond perceptions of scarcity and competition, co-creators build new structures and protocols based on abundance and cooperation. Shared purpose and appreciation for each individual's unique contributions leads to positive change and expansion.

Principle 9: There is always a decision that is mutually beneficial.

As all life is interconnected and inter-dependent, the action of any individual part affects the whole. In co-creative organizations everyone's needs are considered and there is always a decision that supports the whole.

Principle 10: Focus on the whole, as well as the self.

A key to releasing the best decisions is that each of you is responsible for your own needs. Assessing what is right for you (honoring your needs and living a balanced life) and communicating clearly is the responsibility of each member of the Core Group.

Establish a protocol of "check-in" times in which each of you can communicate your thoughts and feelings about the pending decisions; however, do not hold anything back in the moment because it is not an official "check-in" time. Use the protocol of "check-ins" to enhance, and not replace, ongoing communications.

Principle 11: Communicate with integrity.

While engaged in the decision-releasing process, consider whether what you are about to say moves the decision forward or stops the flow. If it may stop the flow, rephrase it before speaking. Communicate the truth for you, clearly and without unnecessary drama. Take responsibility for your emotions by being authentic in your expression.

Principle 12: If decisions are not forthcoming, it may be time to re-establish your group's alignment.

If you notice undue struggle, effort, or drama in releasing the decision, take time to re-establish your relationships with each other and the goal. There may be underlying emotions, unquestioned beliefs or issues of control. You may want to refer to the processes for resolving feelings of separation in Circle 3.

Proceed only when you feel totally aligned again. This may necessitate taking a break and reassembling at a later time or letting the issue rest for a while. Sometimes it is not "right timing" for a decision to be revealed. Perhaps other insights or additional information is needed. Trust the process. When the time is right, a decision will be clear.

Beyond ideas of right doing
and wrong doing, there is a field.
I'll meet you there.
Rumi

A final question:

Before proceeding with your final decision, ask yourself, ***"What would you LOVE do?"***

PRACTICING WHOLE SYSTEMS DECISION-MAKING

As you have probably experienced, in a group setting, we seem to gain access, not only to our own inner voice, but to the collective intelligence of the entire circle. This collective intelligence can access a "template" or pattern of action for the Core Group to discover its function within the larger social body. In a resonant field of love, the synergy of group energy magnetizes higher consciousness and wisdom for all. Each of us is often encouraged by the inspired insights coming forth from the group that can catalyze our own deeper knowing.

Instructions for the Process

The process that follows is an extension of the Group Dialogue of Inspired Insights that you experienced earlier. This practice is particularly useful when dealing with challenging issues and difficult decisions.

Read through the following guidelines before moving into the experiential exercise.

- First get all the facts out on the table and discuss them with as much mental clarity as possible. Honor the rational mind and value the contribution it makes.

- Ask each individual to check in and clear any emotional issues or hidden agendas that may stand in the way of clarity.

- Before beginning the meditative process of inspired insights, frame the question as a group. Speaking the issue or question with clarity, will draw forth clearer insights.

- Decide who will facilitate the process and lead an initial relaxation exercise. It is beneficial to have one member of the circle take notes or to tape record the session.

- Then go within, relax, listen, surrender and allow your awareness to expand. Release the thinking mind and prepare to receive guidance from the Essential Self.

- When the group has entered a meditative state, the facilitator may begin with an attunement that voices the desired qualities for the outcome.

- The question is then offered, with the understanding that the answers already exist.

- Each individual shares what he receives as it naturally arises. Often insights will come through a few members of the group as the others hold the resonant field. It is important to speak when inspired, rather than feeling obligated. If everyone is attuned with one another, usually what is shared will ring true to each member of the circle. If insights come which seem conflicting, it is important to hold the resonant field and allow the process to continue.

- When it appears that all input has been shared, the facilitator gently brings the process to completion. Affirm areas of agreement and synthesize what was shared.

- Take a moment to check in with your body and experience how the agreements feel.

- If alignment has not occurred, re-attune and spend some quiet time alone. It is often beneficial to take a break, walk in nature and be still.

- It is also important that all voices are heard and honored. There can be a tendency to over-ride an inner prompting or bodily feeling if there is a momentum building. It can be challenging to say "this doesn't feel good to me". Have you ever had the experience of denying an intuitive feeling because the rest of the group had excitement and seemed to be aligned? Often clarity comes "after the fact" when we look back on a situation and say, "Why didn't I listen to my intuition?"

- When all feel that clarity has been achieved, make appropriate choices that will move the decisions into action. Remember that this is not a vote, but an attunement.

- Always aim at coming into a deep level of alignment. Seek to arrive at a collective 'ah-ha' that everyone can stand solidly behind.

The Process

Select an issue that is important to you as a group. Begin by checking-in and then discuss the facts related to the issue you have selected. As a group, frame this issue as a question. Finally, choose one member of your circle to serve as the scribe who will write down the insights that emerge.

The facilitator slowly reads the following, remembering to pause between phrases. You may want to play soft beautiful music in the background.

Gently close your eyes and invite your body to relax. . . Take a few deep breaths and observe the activity of your mind and the flow of your feelings. . . There is no need to change your thoughts or feelings. . . just observe them.

(Pause)

We call forth those insights that will lead us to a decision that serves the highest good of each individual involved. . . We ask to be connected heart to heart. . . to have mental clarity and compassionate understanding. . . Guide us in the way of truth, love, and wisdom.

The facilitator then poses the question that the group has selected. Then he continues:

Now, tapping into your deeper knowing, allow Spirit to respond, and speak as you feel moved to do so.

Members of the group speak at this time. When there is silence and it appears that everyone who feels called to do so has spoken, the facilitator says:

We give thanks for the insights we have received and the inspiration we experience. . . We acknowledge that all wisdom lies within and is available when we quiet our minds and surrender to Source. . .

(Pause)

Take another few deep breaths and gently move your hands and feet. When you're ready, open your eyes. . . If you wish, take a few minutes in silence to write about your experience.

_____

_____

_____

_____

When everyone has finished writing, share in the larger circle. If you wish, you may ask the scribe to review what was spoken into the circle.

MOVING FROM INSPIRATION INTO ACTION

Often an inspiration will come, and it feels like clear guidance. This may provoke a desire to "jump into action" and move full speed ahead on the guidance.

It is usually beneficial to re-evaluate priorities and review the inspiration by checking it out with the whole body. This refers to individually examining a decision with the mind and feeling it in the physical body. It also refers to tuning into the larger configuration of individuals who will be affected by the decision and determining if it is accurate for this "whole body". By tuning into right timing, that which feels immediate may be better to consider at some point in the future. Or perhaps there needs to be a more solid foundation in place in order for the vision to successfully manifest. The inspiration might be reviewed as to the stages of development necessary. If an inspiration is held without attachment, the process of attunement will reveal right timing and right action.

Process: Reviewing Your Decision

A useful exercise in coming into a whole systems decision is to review an inspiration through the perspective of time, space, and right relationship. Consider an inspiration that has come to you as a group and review it using the following process:

- Examine the action and determine who is affected by and involved in the activity.

- Next, draw a flower with the number of petals representing all areas of your life that are influenced by the decision. Write in the names of people or aspects of the collective that are affected by your decision and tune into how each of them would respond and might be affected by a certain action.

- After moving an inspiration through this process, sit in circle and open again for guidance. Clarity is revealed as you take all aspects of the whole into account.

For example, if you were deciding whether to take a trip, you might fill in each petal with the names of all those individuals and situations that would be affected by your leaving town. By creating a timeline of what needs to happen before you could take the journey, it may be revealed that making a decision to go would be too stressful at this time.

Note: While it is desirable to bring all of the information into conscious awareness, don't become so overwhelmed by details and logical thinking that you remove all passion and pleasure from the inspiration!

Developing Criteria For Whole Systems Decision Making

Process

Using the process of inspired insights, access criteria for decision making that you feel aligned with as a team. Select a facilitator and a scribe. The facilitator leads the group in an attunement which enhances the experience of inter-connection and opens the field for what "wants to be revealed."

Then the facilitator poses the question: *"What is most important to each of us as criteria for decision making?"*

The scribe records the inspired insights as they are spoken into the circle. The facilitator tunes into when the process feels complete (usually after there has been a long period of silence). He invites everyone to open his eyes and re-connect visually with each person in the circle.

Then the scribe reads what has been revealed. From the inspired insights a key set of criteria for decision-making is established for the group.

Additional Exercises in Whole Systems Decision Making

There are a number of very creative processes for gaining insights and arriving at decisions that are being used in both business and education. The following ideas can be incorporated into your decision-making process as it feels appropriate.

360 Degree Imaging

In her book, *Quantum Leaps*, Charlotte Shelton speaks of *360 Degree Imaging*. It employs the right brain which operates holographically rather than in a linear fashion. "Imagine putting a current life problem/issue/decision into the middle of a large circle. The point of the exercise is to take an imaginary walk around the circumference of the circle, viewing the issue from a wide variety of perspectives. Upon completing this symbolic walk, step back from the circle and imagine viewing all the options with fuzzy eyes, allowing them to superimpose one-upon the other in a kaleidoscope of ever-changing possibilities."

Process

Using *360 Degree Imaging*, resolve either a personal or collective issue. Sit in a circle and have each member of your team be the voice for a particular perspective. It may prove to be useful to have individuals speak from positions that are not necessarily their personal opinion. Honor all voices, releasing judgment as to what is desirable or undesirable. This is similar to parts dialog where one speaks from the perspective of different aspects of himself. Be creative with the process, so that it is most beneficial.

The Way of Council

A book called *The Way of Council*, which reflects many qualities inherent in the Core Group Process, is being widely used in schools throughout the country. The council process has its roots in native traditions and Western culture. Council provides a process for an individual to speak his perspective on any given situation, feeling safe and truly heard in a spacious and loving environment. The Council Process is described in detail in the introductory material of the Handbook. Please review the guidelines for council as they are described there.

> *Perceive all conflict as patterns of energy*
> *seeking harmonious balance*
> *as elements in the whole.*
> Dhyani Ywahoo

The processes that follow were chosen from *The Way of Council* as several options for dealing with conflict, making decisions with a large group, or deepening understanding of divergent points of view.

Processes

Multilogue: The Fishbowl

The fishbowl is a double circle format, where those who are sitting in the center circle are actively engaged in the council process and those who are in the outer circle are actively witnessing the process.

The inner circle may be made up of representatives of the larger group or it may consist of a select group—for example the elders, or those who have more experience in council. It might also reflect a cross-section of people who represent different perspectives around a particular issue. This process is also very effective as a way to increase understanding between genders. For example, a circle of women may sit in the inside circle and share about issues and concerns which are important to them while a circle of men surrounds them, practicing deep listening. Then the circles are reversed with the men speaking and the women listening and maintaining resonance. After the inner circle is complete, the outer one can offer witness comments.

If your group is large enough, select an issue that concerns all of you and divide into two groups, based upon your alignment (or lack of alignment) around the issue you have selected. Those in the inner circle hold hands and attune in silence for 2 - 3 minutes. As you begin to share your ideas and insights, those in the outer circle will listen respectfully. After the inner circle is complete, reverse circles and repeat the process.

When you are finished, share your experience with one another. Was one position more comfortable or natural for you than another? Do you see how this exercise might be useful in your community, your country and between nations?

The Spiral

The Spiral can be very useful when making decisions with a large group. It allows participation from all who would like to be involved without becoming burdensome and lengthy.

Four to eight places are set in the center of the larger circle, depending upon the size of the group. Then after framing the topic, one of the council leaders introduces the process:

We're going to use a spiral format to explore this issue. When we start, those of you who are ready to speak are invited to take one of the empty seats in the center. After the inner circle fills, the council is dedicated and anyone in the center can pick up the talking stick and begin.

When the person who speaks after you has finished, you leave the inner circle and return to your place in the outer one. Then another person from the outer circle takes the empty seat. In this way individual voices spiral into the center and then return again to the outer circle, which acts as a continuously changing ring of witnesses. We'll stop when we run out of time or we see that the process is ready to end.

The flowing movement of the spiral helps a group avoid polarization or factionalism, as participants begin to hear each voice express a different facet of the truth of the situation. Soon a "larger picture" emerges, encompassing all the views expressed with a clarity that is rare in ordinary discussion groups.

If your group is large enough (more than 25 or so), and if you feel so moved, practice the Spiral to explore an issue of concern or importance to your group. At another time you may want to share this process with members of your church or other groups with which you are affiliated.

Council of All Beings

John Seed and Joanna Macy use the council process as a tool for humans to understand the plight of different species and deepen the experience of our interconnectedness. "The Council of all Beings" invites you to drop into the projected consciousness of a particular aspect of creation (animal, bird, insect, spirit of the mountains, oceans, wind, etc.) and speak from that perspective. In so doing, it moves you out of your egocentric, human-centered perspective into a broader understanding of the collective. This is a powerful process to do with children or with groups of all ages, particularly when done in nature. You may want to create a costume that reflects the voice that you are representing.

You can refer to the book *Thinking Like a Mountain*, listed in the Appendix for a more in-depth description of this process.

SELF-GOVERNANCE: A NEW FORM OF GOVERNANCE

Living from the perspective of whole systems requires a shift from local self to Essential Self decision-making. True freedom in a co-creative society is possible when individuals operate from a sense of choice, personal responsibility, and unlimited possibility. While honoring commitments and agreements, each person is free to follow internal guidance rather than to respond from a sense of duty or obligation.

John Hagelin in *A Manual for a Perfect Government* speaks of the properties of nature's government and explains how the ideals of self-governance are based on the principles of natural law.

In comparing nature to the highest order of self-governance, he suggests that both are:

- Profoundly orderly (like snowflakes and atoms)
- Maximally efficient and
- Inherently evolutionary and life supporting.

Self-governance emerges as the Self takes dominion in our lives and each of us takes full responsibility for our thoughts and actions. It requires a high degree of maturity and a willingness to dive deeply into our authentic nature. Through alignment with the Essential Self, we attune to the design of creation and allow life to live itself through us, effortlessly. We surrender to a benevolent wisdom and are guided to find our right relationships in perfect timing.

As Universal Humans, we lay aside our local self desires, attune to a larger pattern, and cooperate with others to build integrated teams that are playing their part to build a better world.

Discussion

Share your thoughts about the emergence of self-governance in your personal life, within your Core Group and in the greater culture. Imagine a world where the consciousness has evolved and all beings are taking full responsibility for their lives. In what areas of your life do you need the support of your teammates to be self-governing? How can your Core be a model of self-governance in the world? Come into alignment as to how you want to apply the principles of self-governance as you pursue your shared destiny.

DAILY PRACTICE
Exercises to be Done Outside the Group

Applying Whole Systems Decision-Making Principles to Daily Life

Be conscious of each of your day-to-day decisions. Consider the ways you can make better decisions by using the whole systems decision-making principles both individually and in group situations.

If you are with a committee or other group of people who are "stuck" and not going anywhere, you can suggest that people refocus on the goal. You can also suggest that the group stop talking for a few minutes. Often this gets people away from their personal agendas just long enough to get things back on track. You might also use an inspired insights process. Read the Twelve Principles again and consider ways you can both model and seed these ideas in any group situation.

As a co-creator, you can remind people of the things they knew all along but may have forgotten. An example is always considering the "wins" for everyone in a particular situation. In a society that emphasizes competition, people may forget their basic instincts for cooperation. You can support them by asking questions and gently coaching them.

Spend time in nature and remember to exercise, relax, and play. Allow the design to emerge naturally and effortlessly.

Journal

Observe how synchronicity shows up in your life. Make notes in your journal and share with your Core Group at the next meeting.

As you make decisions, practice going within. Pay attention to how your body feels. Trust the Self and act on the guidance you receive. Keep track of how your process of making decisions evolves. Record in your journal any insights you receive.

Self-governance

Practice mindfulness and observe how on track you are with being truthful and in integrity. This can become very subtle as you monitor yourself through time. Be compassionate and non-judgmental as you move into greater self-governance. You may want to check in with a partner between meetings to reflect together on the challenges and satisfaction inherent in self-governance.

Acknowledgments

We are grateful to the following individuals for their contributions to this Circle:

Tim Clauss for co-creating the **Principles of Whole Systems Decision-Making**

Charlotte Shelton for the **360 Degree Imaging Process**

Jasmine Boswell for sharing information about the Council Process

Virginia Coyle and Jack Zimmerman for **The Way of Council** and for their dedicated work in bringing council to schools, communities and business organizations as well as modeling new possibilities in governance and conflict resolution

Circle 9

GIVING BACK TO THE WHOLE

When we think of economics, we usually think of the exchange of goods, services and money. The goal of this economics is often seen as enrichment. There is a spiritual economics as well, which is the exchange of energy to enhance the potential for creativity. Its goal is empowerment. Both economics seek to create a condition of abundance, but the nature of that condition—even the definition of abundance itself—is different for each.

In an economy of material goods, abundance is a quantitative idea:
we have abundance if all our needs can be met and we have a surplus left over.
The extent of our abundance can be determined by evaluating or counting that surplus.
In the economy of spirit, abundance (or profit) is a qualitative image:
we have it when we have no obstructions within us to the presence of God and to the empowering and creative flow of life.
Physical abundance may come through hoarding and accumulation;
spiritual abundance comes through utilization and giving it away.

David Spangler

As living cells in the planetary body,
we are being called to collectively express our unique magnificence
through meaningful and chosen work in service to the greater whole.
It is our natural desire to contribute to the evolutionary impulse.
Once we have discovered our soul's purpose and aligned with our Core Group
around a shared destiny, we want to play our part in stabilizing
a sustainable co-creative culture.
We step forward as social architects birthing whole systems based on natural law.

Our "giving back" may express itself in a myriad of forms—be it an entrepreneurial ven-
ture, a not for profit organization, or a social, environmental, or political movement.
All expressions contain the seed of a new social form which combines
the principles of co-creation with the self-organizing laws inherent in nature.

For Universal Humans, our greatest pleasure is to fully express the Self by sharing
our gifts with others. Our reward is the freedom to be authentic,
working cooperatively with those we love and respect. The distinction
between work and play dissolves as all actions are offered as a service and blessing.

We create from a consciousness of "being."
We focus on our internal values rather than external results.
Decisions are derived from tuning into "what wants to happen" and right relations,
being guided by love rather than driven by fear.

The essence of co-creation—working from the inside out, combining the spiritual practices
of resonance, love and inner wisdom with outer actions in the world—
manifests as collective positive change.
Cooperative entrepreneurship releases creativity and provides a vehicle
for our soul's purpose and shared destiny.

As our actions are aligned with our inner values
we consciously evolve a caring economy.
Money becomes the outer reflection of the way that love works.
Gifting and sharing emerge as new forms of economics. Giving back in the form of
conscious investing, philanthropy, volunteerism and tithing occurs naturally.

Powerfully committed beings functioning together in resonance and harmony,
we come together to create the acts that call forth our deepest creativity.
It is the state of consciousness that magnetizes resources, heals communities,
and builds a new co-creative culture.

~ ~

Circle 9

GIVING BACK TO THE WHOLE

We have begun to awaken to the fact that our living planet is the source
of all real wealth and the foundation of our own existence.
We must now look to living systems as our teacher,
for our survival depends on discovering new ways of living—
and making our living—that embody life's wisdom.

David C. Korten

Institutions must balance the need to make a living with a natural ability to change.
They must also honor the souls of the individuals who work for them and the soul
of the natural world from which they take their resources.

David Whyte

The practical test I give people is this: ' What joy do you find from your work?' and 'what
joy do others derive as a result of your work?' We need jobs, but I think the key is, how can
others derive blessings from our work? Because that is what work really is; for human
beings it's a return of blessing from blessing.

Matthew Fox

Give of your hands to serve and your hearts to love.

Mother Teresa

We are living in a time when the whole paradigm is shifting, affecting all aspects of our lives. We may find ourselves in the precarious situation of walking in two worlds, trying to navigate in the existing social structures while simultaneously creating a new culture. As we bring our dreams into full expression in the world, we are required to use our gift of discernment. How do we fund our projects and support our families, while staying true to our ideals? What has value in the world of business and is beneficial to continue and where is there the need for radical transformation? How do the values which we hold dear to our hearts translate into business transactions and economic decisions? How does our conditioning limit our ability to bring our dreams into successful manifestation?

Each of us has his own unique calling in response to this great wave of change. As both our internal and external worlds are shifting, it is necessary to turn our attention to a future of unlimited possibilities rather than trying to fix that which is basically dysfunctional and decaying. This shift calls for nothing less than a fundamental change of consciousness, requiring an in-depth review of our worldview, principles and values.

The transformation of business is critical to ensuring the quality of life for future generations. In this Circle, we will focus on Cooperative Entrepreneurship as the most effective way to fund our projects and fulfill our dreams. In addition, we will examine our relationship with money and explore the areas of conscious investing, conscious consumption and philanthropy to align our values with our financial transactions. Through conscious investing we put our financial resources into that which supports all aspects of life. Conscious consumerism is the vehicle for using our power as consumers to affect positive change. Every dollar we spend is a vote for or against sustainable living.

Drawing upon the inherent wisdom of nature, we co-create organizations that are living organisms: dynamic, flowing and connected. Self-organizing systems enhance both the creativity and effectiveness of all involved. Nature also serves to model circular production where all products and by-products are used and re-used. Our rapidly diminishing supply of finite resources calls us to incorporate this model into every aspect of the production and distribution of goods.

It is heartening that innovative thinkers in all echelons of society are brilliantly expressing solutions for radical transformation—those which are necessary for our survival as a human species. Creative innovations are successfully manifesting throughout the world, modeling new economic possibilities.

Joanna Macy speaks to how swiftly *"new structures, institutions, agreements, and ways of doing things are springing up like green shoots through the rubble of our dysfunctional civilization. I don't think there has ever been a time in human history when so many new ways of doing things have appeared in so short a time. They reveal an amazing degree of ingenuity, an awesome readiness to experiment and create. Even though these emergent and often embryonic systems sometimes look fringe, perhaps, or marginal, they are the seeds of the future."*

New institutions and entities are being birthed daily around the globe, blending the characteristics of chaos and order—what Dee Hock, the founder of VISA, calls a chaordic organization. Self-regulating, self-governing, flexible and able to adapt to change swiftly, these organizations are contributing to the birth of a new economic and social paradigm. By aligning groups around shared purpose and ethical principles, chaordic organizations are able to create and govern diversity and complexity in ways that a centralized system or bureaucratic structure cannot readily manage.

MOVING FROM THE EXISTING INTO
THE EMERGING CULTURE

In his article, "Evolution and Business," Gary Zukav has the following insights to share about the new way of doing business:

In the place of the pursuit of external power—the ability to manipulate and control—humanity is now evolving through the pursuit of authentic power—the alignment of the personality with the soul. Alignment of the personality with the soul automatically brings with it a set of values and behaviors that are different from those that are based upon the perception of power as external. The soul always strives for harmony, cooperation, sharing, and reverence for Life. As the deep and sometimes difficult inner work of aligning the personality with the soul through the mechanism of responsible choice begins to produce authentically empowered individuals, the values and behaviors that these individuals bring to the business community will both strengthen and foretell the major shift that is underway, and attract others in whom this process is becoming conscious. As entrepreneurs, employees, investors, and philanthropists move toward their own authentic empowerment, they will create commercial structures which reflect an economic reality that is strikingly different from our present experience.

The following chart depicts the differences between the existing paradigm and the emerging co-creative culture.

Existing Paradigm	Emerging Co-creative Culture
Power	
External power	Authentic power
The ability to manipulate and control	Alignment of personality and soul
Five sensory perception	Multisensory perception
Attitude	
Exploitation	Contribution
Competition	Cooperation
Need to control	Desire to co-create
Commerce	
Primary source of data and strategy development: analytical mind	Primary source of data and strategy development: intuition
Competition, hoarding, focus on personal needs and ownership	Cooperation, harmony, sharing reverence for life

Productivity

Defined as ability to transform material resources and human creativity into products

Defined as empowerment of the individuals participating

Focus on physical/body needs

Focus on spiritual/soul needs

Choices and acceptance of responsibility relegated to upper levels of the hierarchy

Freedom to choose and acceptance of responsibility prevalent at all levels in the organization

Economics

Assumption of scarcity
Focus on exploitation
Goal: maximal extraction from the environment

Assumption of abundance
Focus on contribution
Goal: maximal contribution to the environment

Profits/Benefits

Bottom line: currency (dollars, marks, yen)

Multiple bottom lines: spiritual growth, material well-being, support and empowerment of all

Experience of Work

Necessary
Done from need

Engaging, stimulating, fulfilling
Done from choice

Business Relationships

Defined by what is owned and controlled

Defined by the ability to contribute to life

Business-Employee Relationships

Value of employees is what company can extract from them

Focus on empowerment and well-being of employees

Relationship to the Environment

Assumption that life exists only as humankind recognizes it

Recognition that there is life/consciousness in everything

Humanity perceived to be at the pinnacle in hierarchy of life

Reverence for all forms of life as having equal value

Suggested Process Sequence

- Open your session with the Visualization that follows—or create your own attunement process.

- Remember to check-in.

- Read The Co-Creator's Agreements aloud.

- Read the Introduction to the Circle. Take a moment in silence to reflect on this. Then share your inspired insights with the group.

- Select one or more of the Experiential Exercises that follow.

- Take a break! Move around and stretch.

- Complete any "old" business from your last meeting.

- Tend to any new business.

- Select who will fill the key roles at your next meeting.

- Complete your meeting with a closing exercise.

Note: There are a number of co-creative exercises in this Circle. It will take several meetings to complete all of them. The facilitator should read through this chapter before each meeting, as you will need art materials for some of the exercises.

GUIDED VISUALIZATION

Before beginning, make sure to have your journal and pen handy to record insights. You will want to allow 60 to 90 minutes for this exercise and the check-in that follows. Choose a scribe who will record insights during the check-in process.

The facilitator slowly reads this aloud, remembering to pause between phrases. You may want to play soft, beautiful music in the background.

Close your eyes and tune into your breath.   Breathe in deeply and on the exhale release any tension that is held in the body . . .

(Pause)

Breathing in and letting go. . . Drawing from the source of life and releasing back to the One. With each breath allow the body to soften and relax.

(Pause)

Allow your attention to travel back in time to your childhood. . . Call forth different situations which may have influenced your conditioning around money. . .What are the predominate beliefs?. . . What is being said or modeled?. . . How do you feel in your body as you tune into these influences?

(Pause for 1 - 2 minutes)

What was valued in your family in regards to financial transactions?. . . Did money flow easily or was there a tightness or contraction around spending money?. . . As a child, what was your pattern? Did you spend your allowance the moment it reached your pocket or did your piggy bank overflow with pennies?. . . Was buying something for yourself easy or difficult?

(Pause for 1 - 2 minutes)

Bring your attention to the present. Do you tend to experience abundance or scarcity in your life?. . . Is creating money a struggle or does it occur with ease?. . . What is your greatest fear in regards to money?

(Pause for 1 - 2 minutes)

What do you feel is the most limiting belief that you hold in relationship to your ability to create abundance?. . .What would need to change in your current life situation for you to experience financial freedom?

(Pause for 1 - 2 minutes)

Notice what emotions have arisen as you have focused on these questions. How do you feel in your body?

Take a deep breath and release any tension that may be present. Know that all conditioning and beliefs can shift and that you can create the reality you choose. . .Take a few moments to bring your awareness back to the room. . . Slowly open your eyes and join together as a group.

Check-in

Note: This exercise may have stirred up strong memories or emotional responses. Be sensitive to the needs of each member of your Core. Begin the check-in with the indi-

vidual who feels most ready to speak. Use the Council Process, passing a sacred object (the "talking piece") to ensure deep listening.

This process is an in-depth check-in allowing each person to reflect and share what was revealed during the guided visualization. Questions to bring to focus include:

- How does your childhood conditioning effect your current beliefs and attitudes as you operate in the material world?

- Are you modeling the consciousness of abundance in your life? Where do you get caught up in scarcity consciousness?

- What is your greatest fear in regards to money in your life?

After each individual has responded, take 15-20 minutes to do the following re-alignment technique. When you have completed, share any insights with a partner.

Re-alignment Technique

List below some of the disabling or limiting beliefs you have in regards to money.

_____

_____

_____

_____

_____

What does having this belief in your life cost you?

_____

_____

_____

_____

_____

What are the payoffs or rewards?

_____

_____

_____

_____

_____

What results do you want in this area of your life?

_____
_____
_____
_____
_____

What shift in perspective or context do you choose? (Create an affirmation; for example, "All my material and financial needs are met effortlessly.")

_____
_____
_____
_____
_____

As you state your creating intention, what reaction does your mind offer? (For example, if you affirm, "I live abundantly," does a little voice say, "Then why are you so careful about how you spend money"?) What kind of support do you choose to assure this shift and create these results? (In the near future, you may want to work with a partner or dialogue in your journal to release the reactive mind that sabotages your intentions!)

_____
_____
_____
_____
_____

In 1996 a small core group within Global Family co-founded a community in northern New Mexico called Hummingbird. They purchased the land and are modeling a new form of economics, where consciousness rather than money is experienced as the source of power. Every individual is valued as a divine being and has equal influence in the creation of the community. There is a wide range of financial contributions, with each person contributing according to their inner guidance and ability. This is reviewed on an annual basis.

This community has engaged in numerous processes together with the intention of revealing the deeper conditioning in regards to financial interactions. They have also discovered where there is a field of alignment. Through this process they have articulated a set of co-creative financial agreements. A sampling of the agreements follows:

Co-Creative Financial Agreements

- We know that Spirit, which embodies all of creation, is the source of our supply.

- We aspire to gain freedom in our relationship with money and to experience money as flow.

- We give our gifts freely and as we feel guided, knowing that money is a by-product of our creativity and service.

- We aspire to make conscious choices in our purchases, differentiating between true needs and wants.

- We affirm that money is here when we live our guidance. We know we are taken care of, and we receive what we need.

- We invest in those activities that are aligned with our values and contribute toward birthing a co-creative culture.

- We contribute to those activities that support our soul's purpose and shared destiny.

- We share our financial resources with those activities and organizations that are working to create a better world.

Process

In the previous exercise you began to explore your beliefs and attitudes around your relationship to money and economics. Now it would be beneficial to focus on your alignment (or lack thereof) around financial principles and agreements.

Take a few minutes to reflect on these Co-Creative Financial Agreements. Then choose a facilitator to guide you in a brief centering process. Have each person respond to the following questions, as a scribe records the reflections.

- *What are your present values in relationship to money and what do you aspire toward?*

- *Is there a discrepancy between your beliefs, ideals, and actions?*

- *What does taking financial responsibility really mean to you?*

- *What ideals are most important to you for your group to align around?*

After each member of the Core Group has spoken, reflect on where there is alignment and discrepancy in the values and priorities of your group. For example: how does everyone feel around the value of paying bills on time? How does the experience of trust vary? What are the different comfort levels in regards to the assumption or knowing that you will be taken care of as you express your soul's purpose? What does financial responsibility really mean?

A rich diversity of perspectives and belief systems can be beneficial or detrimental. Do you feel that the discrepancies will effect your group's ability to successfully manifest?

Alignment and clarity—combined with right action—are a magnetic force that will attract the resources that are necessary for success. Be united in the message that you are putting out to the Universe. Be conscious and deliberate as to your intentions and ideals. Then release expectations and projections and allow Spirit to handle the details.

> *If enough of us value life more than money, we have the means and the right to create an economy that nurtures life and restores money to its proper role as life's servant.*
>
> David C. Korten

Articulate the points of alignment as you create your own Co-creative Financial Agreements. Review these often as you proceed with your project or venture.

Discussion

Review the chart, a few pages back, comparing the Existing Paradigm and the Emerging Co-Creative Culture and make any changes or additions based on your knowing and experience. Then discuss how these paradigms operate in your life. Are you living between worlds? Is there a transitional paradigm that is serving as a bridge between these worlds? How would you describe the qualities of the transitional paradigm? Have compassion for yourself and others as we move collectively from the old into the emerging co-creative economic paradigm!

The more we are aware of the things going right, and the more we make gratitude a part of our everyday experience, the more likely we are to express generosity as well. Generosity and gratitude dance together and support each other. The presence of both depends upon an open compassionate heart, a willingness to share life's bounty, and a basic belief in life's abundance. An abundant state of mind assumes we will have what we need, even when we haven't a clue from where it will come.

Nancy J. Napiez

FULL CIRCLE ECONOMICS

In order for our businesses to be sustainable and trustworthy in the world, we must address not one, but multiple bottom lines. The traditional "bottom line" has been to make a profit. Profitability takes on a new meaning in a co-creative society. It no longer refers to the amount of money remaining from sales or other activities after all expenses and taxes are paid. The more critical question is, "Who wins as the result of the decisions we make?"

> *The universe operates through dynamic exchange ... giving and receiving are different aspects of the flow of energy in the universe. And in our willingness to give that which we seek, we keep the abundance of the universe circulating in our lives.*
>
> Deepak Chopra

True and sustained financial profit can only come through addressing and honoring a holistic model which benefits all aspects of our lives. Thus, profitability includes how well we've protected or enhanced our environment, our health, and our family and community while creating and implementing our project. Profitability broadens its focus from short term monetary gain to long term, life sustaining value. The economy shifts from a product-orientation to a service and flow orientation. Relationships and processes become key considerations. Everybody "wins" and every sphere of activity in society is enhanced.

> *The hard truth is that our (free market capitalist) economic system is partially blind. It "sees" some things and not others. It carefully measures and keeps track of the value of those things most important to buyers and sellers, such as food, clothing, manufactured goods, work, and indeed, money itself.*
> *But its intricate calculations often completely ignore the value of other things that are harder to buy and sell: fresh water, clean air, the beauty of the mountains, the rich diversity of life in the forest, just to name a few.*
>
> Al Gore

Process

A business within Global Family created the following eight bottom lines as a guideline for the creation and operation of their business. Read and discuss them. Do an inspired insights exercise reflecting on the "wins" that are important to your team.

Create your own version of the "Eight Bottom Lines." As you continue to evolve your business or project, refer to your bottom lines often to guide you in planning and making decisions.

Eight Bottom Lines

1. **Co-Creational:** We recognize our interconnectedness with all life and honor the unique gifts which we each have to offer. We are committed to creating an organizational structure that empowers each individual and enhances our ability to work in co-creation. This co-creative relationship extends beyond our team to other businesses, other countries and other forms of life.

2. **Generational:** We are committed to making every decision with regard to the well-being of the next seven generations.

3. **Educational:** It is our intention to draw forth and honor the inherent wisdom that is within each individual. In a field where each person's wisdom is respected, the group genius will emerge. It is our intention to share our experiences with other businesses who are seeking to shift to a holistic approach and to educate the public, wherever possible, to being environmentally aware and making conscious choices with every purchase.

4. **Economical:** It is our intention to model an economy of abundance which supports all aspects of the organizational matrix, as well as inspiring a wheel of wealth for the greater community. We recognize that we are true co-creators of our abundance, which will lead us to experience balance and the reality of infinite supply.

5. **Multicultural:** Honoring our global family, we are committed to creating economic, empowering opportunities for individuals from a wide variety of cultural and economic backgrounds throughout the world.

6. **Individual:** We strive to recognize and honor the physical, emotional, mental and spiritual needs of each individual within the organization, thus drawing forth the full potential of every member of the team.

7. **Occupational:** It is our intention that each member of the team be fulfilling their soul's purpose, doing what they love to do and being financially rewarded for their gifts. This generates passion and joy, while serving the greater whole.

8. **Ecological:** We are committed to the creation of products and services which are environmentally sound and contribute to enhancing the quality of life on the planet. To assure sustainability, we acknowledge that the waste of one organization is a resource for another.

Profit is not the legitimate purpose of business. Its purpose is to provide a service needed by society. If you do that well and efficiently, you earn a profit.

Corinne McLaughlin and Gordon Davidson

Full Circle Economics also addresses how finances flow within the system. Are all participants being financially honored and compensated accordingly? Do we fully value ourselves and each other? When we truly recognize that each person's part is essential, whether they make a product, provide a service, or are the visionaries, administrators or workers of a business, then we naturally desire to share profits in an equitable manner.

Shocking statistics reveal the growing disparity between workers and top management in the U.S. (and in virtually every country around the world).

In 1980, the ratio of CEO pay to non-management worker pay at the 365 largest U.S. corporations was 42 to 1. By the year 2008, that ratio had become over 500 to 1!

During the same period, the share of wealth held by the top 1% of households in the U.S. had gone from 24.8% to 40.1% and 80% of the population held only 8% of the wealth.

To many people, this gap between rich and poor is deeply troubling. A spirit of egalitarianism, that set this country apart in its early years, is rapidly changing! Many economists are coming around to the belief that the advent of the information age, echoing that of the industrial age, portends a pattern of steep and possibly rising inequality for a long time to come.

U.S. News and World Report

Creative systems of compensation can be incorporated into any form of cooperative entrepreneurship. Establishing a ratio between the highest and lowest paid person prevents the possibility of such disparity. Two examples of this are the Mondragon Cooperatives in Spain and the original Ben and Jerry's (before it was purchased by a large corporation), where the ratios were 5:1 or 7:1 depending on the size of the business.

As you take your project or entrepreneurial venture out into the world, what is your team's commitment to modeling this financial principle?

Challenges Along the Way

The history of organic organizations to date is that they work well when they are small. As such organizations grow, they get to the point where they must hire people who are not committed to the larger mission and are there just for the paycheck.
When this happens, the bureaucracy is just a step away.

How can a company grow and still maintain an organic form? Apparently, we have not progressed far enough in the paradigm shift to be able to produce a large organic organization. What will it take? Clearly, the key ingredient is a nucleus of truly mature, cause-oriented individuals aligned with a purpose greater than themselves.

*With self-centeredness pushed to the background and a perspective
of transcendent purpose (one of service to the whole), the organization
can theoretically remain organic in form, and its effectiveness,
flexibility, and resilience can continue unabated.*

David K. Banner and T. Elaine Gagne

As your venture evolves, discuss how you can expand your team without losing the organic nature of your enterprise.

Cooperative Entrepreneurship

Cooperative entrepreneurship provides a powerful initiative for re-integrating human culture into its natural environment, by always considering the effect of human effort on the larger community.

The world of business and non-profit organizations is being transformed through the practical application of win/win practices and the expanded awareness that humanity is bringing to this arena. We can no longer—nor do we want to—rely on government or large bureaucracies to support our creativity. In a conscious business, co-creators express themselves fully, responsibly, creatively, and joyfully, and make valuable contributions to the greater community. We learn to become self-supporting and self-generating. The organization becomes a living organism—shifting and transforming to meet the needs of a rapidly changing world. People find their perfect place based on right relationship, going where they are invited and trusting their inner guidance.

To manifest successfully, basic principles of good business are needed: integrity, service, perseverance, excellence, commitment, vision, strategy, communication, efficiency, and more. Some Co-creative Cores, when they have accepted a shared purpose, evolve into entrepreneurial enterprises, so that they can support themselves. Although there is risk involved, we can look beyond our personal talents and call upon the creativity of the group. If the team is balanced and all functions are represented, the possibility of achieving financial success and personal fulfillment is optimized.

To paraphrase James Michener, masters in the art of living make no distinction between their work and their play, their labor and their leisure, their mind and their body, their education and their recreation, their love and their religion.
They hardly know which is which. They simply pursue their vision of excellence through whatever they are doing and leave it to others to determine whether it is work or play. To themselves, they are always doing both.

Charlotte Shelton

In cooperative entrepreneurship, the dichotomy between work and play ends. Gone are the barriers between inner and outer work, and between spiritual and secular life. Cooperative entrepreneurship transforms the workplace from an arena of effort and struggle to an oasis of cooperation and creativity.

As a Core Group begins to practice this new social form it is important to choose, affirm, and declare the success of your work as a model of the change you would like to see in the world.

Some components of cooperative entrepreneurship include:

- self-actualizing all members
- providing a quality product or service of true value
- oriented for social good
- tapping group creativity
- applying good business skills
- responsibly rewarding everyone
- financial profitability
- providing transformational experiences
- being self-regenerating and sustainable
- reward comes from the satisfaction of participating
- being stimulating and expanding
- feeling good, joyful, and passionate
- enhancing all relationships

Discussion

Discuss the characteristics of cooperative entrepreneurship. Modify or add to the list above, to reflect your own understanding and experience. What do you feel is important for the success of a business or project that embodies the principles of co-creation and is reflective of the emerging paradigm? Use your list as criteria to guide your group's venture and assist you in your decision-making process.

_____

_____

_____

_____

_____

_____

_____

_____

There is a great need to bring spiritual values into the corporate setting.
Persuading your organization to shift from a paradigm of competition, exploitation
and self-interest, to cooperation, empowerment, and the common good
is one of the greatest gifts you can give society.

Richard Barrett

Empowering Leadership

*True leaders are those who epitomize the general sense of the community—
who symbolize, legitimize, and strengthen behavior in accordance with the sense of the community—who enable its conscious, shared values and beliefs to emerge, expand, and be transmitted from generation to generation—
who enable that which is trying to happen to come into being.
The true leader's behavior is induced by the behavior of every individual
who chooses where they will be led.*

Dee Hock

Empowered leadership refers to the ease of assuming authority as appropriate. Each person will lead when he knows best, and others will support him to do so. For example, the Connectors will lead the way for your Core Group in reaching out to other networks; the Instructors will guide the team in developing goals and creating the necessary strategies; and the Producers will lead the group in taking the action steps necessary to achieve your mission. In the co-creative model, we are all simultaneously leading and following!

Empowering leaders foster the experience that each member of the team is equally unique and vital to the whole. Empowering leaders have a gift for focalizing, facilitating, and bringing the best out of everyone. They relate as well to each of the parts as they do to the whole.

Empowering leadership co-creates and maintains the vision and spirit of the Core, and assures that both community and individual mastery are valued.

While traditional managers are expected to "do things right," the evolved leader "does the right thing." He earns the Core's trust by being consistent and by making intentions evident. Mistakes are forgiven, even encouraged. Failures of the past are re-contextualized as "learning experiences."

True leaders bring the Core's vision to life. Through their dedication and commitment to the goal, they attract other like-minded, like-spirited individuals to the enterprise.

Process

Take a few minutes to discuss these ideas. Then use the process of inspired insights to share what you know about inspired leadership.

To begin, the facilitator will guide the group in a brief centering exercise. You may want to hold hands and use the Heart Meditation.

After a few minutes, the facilitator will ask the group:

"What do you know about co-creative leadership?"   "What qualities would you desire to have as an ideal leader?"

When group members feel guided to do so, speak as the Essential Self and respond to the questions. When you have finished speaking, gently open your eyes and take a few minutes to write down your insights.

_____
_____
_____
_____
_____
_____
_____

Before completing the exercises in this Circle, refer to the Ceremony of Empowerment in Circle 5 to determine if it would be appropriate to honor some individuals on your team at this time.

This might be a good time to take a break. You may want to play some lively music and dance.

Creating a Picture of Your Living Organism

In the old hierarchical organizational model, the organizational chart had boxes that showed who had power over whom. In Circle 7 you created a new kind of organizational chart, depicting the organism as a pie-shaped hologram, cut into equal sections—which represent the various functions or roles of the team players.

Process

You will need art materials, scissors, colored paper and a large piece of butcher paper. Allow at least 60 - 90 minutes for this exercise.

Create a picture or diagram of your team's organization that reflects the equality and value of all players, the interconnectedness of the parts and the power of synergy. You might see your Co-creative Core as a body, with each person representing a different part. The objective would be for each part—the ears, eyes, hands, lungs, and so forth—to be outstanding in their particular functions within a healthy, growing body. This structure shows the obvious: we cannot perform our particular role if the body as a whole is not vital and healthy.

You could also depict your organization as a tree with branches—a living organism. By showing your structure as a tree that feeds and is fed by the leaves on interdependent branches, rather than a series of boxes, you will be laying the foundation for seeking decisions that positively effect the whole, rather than only a part.

A third way of drawing your organization might show circles within circles, much like the graphic used to model the Circles of Co-Creation! Let your imaginations soar! Be co-creative and have fun with this process. When your "chart" is complete, hang it in a place of honor at future meetings or at your place of business.

Clarity and Focus

As you prepare to embark on grounding your vision in action, remember to set up a number of basic systems to assure that your team is able to communicate effectively and that all members are clear, aligned and focused on your mission, objectives and goals.

Co-creative communication is accurate, complete and frequent. Documentation and distribution of all decisions, periodic internal newsletters, memos, emails, and meetings can foster aligned movement. Applying the Co-Creator's Agreements becomes more important as you move into joint action.

Weekly meetings that focus on "what worked?" and "what needs improvement?" provide encouragement and may improve the morale and productivity of your team. Refer to the communication processes in Circle 3 if you find yourselves moving into dissonance or serious disagreement.

For cooperative entrepreneurship to thrive, people must feel connected to one another at a level beyond personality—and they must feel free, and even encouraged, to express that connection. Telling stories that reflect the movement and growth of your organization or enterprise is invaluable. Trials and tribulations, successes and "learning experiences," celebrations and personal transformations are all part of the culture of an organization. New teammates are instructed by these stories, and all are empowered and energized by them. Make sure that someone on your team is maintaining a chronicle of your collective story!

A STATEMENT OF CLARITY

Co-creative entrepreneurs know that clarity up-front, combined with deep conviction of purpose, is a vital part of the foundation for aligned action. Clarity reduces all types of misunderstandings later and saves energy that can be better directed toward fulfilling your mission. For that reason, a new tool, called a Statement of Clarity, is useful for all forms of our work relationships—whether for a partnership, business-client or employer-employee relations. A Statement of Clarity can replace or augment contracts and agreements written in "legalese." It is always written from a win-win point of view and from the heart. This Statement documents and clarifies all agreements made between group members, in language that is positive and empowering. This protocol empowers all participants to "live as their word."

The elements include:

- Who is involved.
- What you agree to do and by when.
- What compensation you will give or receive.
- A statement of acknowledgment and trust.
- Your signatures.

If you are working on a specific project, practice writing a Statement of Clarity now.

YOUR BUSINESS PLAN

Every successful enterprise has a clear business plan. Your plan will help you clarify and develop your business ideas, align your actions, and strengthen your bonds with one another.

Your Success Statement, which articulates your vision, mission, passion, and action steps forms the heart of your business plan. To this you will add:

- Your objectives and goals
- The list of team players, highlighting their functions
- Your budget

The work that you did in Circle 7 will make this task relatively easy!

Keep your plan as simple and clear as possible. Be sure you have prioritized your action steps. Perhaps two or three people can write the initial draft and then share it with the remainder of the team. (Business plans are best written by people who have logical minds and a gift for clear, precise writing. Jim Horan's *One Page Business Plan* is a valuable tool to assist small teams in completing a clear plan. For information, go to www.onepagebusinessplan.com.

Adequate Capital

Every enterprise, no matter how large or small, requires capital to initiate it and capital to maintain it. The best position to be in to start a project is to use your own money. By everyone on the team contributing, it gives you high stakes to succeed.

The aim, of course, is to become self-sufficient at the earliest time possible. This means that your product or service is designed to pay for itself and that your project or business is sustainable. Until that time you may have an investment or fund-raising plan that allows others to participate financially in the venture.

Should you elect to use money from investors, or donations (for non-profits), know that these people are co-creators with your team. Make sure that their values are aligned with yours and that they honor the process of co-creation. One of the gifts they bring is financial sustenance; another is their creativity, expertise, and passion. Invite them to participate fully. Maintain a high level of communication with them, defining the responsibilities you have to one another.

Staying Focused

Regular alignment meetings at which you review key elements of your Business Plan will help to keep your Core focused on your shared purpose and goals.

Place your attention on your purpose and on one objective at a time. If there are too many items on your agenda, the lack of focus will disperse your energies and leave you without the momentum needed to carry any of them through to completion. Remember to verbalize and align your intentions and call on your Quantum Partners to assist with the fulfillment of your mission!

If you have a "bias for action," your project will move further faster than spending inordinate amounts of time planning. Once you take action, review the results and then correct before taking the next action.

Semi-annual "advances" (in contrast to "retreats") where you review your mission, your objectives and your actions give you the opportunity to confirm or change direction as you, your Core Group, your enterprise and the world continue to change!

Assess Your Team

In his excellent book, *The E-Myth Revisited*, Michael Gerber suggests that every successful entrepreneurial venture has an entrepreneur, a manager and a technician on the team. In a small business, these functions are often held by one person. In the co-creative model, at least two people would carry these functions. According to Gerber, the entrepreneur holds the vision, thrives on change and dreams of the future. The manager is pragmatic, has learned from the past, craves order, sees the problems and loves to quantify and plan. The technician is the doer who lives in the present and loves to be "hands on."

Reflect on the strengths of your team, using Gerber's system as a criteria, and ask yourselves:

- Do we have an entrepreneur?
- Who is our manager?
- Who are the natural technicians?

- Have we asked the right questions to ground our vision?
  - Where do we want to be in one year? In three years?
  - What is our primary aim?   Service? Providing hope? Demonstrating care?
  - Are we being realistic about the amount of capital needed to fulfill our mission?

THE CARING ECONOMY

As we co-create a new economic paradigm, our focus shifts from money first to care first. We remember that the Earth and every part of the material world is a gift and that we are here to share with one another. As temporary stewards of the money that moves through our lives, we support a circular flow based on sharing, caring, loving, giving and receiving. Remembering that we are all one human family, we trust that there is enough for everyone and that we can take care of each another. We give our power to Spirit, rather than to money.

To me a 100% sustainable economy is the economy of love.
When love is a part of every action we take with goods, services and money,
all those actions are sustained by the love we put into it.

Louis Bohtlingk

To live is to give, to share is to care.
Love is the deity of all life. There are no beginnings and no endings. There is just now— forever and ever.

Makasha Roske

Discussion

Discuss and co-create your own operating principles of the new caring economy, using the statements that follow as guidelines:

- Put care first! Care about your customers. Care about your staff. Care about all those connected with you. Put people first!

- Empower all those connected with you and where appropriate, organize around the people you serve, rather than around a product.

- Champion and support the elderly, women and children—who are often sources of inspiration in The Caring Economy.

- Focus on niches and communities of interest, delivering unique products and services: specialize.

- Let your information flow; share your knowledge with others.

- Keep your communications as simple as possible.

- Protect and build your good name. Trust is not easy to establish and those who gain their customer's trust will reap the long-term rewards.

- Focus on the value you deliver, not just the costs you save.

- Have a long-term vision of where you want to go. Remember that we are citizens of an increasingly connected world. For the long-term stability and prosperity of our world, we cannot continue to ignore the injustice, poverty and famine that so many of our fellow citizens must daily endure.

- Learn to play, think the unthinkable and encourage the heretic. Embrace change and flow with life.

- Remember that money flows in a non-linear way. There are times when giving precedes receiving—and vice versa.

Money is the visible sign of a universal force, and this force in its manifestation on Earth works on the vital and physical planes and is indispensable to the fullness of the outer life. In its origin and its true action it belongs to the Divine.
Sri Aurobindo

In the corporate world, job sharing, flex time, telecommuting, working at home and sabbaticals are current examples of the emerging Caring Economy. As more of us acknowledge that the world is a global village and put care first, we are building a strong economic foundation for future generations to come.

"The Blue Bowl Ceremony"

The following ceremony can be done by an individual or by your entire team. You may want to do it with your family. The purpose is to release all wounds from the past regarding money and to empower the financial prosperity of your household, your enterprise and your global family. It is a way to focus intention and express gratitude, opening the gateway of financial flow.

You will need three blue bowls—representing your household, your Core Group enterprise, and the world community. In addition, each participant will need some money to place in the three bowls. The amount of money is not important; the symbolic gesture of giving provides the power behind this ceremony.

Begin by creating sacred space. Place the three bowls on a table or on the floor in the middle of your circle. You may want to add flowers, candles, and sacred objects to create a beautiful altar.

Start with an attunement. The facilitator might create a guided visualization, or you may wish to hold hands and sit together silently for a few minutes. Each person who feels guided to do so can say a blessing as part of the attunement. Then, one by one, each person comes forward and puts money into each of the three blue bowls. As you do this, say a prayer for abundance for all or ask for a healing in your personal relationship to money. Say whatever feels appropriate in that moment.

This ceremony creates an opportunity to shift your limiting beliefs and affirms the values that you hold true in your heart regarding giving and receiving money. As a group, it is a time to align more deeply and collectively create a chalice for the flow of personal and planetary resources.

Conscious Consumerism

The Caring Economy demands that we are ever mindful of our place in the whole of creation, acknowledging that the resources of this planet are finite. As many of us move toward voluntary simplicity in our lives, our focus is on attaining a balance of sufficiency—avoiding excess deficit and material excess. We differentiate between genuine needs, which are essential to our survival, and wants that gratify our desires. Balanced simplicity creates a life that is clearer, less complicated, and more soul-satisfying. We are empowered, rather than depleted or distracted, by our material circumstances.

> *As we gradually master the art of living, a consciously chosen simplicity emerges as the expression of that mastery. Simplicity allows the true character of our lives to show through—like stripping, sanding, and waxing a fine piece of wood that had long been painted over. Bringing simplicity into our lives requires that we discover the ways in which our consumption either supports or entangles our existence.*
>
> Duane Elgin

Discussion

In your group, discuss the following questions:

- Are your consumption patterns satisfying and fulfilling, or do you buy items that serve no genuine needs?
- Are you aware of the choices you are making every day when you go into the marketplace?
- Do you consider the impact your consumption patterns have on other people and on the Earth?

If you oppose the business ethics of a particular company, you can choose to boycott their products. Remember that every dollar you spend is a vote for or against a sustainable lifestyle.

As a team, you may want to create a group intention to practice balanced simplicity in your daily lives.

Conscious Investing

The first place for a conscious investor to consider placing his personal resources is into that endeavor which empowers his unique vision and purpose. If you and your Core Group have created a not-for-profit organization, a community project, or a business enterprise—invest in that first! By investing in yourself, you will empower your entire team and enhance the possibility of fulfilling your shared destiny!

If you want to invest in the larger economy, there are dozens of socially conscious mutual funds that have emerged over the past two decades. These publicly held companies allow the conscious investor to "do well and do good" as he invests in birthing a new economy. By 2007, roughly one out of every nine dollars under professional management was involved in socially responsible investing.

Most of these funds focus on a broad range of social concerns, screening out firms that profit from tobacco, fire-arms, military weapons, fossil fuels, alcohol and gambling. They also examine corporate records on the environment, human rights and product safety.

For additional information, go to www.socialinvest.org, which lists the issues that each fund emphasizes. As a conscious investor, you are in a position to support the new economic paradigm as you generate personal resources and free yourself financially to focus on your soul's purpose!

Conscious Philanthropy

There are thousands of worthy organizations around the globe working for positive change. If you are in a position to donate money to one of them, be sure to conduct research on the Internet or talk with your friends to discover the group(s) whose mission is aligned with your vision and values. Using small funds intelligently and insightfully can often result in achieving big results!

The only ones among you who will be truly happy
are those who have sought and found how to serve.

Albert Schweitzer

One of the deep secrets of life is that all that is worth doing is what we do for others.

Lewis Carroll

Volunteering your time and talents is another excellent way to support worthy causes. This service need not deplete your pocketbook nor distract from your co-creative endeavor! As you move into the next Circle, you will be connecting with other Co-Creative Cores to fulfill your mission. Many of the connections you can make with others who support the new paradigm will enhance your Core and your unique purpose.

A New Business Model

In June, 2008 a new organization was launched in the U.S. called Humanity Unites Brilliance (HUB). This is a for-profit business and a social movement that is committed to personal and planetary transformation and to creating a society based on sharing and caring. HUB brings people and organizations together to move the world from survival to self-empowerment to sustained abundance on all levels. It provides income and empowerment for its members and delivers humanitarian aid and sustainability to those in need around the world. For more information: www.globalfamily.hubhub.org.

In Summary

In the new economy, people are electronically connected and globally oriented.   Enterprises are owned by people who co-create them, invest in their products or services, and are sustained by them.   Individuals receive a fair return on their labor and their investment, as they are empowered to fulfill their souls' purpose.   Some communities even have their own speculation-proof currencies to facilitate local exchange!   They're redefining and recreating how business is conducted locally and globally.

Mindful businesses are being matched by the mindful consumption choices fostered by the rapidly growing voluntary simplicity movement. Tens of thousands of socially responsible investors are making mindful investment choices.

These and countless other positive initiatives are creating the outlines for self-organizing, life-sustaining economies that are: radically democratic; comprised of human-scale firms, owned by and accountable to people with a stake in their function and impacts; frugal with energy and resources, allocating them efficiently to meet needs, recycling the "wastes"; culturally, socially, and economically diverse, supportive of innovation and the free sharing of knowledge; mindful of responsibility to self and community.

David C. Korten

Discussion

What businesses do you know about that are taking an active role in modeling new paradigm values? How could you imagine working in collaboration to be a collective voice for change?

Discuss what actions you might take as a Core Group to work in collaboration with other projects or businesses, supporting one another through these exciting transitional times.

As you step forward in your community with your new enterprise, know that you are contributing to a transformational shift that is touching the lives of people around the globe and will effect positive change for generations to come.

Imagine an association of businesses, referred to as Conscious Commerce, who are committed to co-creating a paradigm shift from a world economy of decline and taking, to an economy of restoration and giving. What if business leaders who understand the interconnectedness of all life were to support one another in the full expression of their mutually held values.

An association of conscious businesses has the potential to mobilize the collective voice of the people, impact change in all aspects of society and produce new models of social and environmental regeneration. Let's continue to imagine this association into reality.

Makasha Roske

DAILY PRACTICE:
Exercises to be Done Outside the Group

Something to Ponder

If you woke up this morning with more health than illness—you are more blessed than the millions who will not survive this week.

If you have never experienced the danger of battle, the loneliness of imprisonment, the agony of torture, or the pangs of starvation—you are ahead of 500 million people in the world.

If you can attend a church meeting without fear of harassment, arrest, torture, or death—you are more blessed than three billion people in the world.

If you have food in the refrigerator, clothes on your back, a roof overhead, and a place to sleep—you are richer than 75% of this world.

If you have money in the bank, in your wallet, and spare change in a dish someplace—you are among the top 8% of the world's wealthy.

If we can shrink the world's population to a village of only 100 people, keeping all existing ratios the same, that village would look like this: There would be 57 Asians, 21 Europeans, 14 from the Western Hemisphere-north and south-and 8 Africans; 52 would be female; 70 would be nonwhite and 30 white; 70 would be non-Christian and 30 would be Christian.

Six of the 100 people would own 59 percent of all the wealth in the world, and all 6 of those people would be from the United States. Eighty of the 100 people would live in substandard housing. Seventy would be unable to read and write. Fifty would suffer from malnutrition. One would have a college education.

Julian Bond

Journal

Visualize the success of your project or venture and the fulfillment of each member's soul purpose. Clarify your intentions and write them in your journal.

Be Mindful

Pay attention to the choices you and your family are making in your daily lives as consumers. Do you buy from independently owned local businesses instead of national chains? Do you buy organic produce and environmentally positive products? When you go to buy something, ask yourself: Is this fulfilling a need or a desire? Will this item enhance my life or deplete my energy?

When making a decision regarding money, feel into your body. What is it telling you? Do you feel expanded and relaxed or contracted in some way? Allow your body to serve as a guide for you in making financial choices. Your mind may play tricks on you; your body will tell you what's true for you!

Share Your Knowledge and Insights

Speak with your friends and family members about conscious choices around money—including investing, consuming, and philanthropy. By speaking out and modeling new behavior, you are doing your part to build a sustainable economy!

I believe that if we are to achieve genuinely sustainable development, we will first have to rediscover, or re-acknowledge, a sense of the sacred in our dealings with the natural world and with each other. Fundamentally, an understanding of the sacred helps us to acknowledge that there are bounds of balance, order, and harmony in the natural world which set limits to our ambitions and define the parameters of sustainable development.

So do you not feel that, buried deep within each and every one of us, there is an instinctive, heartfelt awareness that provides...the most reliable guide as to whether or not our actions are really in the long-term interests of our planet and all the life it supports? This awareness, this wisdom of the heart, may be no more than a faint memory of a distant harmony rustling like a breeze through the leaves, yet sufficient to remind us that the Earth is unique and that we have a duty to care for it. ...it is only by employing both the intuitive and the rational halves of our own nature—our hearts and our minds— that we will live up to the sacred trust that has been placed in us by our Creator.

Prince Charles

Acknowledgments

We are grateful to the following individuals for their contributions to this Circle:

Gary Zukav for his description of the existing and emerging paradigms of business, as it appears in a business anthology edited by Professor Michael Ray and Alan Rinzler: *"The New Paradigm in Business: Emerging Strategies for Leadership and Organizational Change."*

Amayea Rae for creating the chart, **Existing Paradigm and Emerging Co-creative Culture**, based on the work of Gary Zukav.

Duane Elgin for his pioneering work in the arena of voluntary simplicity and for inspiring the process on conscious consumption.

Marion Culhane for her work in releasing limiting beliefs.

Michael Gerber for the information from his book *The E-Myth Revisited* concerning the creation of successful entrepreneurial ventures.

The partners of Global Family Enterprises for their work on the **Eight Bottom Lines.**

Makasha Roske for his pioneering work and holding the vision for Conscious Commerce and Conscious Investing.

Wayne Umbertis for his guidelines for the **Caring Economy.**

Louis Bohtlingk for his vision of putting Care First and for **"The Blue Bowl Ceremony."**

Circle 10

BIRTHING A CO-CREATIVE CULTURE

Life from its beginning more than three billion years ago did not take over the planet by combat, but by networking, by cooperation, by partnership.

Fritjof Capra

In a Hindu myth, Indra once wore a net to encompass the world, and at each knot he fastened a bell. Thus nothing could stir—not a person, not a leaf on a tree, not a single emotion—without ringing a bell, which would, in turn, set all the others to ringing.

Greg Levoy

We are at that very point in time when a 400-year-old age is dying and another is struggling to be born—a shifting of culture, science, society, and institutions enormously greater than the world has ever experienced. Ahead lies the possibility of the regeneration of individuality, liberty, community, and ethics such as the world has never known, and a harmony with nature, with one another and with the divine intelligence such as the world has always dreamed.

Dee Hock

With the support of one another, we are learning how to stabilize as Self,
discover our unique purpose, express our shared destiny and build a society based on the
innate values of love and creativity. Through the Co-creative Core,
we are exploring the next stage of self-government by attunement
to the universal pattern within each person.

Like seedlings emerging from fertile soil, all over the world
individuals gather in every sector of society to birth new forms
which are a reflection of whole systems understanding.
As people converge in Core Groups or chosen family units, learning to be
entrepreneurial and self-sufficient, there is a natural tendency for each Core to seek out
other teams and to join or cluster with them, to fulfill their purposes.

Much as pioneering families on the frontiers joined together for mutual support,
so social pioneering Core Groups come together in larger groups to be more fully actual-
ized. By coming together we tap the power and resources available in each group.

Each team is performing a unique and vital function within the body of humanity.
As it finds and attracts other Cores performing similar functions, alliances of Cores
begin to form. These could be likened to organs within the social body.
Heart cells join with heart cells, kidney cells with each other,
and brain cells link and form the organism of the emerging social body.
The whole is formed by its parts, yet it is the whole which is informing
the parts so they know how and what to build.
The whole itself is invisible until a certain stage,
when the work of the parts converges and interaction is
sufficient for the whole to be seen.

Such clusters of Cores are occurring simultaneously around the world right now,
independent of one another. They are forming because of evolutionary drivers
such as the environmental crises, hunger, homelessness, economic necessity
and other challenges that are needing solutions from the collective.
In business these clusters are called strategic alliances and their purpose
is to enhance the whole and benefit each part.
Many teams are coalescing without yet knowing what the other is doing,
yet all motivated by similar purposes.
From an evolutionary perspective, we are approaching a quantum jump in
self-organization and transitioning from a competitive into a cooperative society.

~ ~

Circle 10

BIRTHING A CO-CREATIVE CULTURE

*Humankind has experienced more change in the last 20 years
than it has in the 2,000 that preceded them.*

Michael E. Gerber

*The task of showing whether or not humanity is viable rests with us—each of us. Unlike
other species, humanity can anticipate the future, make conscious choices and deliberately
change its own destiny. For the first time in the whole history of evolution, responsibility for
the continued unfolding of evolution has been placed on the evolutionary material itself.
We are no longer passive witnesses to the process, but can actively shape the future.
Whether we like it or not, we are now the custodians of the evolutionary process on Earth.
Within our own hands lies the future of this planet.*

Peter Russell

In a fully functioning social body, whether at a community, organizational, regional, or eventually global scale, Core Groups join center to center. This connection is beyond time and space, because at the center each is already at one with the unifying pattern of creation. The center of each group is at one with the center of every other Core, which is at one with Spirit. Simultaneity and synchronicity link them so that they seem mysteriously to operate as one, as though connected by an invisible thread. To the extent that they maintain resonance, harmony, and love with each other and with the patterns of life that are motivating them to cooperate, they become empowered as a living system. The capacity of this system is a quantum jump from the capacities of the individuals and Core Groups separate and alone.

This process of convergence is encoded in our cells and offers us the opportunity to build social forms that can transform people, governments, businesses, economies, and whatever other systems need assistance on the planet. All we need do is consciously choose to converge. Inspired insights and understanding of what to do next will follow, for how to care for ourselves as a whole is innate knowledge.

In this Circle we will explore new ways of living as we bridge from the old to the new. We will reaffirm our values and focus on emerging forms and institutions that support convergence, community, and cooperation between people, teams, and aligned organizations.

It is our birthright to evolve fully as our potential selves and to experience "heaven on earth."

*We are called to come together in an open and
level place with no boundaries,
a space in consciousness of the universal person,
the sacred precincts of the cosmos itself,
our temple and home.*

Sidney Lanier

By practicing the Circles of Co-Creation, modeling unity and love in our daily lives, and joining with others in a convergence of Cores, we are shifting the collective consciousness on this planet and co-creating the world we choose.

Note: Some aspects of Circle 10 are intended for teams that are actualizing their shared destiny and are naturally aligning with other teams to fulfill their mission. If your Core Group has not evolved to this point, you may want to read through and discuss some of the information in this Circle, but save the processes that relate to teams that have a shared purpose until you are ready to link with other Co-Creative Cores.

Suggested Process Sequence

- Open your session with the Visualization that follows—or create your own attunement process.

- Remember to check-in.

- Read The Co-Creator's Agreements aloud.

- Read the Introduction to the Circle. Take a moment in silence to reflect on this. Then share your inspired insights with the group.

- Select one or more of the Experiential Exercises that follow.

- Take a break!

- Complete any "old" business from your last meeting.

- Tend to any new business.

- Acknowledge and celebrate the evolution that has occurred for your group.

EXPERIENTIAL EXERCISES

GUIDED VISUALIZATION/INSPIRED INSIGHTS

Note: The following process is a combination guided visualization and inspired insights exercise. It is helpful for the facilitator to read through this exercise in advance to become familiar with the content. Be sure to leave enough time between questions for members of the group to respond aloud.

The facilitator slowly reads this aloud, remembering to pause between phrases. You may want to play soft beautiful music in the background.

Gently close your eyes and take a few deep breaths. . . Feel your body relaxing as you let go of all plans for tomorrow and memories of yesterday.

(Pause)

Breathing slowly and deeply. . . feeling the energy of life moving through every cell of your body. . . bringing a sense of deep peace and well-being. . .

(Pause)

In your mind's eye, begin to imagine a new world unfolding before you. . . a world of justice, beauty, and fulfillment for all. . . a co-creative culture. . . Take a moment to look around you. . . drink in the beauty of your environment. . . Notice how clean and conscious everything appears to be.

(Pause)

Now, place yourself in this environment. . . Be aware of the Co-Creative Self that you are. . . radiant, vibrant, centered, whole. . . Feel your being in perfect resonance with all your surroundings. . .

(Pause)

Now, see yourself fulfilling your soul's purpose. . . expressing your mastery . . . sharing your gifts and talents. . . What are you doing?. . . Share this with the rest of the group . . Just speak it into the circle when you are ready.

(Pause for a few minutes here and allow the group members to speak out loud.)

How does this feel?. . Notice any sensations in your body.

(Pause)

Sense yourself joining with your perfect partners. . . those who share your destiny. . . your ideal teammates. . . Notice that your team is perfectly balanced, whole and complete. . . All the gifts and resources that are needed for your success are available. . . You feel excited and grateful.

(Pause)

In this new world every field of endeavor has shifted to a higher frequency. . . All of humanity is empowered and supported. . . every true need is being filled. . . There is no hunger. . . no homelessness. . . no refugees. . . Creativity abounds. . . The division between work and play is gone.

(Pause)

What do you know about health and relationships in the new co-creative culture?

(Pause for a few minutes here and allow the group members to speak out loud.)

What do you sense about new forms of education?

(Pause for a few minutes, allowing group members to speak.)

Describe spirituality and religion in this new society.

(Pause again for a few minutes.)

What is unfolding in the arena of government and law? . . Describe the new forms of governance.

(Pause again for a few minutes.)

What is occurring in the fields of business and economics?

(Pause again for a few minutes.)

Share what you see about the environment.

(Pause again for a few minutes.)

What is new in the fields of science and technology?

(Pause again for a few minutes.)

And, finally, what do you know about the new media? What stories are being reported in the press and on the radio, television, and the Internet?

(Pause again for a few minutes.)

Take another deep breath, relaxing into this feeling of satisfaction and well-being. . . Know that as you envision, you are bringing this new culture into reality . . . Feel the radiance of your heart overflowing, sending love to every member of our human family . . . to every village on the planet. . . Affirm that what you have seen, felt, and declared is happening now! Feel the presence of Spirit moving through you and this group, rekindling hope, faith and trust in all of humanity.

(Pause for about one minute.)

Now, with another deep breath, become aware of yourself seated in this room and, when you're ready, open your eyes and connect with each person in the circle in silence. . . See the One in every person in this circle.

You may want to take a few minutes to write in your journals and then share your insights in the larger circle.

Check-In

As you check-in this week, take a few minutes to share any shifts that have occurred within you since you first began meeting and going through the exercises in this Handbook. How are these changes reflected in your home, your work, your relationships, and elsewhere in your world? What are the most important lessons you've learned about yourself?

LIVING BETWEEN WORLDS

Worldwide, more than 1,000,000 citizens' groups, non-governmental organizations, and foundations are addressing the issue of social and ecological sustainability in the most complete sense of the word. Together they address a broad array of issues, including environmental justice, ecological literacy, public policy, conservation, women's rights and health, population growth, renewable energy, corporate reform, labor rights, climate change, trade rules, ethical investing, ecological tax reform, water conservation, and much more.

If you ask these groups for their principles, frameworks, conventions, models, or declarations, you will find that they do not conflict. Never before in history has this happened.

Paul Hawken
www.wiserearth.org

We recognize that we are in a transitional phase between paradigms. We live in an era when outer forms and structures do not reflect our inner knowing. The institutions and systems that we interact with on a daily basis most often do not support the values and ideals we cherish. This paradox requires a skillful navigation between worlds. It becomes necessary to simultaneously deal with the increasing demands of our modern society (with the onslaught of technological advances) while opening to radically new ways of being. We are learning how to embrace what has come before, honoring the gifts of each stage of our personal and collective evolution.

As we awaken as our Co-Creative Selves, there is a reconfiguration of our individual behavior. Simultaneously a new world is seeking to be born through us, one that reflects a synthesis of the wisdom of the past and unlimited possibilities of the future. It is invisibly growing while the world we have known is breaking down. Like new shoots awaiting birth in the springtime, the seeds of this new world are gestating, awaiting right timing to become fully visible.

Discussion

Recognizing the transformational nature of these times, we are called together in compassionate understanding both for our personal journey and the lives of others. Hold council as a Core Group to address the challenge of "living between worlds". Have each person share in response to the following topics, one topic at a time.

Pass the talking piece around the circle at least three times as you speak to these issues:

- What is most challenging to you as you navigate between the worlds?
- What do you need from your Core Group to support you in this transitional time?
- What have you learned that you feel is the greatest gift you have to offer to assist others as they experience an inner awakening?

Allow time at the completion of the council circle to write in your journal or in the space provided below.

_____

_____

_____

_____

REAFFIRMING YOUR VALUES

In their book, *The Cultural Creatives*, Paul Ray and Sherry Anderson offer important insights into the U.S. culture and how we—and the millions of others around the world who share these values and state of consciousness—might organize to change our future. They have identified three major groups in our society: Moderns, Traditionals, and Cultural Creatives.

The Cultural Creatives are responding to the world's overwhelming challenges
by creating a new culture. They are constructing a new world in our midst, largely ignored by the media!

Together, they are beginning to rebuild the industrial infrastructure of the western world!

Paul Ray and Sherry Anderson

In brief, Moderns are the dominant subculture who make the rules we live by. They control the civil service, the military, the courts, and the media. They see growth as essential, support progress and value financial success and technological progress. They are found in every country and comprise 48% of the U.S. public. Traditionals, who number 24% of U.S. citizens, are proud to serve in the military, value the patriarchy, family and church, and believe that the freedom to carry arms is essential.

Cultural Creatives, who are a minority in every country, are a third subculture numbering approximately 50 million—26% of all adults in America. They share the following characteristics:

- A love of nature and a concern for its destruction

- Awareness of the problems of the whole planet and a desire to solve them by limiting economic growth, family planning, cleaning up the environment, etc.

- Give importance to maintaining relationships and place great importance on helping other people

- Volunteer for good causes

- Look to support themselves through "right livelihood"

- An interest in complementary medicine and holistic ways of thinking

- Want more equality for women at work and in business and politics

- Are concerned about violence and abuse of women and children around the world

- Emphasize education, rebuilding neighborhoods, and the creation of an ecologically sustainable future

- Like people and places that are exotic and enjoy variety in their life's experiences

- Want to be involved in creating a new and better world

Discussion

Discuss the characteristics and values of Moderns, Traditionals, and Cultural Creatives, as defined by Ray and Anderson. Which are you aligned with? Which values do you aspire to align with? You may want to review the values you listed in Circle 7. Take a moment to add to this list of values now, if you wish.

How would you characterize your Core Group? Are you Moderns, Traditionals, or Cultural Creatives—or does your membership represent a mixture of all three groups?

HOW TO CONVERGE CORES

We must be the change we wish to see in the world.

Mahatma Gandhi

I believe in rain, in odd miracles, in the intelligence that allows terns and swallows to find their way across the planet. And I believe that we are capable of creating a remarkable future for humankind.

Paul Hawken

Every group has natural, multiple connections. As part of a living system, each Core will begin to seek out, by attraction, other Cores that are complimentary to its function. Often this link-up occurs through a connecting point, such as shared purpose, or through a connector who holds membership in several groups at once. Regardless of how this occurs, Cores must carefully blend during the early, delicate stages of convergence so as to not become disempowered, overshadowed, or dysfunctional by this merging. Eventually, a balance will occur where all converging Cores find their right place in the whole.

The following steps are a guide to this process:

- Bring representative members of existing Cores together around shared purpose or though a person or people who are members of all Cores.

- Create a field of resonance, trust, and co-creative love together.

- Have each person share his purpose, vision, goals, and function as part of a whole system.

- Take your time building relationship, keeping your hearts and minds open to one another. This convergence process is much like the courtship period you may have experienced with members of your Core Group. Treat it with sensitivity and respect.

- Look for points of convergence such as complimentary vocations and functions. Cluster members around these points. Allow for sharing and differentiation; then converge once again. Don't rush the process. Surrender to what wants to happen and don't try to force or control the convergence process.

- Create structural forms for ongoing communication and working together to fulfill a shared purpose or function. Synergy and radical empowerment will take over. Use inspired insights to guide your actions.

- Manifest results for the good of the whole and for the total fulfillment of each individual Core. Allow this ability to be a demonstration of your true success!

- Affirm that an organic federation has been born, a quantum jump in self-organization. Use what worked to converge additional Cores for greater support and actualization.

If you find that there are other Cores in your community who are attracted to converging with your group, your next step might be to create a local SYNCON.

BRINGING YOUR LOCAL COMMUNITY TOGETHER

The SynCon

In a new kind of town meeting, individual people and groups come together to collaborate and share information and resources. Devised by Barbara Marx Hubbard, participants in a "**syn**ergistic **con**vergence" experience first-hand that the whole is greater than the sum of its parts. Participants enter a social "wheel of co-creation" representing vital functions of the community. (See Circle 7.) Small groups form in each area of interest to share their passion, needs, and resources—seeking common goals. Gradually, an Assembly of the Whole is formed in which each sector presents its composite goals, needs, and resources. A facilitated sharing encourages multiple connections, based on unique purpose and shared destiny. Through the SynCon, participants experience, in microcosm, the co-creative culture we are choosing to build!

Discussion

Discuss which groups in your area are aligned with your vision and values and might benefit from sharing the SynCon Process. Contact those groups, and create your own SynCon!

(For advice or support about how to proceed, contact The Foundation for Conscious Evolution in Santa Barbara, California. For more information, go to www.barbaramarxhubbard.com.)

The natural next step after a SynCon might be to create a Citizen Solutions Council in your community—to scan, map, connect and communicate the good news about the innovations that are occurring locally. These Councils would be operated by a cluster of Cores who are themselves practicing resonance and modeling co-creative practices and whose shared destiny is to perform this function. Eventually, local Councils are connected all over the world, creating an invisible field of unity and love that is birthing a co-creative culture!

Discuss within your group whether you feel called to link with other groups to perform this function in your community.

NEW WAYS OF LIVING: BUILDING CO-CREATIVE COMMUNITY

As the self is repatterned, the ways we relate to each other are necessarily shifting as well, toward the discovery of new styles of interpersonal connection and new ways of being in community, given a global society. The movement seems to be from the egocentric and the ethnocentric to the world centric—a fundamental change in the nature of civilization, compelling a passage beyond the mindset and institutions of millennia.

Jean Houston

As we move through a whole-system transition toward the next stage of human evolution, small groups of innovative social pioneers are creating new structures to provide for a more sustainable, compassionate world and to build true community.

True community encourages diversity and authenticity. It is a place to share common ideas, beliefs, values and traditions. Although there are many new forms associated with community, they have the following in common: it feels like home—a place to be held and to be challenged; a place to learn about self and others; a place to deepen, evolve, and be.

A sustainable community designs its businesses, culture and institutions to align with nature's ability to sustain life. It thinks in terms of process, pattern, context and relationships—in other words, whole systems. Thus co-housing, convergence centers, intentional communities, eco-villages, and the Internet are providing new structures that facilitate connection, enhance cooperation, provide mutual support, and build co-creative community for many members of our human family.

Urban Communities

The Co-housing Model

This type of housing, which began in Denmark in the late 1960's, attempts to balance the traditional advantages of home ownership with the benefits of shared facilities and the experience of true community. Private dwellings have their own kitchens, bedrooms, living and dining rooms, but there are also extensive common facilities. The latter may include kitchen facilities, lounges, meeting rooms, workshops, a library and childcare facilities.

Usually, cohousing complexes are managed by the residents and all families are committed to live as a community. Thus, the process of designing and directing their management is participatory, the physical design encourages a sense of community, common facilities are designed for daily use, they are non-hierarchical, and decision-making is shared equally by all. In the cohousing model, there is no shared community economy; that is, the community does not provide residents with their primary income.

There are currently more than a hundred cohousing communities completed or in development in the United States. For many people, this is the perfect solution to feeling isolated and alone in larger towns and cities.

The Citizen Solutions Council

The Foundation for Conscious Evolution has initiated a new social function called the Citizen Solutions Council. The mission of the Council is to identify, connect and communicate what's working in America and the world. The focus of this initiative is to establish the President's Council on Solutions in the White House, an internet television network and local Solutions Councils that will be sources feeding solutions to the White House.

Thus, the Citizen Solutions Council exists in the community and on the Internet making it possible to catalyze and ground new Councils in every town, city and village around the world. (Contact Eileen Workman at 1fearlessmind@gmail.com for more information.)

Discussion

What are the innovations occurring in your area? Have they been linked with one another? Is your local press sharing the good news or focusing on breakdowns? What simple steps can your group take to be a force for positive change in your local community?

THE ECOVILLAGE MOVEMENT

The challenges of our time have demonstrated the need for positive models that can support the transition to a way of living in which all people and all life can enjoy wellbeing for generations to come. The ecovillage model is a response to this need.

An ecovillage is a human scale, full featured settlement which integrates human activities harmlessly into the natural environment, supports healthy human development and can be continued into the indefinite future.
Robert Gilman

A small community of from 50 to 2000 people united by a common goal, the ecovillage can be found in urban or rural areas and in both developed and developing countries. Its purpose is to address environmental, social, economic and spiritual sustainablity. Ecovillages, working with the principle of not taking away more from the Earth than can be given back, often utilize the practices of permaculture, deep ecology, and wilderness restoration. They give priority to ecological building, renewable energy systems, local organic food production, sustainable economics, cultural diversity, inclusive decision-making processes, and holistic health care.

The most evolved ecovillages are:

- self-organizing, self-regulating and cooperative at the local level
- frugal and sharing
- self-reliant and dedicated to offering their residents a means of right livelihood
- committed to maintaining their unique integrity while remaining open to exchange with their larger environment
- nurturing of cultural, social and economic diversity and creativity
- attentive to the needs of other species and life forms

One of the great strengths of the ecovillage movement is its foundation in the understanding that sustainability is not only an environmental issue. True sustainability arises from the balanced interdependence of the physical, social, and personal worlds. Ecovillage life is every bit as much about how we cooperate, make decisions, resolve conflicts, measure and distribute wealth and build community, and about how we find our individual purpose and worldview, as it is about permaculture, appropriate technology and organic farming. In fact, they cannot ultimately be separated from each other.
Jeff Grossberg

The Global Ecovillage Network

The Global Ecovillage Network is a confederation of people and communities that meet and share their ideas, exchange technologies, develop cultural and educational exchanges, newsletters and directories, and are dedicated to restoring the land and living "sustainable plus" by putting more back into the environment than they take out.

GEN was founded to support the development of sustainable human settlements around the world. It facilitates information exchange and cooperation among groups, encourages whole systems approaches which integrate ecology, education, spirituality, participatory decision making and green businesses. For additional information: www.gen.ecovillage.org.

CREATING INTENTIONAL COMMUNITY

What calls individuals to live in communities which they intentionally create as an expression of their values and ideals? What are the common elements motivating a shift in lifestyle that most often requires a departure from the mainstream culture? Is the growing movement of intentional communities a passing trend or an indication of the wave of the future?

As humanity takes an evolutionary leap from one paradigm to another, pioneering souls are modeling new possibilities in every realm of human endeavor. In response to their soul's purpose, some individuals are called to create or be a part of "light centers", islands of hope in a chaotic and confused world. They may be drawn to community life for social, political, ecological, personal or spiritual reasons. Communities that blossom and endure are comprised of members who are magnetized together by resonance and a unified purpose. They desire to be living and working in a co-creative environment that allows for the full expression of their soul qualities.

Emerging at an ever-increasing rate, intentional communities are a natural reflection of the evolution of consciousness. They allow for the modeling of a holistic integrated lifestyle, where the influences of the external culture are minimized. In addition, they can serve as "cocooning centers" for personal and collective metamorphosis. Individuals are held in a safety net of love and acceptance in the midst of inner reconfiguration. The natural yearning to belong is fulfilled as each person remembers his interconnectedness with all life.

Intentional communities also provide a more conscious caring environment for young people whose destiny may be to usher in this new co-creative culture and manifest innovative solutions to the massive problems that confront us. Much of the distress of young people these days is that their brilliance is not seen or supported. They often do not have outlets for their creativity and are blocked in their expression. During this transitional phase communities are vital to providing a highly nurturing living context for these wise young beings.

Hummingbird Ranch

Located on 500 lush acres at the foot of the Sangre de Cristo mountains in northern New Mexico, Hummingbird Ranch was founded by a small group of Global Family members in 1996.   As social pioneers, the members of this community are dedicated to the practices and principles of co-creation and to modeling a loving and compassionate world.   Members of Hummingbird Ranch honor diverse religious and spiritual traditions and are committed to personal and planetary transformation. Hummingbird Ranch aspires to be a place where children and adults live in partnership together, in a spirit of reverence, creating an environment based on cooperation, integrity, trust and love. Community stewards are learning skills for living a sustainable, holistic, balanced and integrated lifestyle. (For additional information, go to www.hummingbirdcommunity.org.)

Hummingbird Ranch is one of hundreds—or perhaps thousands—of intentional communities emerging or established in countries all over the world.

Discussion

Engage in a heart storming session to envision your ideal community.

- What would be the unifying purpose drawing you together?
- Would it exist near a thriving metropolis or in a remote rural environment?
- Would it consist of a small intimate group of friends or a much larger expression of diversity?
- What service might you provide to the larger community or to the world?

Use the process of inspired insights to access your collective knowing. Be open to new possibilities as you explore the potential inherent in community living.

We shall not cease from exploration and the end of all our exploring shall be to arrive where we started and know the place for the first time.

T.S. Elliot

You may wish to use large sheets of paper and different color magic markers to record your insights and inspirations.

BUILDING GLOBAL COMMUNITY

Global Family

The next Buddha may not be an individual, but an enlightened community.

Thich Nhat Hanh

Founded in 1986, Global Family is a non-profit, international network of individuals and groups who are dedicated to shifting global consciousness to unity, love, and cooperation to build a new, co-creative culture. Through Core Group experiences which connect people at the heart, world peace events, and the linking of innovative people and projects internationally for positive change, Global Family provides opportunities for people everywhere to be reunited in spirit as one human family. For additional information on how you can participate, go to www.globalfamily.net or see the Appendix of this book.

The Internet

With the breakdown of walls between people and nations that technology has wrought, we are witness in our lifetime to a massive ontological shift in personal, social and business consciousness. It is a matter of network, relate or perish. We succeed through our networks, our relationships, our win-win attitudes. Otherwise, there is only temporary success followed by failure of one kind or another.

The Internet is bringing about as great an evolutionary change as occurred when people stopped depending on the meandering of the hunt and settled down to agriculture and civilization.

Jean Houston

No other technology in history can match the power and dynamism of the Internet to empower humanity, link our human family, and break down the walls of ignorance, despair, and separation. With over 50,000 people joining daily—one person every 1.6 seconds—the Internet has exploded into a web of invisible connections that is revitalizing and bringing change to every corner of the globe. In 2008 there were over 100 million websites around the world.

Discussion

Discuss how your group can use the Internet to best advantage. You may want to create a web site, join chat rooms, and/or create a bulletin board to share your project and vision with others in neighboring cities and far-off villages. Through cyber-synergy your team can link with others on every continent to more powerfully fulfill your destiny and create the field of convergence that will shift consciousness to unity and love.

The Internet can be a force for nonviolent social change and serve
as a nexus for knitting together global movements to resist injustice,
advance human liberation and build the beloved community.

Coretta Scott King, wife of the late Martin Luther King, Jr.

Finding Your Rightful Place in Community

Discussion

Building on the Discussion/inspired insights experience you have had about intentional community, consider the following:

- Does your current living situation meet your needs for community?
- Are you attracted to the co-housing model? To the ecovillage model?
- Does the thought of living in an intentional community stir your soul? Are you ready to take this quantum leap in cooperative action?
- Do your values and consciousness suggest that you are already a member of Global Family?
- How are you transitioning into a co-creative culture? Are you supporting your circle of influence to do the same?
- What steps might you take to enhance this transition?

You may want to write down your intention and the steps you will be taking to find your rightful place in community. Be open to the possibility that you are living your dream now!

Imagine if your favorite magazine, your daily newspaper,
and your local radio and television stations made community a top priority.
They might help you get to know your neighbors, and yourself, in ways you never imagined.
Your neighborhood might start feeling more neighborly,
with people feeling connected to and responsible for their communities.
Participation in all sorts of activities would increase.
We might even see a revival of direct democracy.

Eric Utne

COMPLETION CEREMONY

To honor the deep internal and external changes that may have occurred for members of your group, co-create a ceremony that reflects the individuality of each member of the Core and the shared values of the whole. You may want to do this inside or out in nature.

Co-create an altar with candles, flowers, and the gifts of the Earth. Be sure that each member of your team places an object that symbolizes his unique purpose and creative expression on the altar.

Devise a meaningful ritual that allows each of you to share what you have learned and where you see yourself in six months, one year, and in five years. Express your gratitude for all lessons—large and small—and for your heartful connection to the members of your group.

You may want also want to include a "Give-away Ceremony" as described in Circle 5, as part of your completion.

Each time a person stands up for an ideal,
or acts to improve the lot of others—
he sends forth a tiny ripple of hope. And
crossing each other from a million
different centers of energy and daring,
those ripples build a current
that can sweep down the mightiest walls
of oppression and resistance.

Robert Kennedy

Close with the Silent Greeting

As your group nears the completion of this phase of its work together, use the Silent Greeting to share your love and respect for one another.

If necessary, refer to Circle 2 for specific instructions. Be sure to play heartful music in the background and speak only with your hearts and eyes. Drink in the magnificence of each person in your Core Group—the Self manifesting as many.

Celebrate!

Either at the end of this session or in the near future, plan a party to celebrate one another. Each person could bring his favorite dish of food and musical instrument. You may want to include special friends and family members as you commemorate the completion of one phase of your collective journey and the beginning of another!

We are in a very special situation, extremely special, without precedent.
We are now witnessing the birth of a new world; it is very young, very weak—
not in its essence but in its outer manifestation—not yet recognized, not even felt,
denied by the majority. But it is here, making an effort to grow, absolutely sure of the result.
But the road to it is a completely new road which has never been traced out.
Nobody has gone there, nobody has done that! It is a beginning, a universal beginning.
So, it is an absolutely unexpected and unpredictable adventure.

The Mother, Mirra Alfanso, spoken in the 1960s.

Let the adventure begin!

May you be richly blessed as you continue on your journey and do your part to birth a co-creative society.

Awakening In Our Dream

Imagine…

An emanation of radiant golden sunlight appears on the horizon as we gaze out onto the world. The birds joyfully sing forth the new dawn. All life is awakening in a world once held only in the realm of dreams.

Imagine…

There is a lightness in the air. It is the springtime of our evolutionary journey…through a long dark night of the soul to the birth of ourselves—unto our true Selves.

Imagine…

We are awakening in our dream.

A time has arrived when there is a generosity of spirit out of which flows a natural desire to share and to care for one another. Diversity is not only honored, it is cultivated as essential. We have come to understand that it is through a rich expression of diversity that nature and thus humanity, survives and thrives. We are able to see beyond the illusion of race, class, age and gender, appreciating and celebrating each individual's uniqueness.

Families, which are now a reflection of resonance rather than based solely on kin, have once again become the nucleus of society. Interpersonal growth and the nurturing of soul qualities have become the primary focus of intimate relationships. As we achieve healthy, functional supportive relationships within ourselves and our families, our communities begin to thrive.

The breakdown of institutions worldwide has become compost for the birth of a global community based on mutual respect, cooperation and love. Beginning at the turn of the 21st century, people gathered in community in response to extreme fragmentation and widespread crises. Out of a deep yearning for a "sense of belonging" and the gifts of true community, individuals everywhere realized that cooperative caring action was the most fulfilling way to interact. Ecological and social disasters served to awaken humanity to the preciousness of our resources and each other. That which was once taken for granted was now appreciated and used wisely. Shortages spawned positive solutions and the rising use of renewable energy.

Building upon the success of programs like Habitat for Humanity, a movement has spread across the globe to engage people of all nations to work together to create shelter for the homeless. Everywhere community has been strengthened as rich and poor, young and old demonstrate an understanding of integrated systems through the application of permaculture, bio-dynamic farming and sacred geometry. Having respect for the ecological web, people desire to live a simple, sustainable, and balanced lifestyle. Genetic engineering is a phenomena of the past as citizens of the world wake up to the devastating effect tampering with nature has had on the integrity of our natural systems.

Community gardens and farming cooperatives are abundant, providing locally grown organic foods to nourish our spirits as well as our bodies. We now understand that rich fertile soil and diversified planting yields the healthiest and most bountiful harvest. Care is taken to learn from the wisdom inherent in nature and apply these principles to the production of our food. The synergistic relationship between plants and animals is honored and all life is held as sacred.

The purpose of education is no longer to train individuals to follow the orders of others and be socialized to fit the needs of a mechanistic civilization. As we have moved from the industrial to the information age, our planetary focus is now toward the rejuvenation of our precious natural resources and the healing of the planet. We have come to a collective recognition of the Earth as a living organism and humanity as inter-dependent and interconnected with nature. Interspecies communication has deepened our understanding and reverence for other life forms, as we are coming into greater harmony with natural law.

The task of education is to nurture the development of creative imaginative individuals who can navigate through an era of tremendous change. Schools have turned their attention to be of service in the community, engaging young people in the restoration of the ecological and social fabric. Their brilliance is honored, as they boldly bring forth elegant solutions to complex problems. Intimately connected with the different aspects of their being (body, mind and spirit), the young people have learned to listen deeply and speak from the heart. Their intuition has been developed in concert with their mental faculties and skills of discernment. Children experience their connection to the stars, while being firmly rooted to Earth, knowing that they are divine beings in a worldly dance.

Young people work in partnership with adults, bringing their fresh creative impulses to wed with the experience and expertise of their adult mentors. They especially draw upon the wisdom of their elders who are now revered, and making a valuable contribution to the transformation of society. Young and old are held in the center of the community in a field of safety, trust, and love. When it is time to complete the earthly journey, the physical form is released at will. There is no fear of death as there is an inherent understanding of the journey of the soul.

It is now common knowledge that babies are greatly influenced by the manner in which they are nurtured within the womb and brought forth into the world. Preparation for childbirth begins before conception as couples consciously call forth the soul. Mothers are encouraged and supported in creating an optimal in-utero environment through a healthy diet, plenty of exercise, and prayerful attention to their inner life. Underwater birthing and other gentle birthing techniques invite the newborn into the world with ease and grace. The elders tune into the "song of the soul" which is lovingly offered as a guiding light for the child's journey through life.

Ecovillages have emerged worldwide, being resource and educational centers for the surrounding towns and villages. As campuses for inculturation into the Co-Creative Culture, ecovillages are hubs of cross pollination between traditions, generations, economic classes and those from urban and rural environments. In these rich centers of exchange new models emerge which reflect a more awakened consciousness. Collaborative efforts among diverse perspectives and understandings give birth to new social forms and structures which serve the greater whole. Knowledge and experiences gained in the ecovillages are shared as participants return to their homelands. Cultural exchange programs enrich the lives of young people as they share their unique traditions in mutually beneficial ways.

When the hierarchial structures collapsed at the beginning of the 21st century, the Core Group Process laid the foundation for a partnership model of empowered leadership. All individuals are now seen as equal in the circle of life and valued for their unique contributions to the whole. Self-governance has replaced domination and control as individuals take responsibility for their choices and actions in life. The wisdom inherent in natural law creates the guiding principles of all nations. Restorative justice and the way of council have become the vehicles for conflict resolution. Leaders come together and access their collective wisdom as they make whole systems decisions on behalf of all life for generations to come.

The power of prayer, clear intention and group meditation is widely accepted and has been integrated into daily life in every sector of society. Back at the beginning of the 21st century, it was clearly revealed that a collective of individuals aligned in prayer and intention greatly impacted peace negotiations and the laying down of arms. Group attunement now precedes all activity and honors beings in other dimensions that are working on our behalf. There is an experience of co-creation with all kingdoms as the invisible realm is invoked for the greatest good of all. Ceremonies and rituals are integral as we honor the passages from one stage of life to another.

A caring economy cultivates generosity of spirit and resources. Full Circle Economics ensures that all individuals are valued first and foremost as humans and honored for their unique contribution to the whole. Individuals experience a renewed sense of dignity and respect as they are supported to fulfill their soul's purpose. The sharing of material resources and local barter economies have become a new mode of economic exchange. The distinction between work and play has dissolved as each person is pursuing his passion and following the guidance of the heart.

Voluntary simplicity is now the trend in the western world and those of the developing nations have come to appreciate their traditional ways and a lifestyle more attuned to the cycles of nature. They are no longer enticed to the frivolous and wasteful ways of the developed nations and capitalistic lifestyle. Instead there is a reverse trend whereby corporate leaders are drawing upon the wisdom of tribal elders.

Understanding the interrelatedness of all aspects of our being (the diversity of systems within our physical body, as well as the relationship between body, mind, emotions and spirit), we address our health and well-being from a wholistic perspective. We have moved from fear-based invasive modern medicine, to a focus on prevention and optimal health as we lovingly take care of our bodies. Periodic check-ups help to fine tune our personal regimens of diet and exercise. Technological advances are interwoven with ancient tribal remedies to create a diversified inter-disciplinary approach to healing. Children are educated from a very early age to healthy eating habits and a diversity of self-healing techniques. The epidemic of degenerative diseases is rapidly declining.

The arts are flourishing, creating a global renaissance as never experienced before. Centers for visual and performing arts are at the heart of every community. Media is transformed and is utilized to inspire, uplift, educate and inform. Singing, dancing, and performing ritual are all expressions of celebration for the gift and the privilege of being alive!

It was with great astonishment during the era of the Great Turning that the general populace of the world experienced the emergence of the co-creative culture. It was as though there was an invisible root system quietly spreading throughout the land. Within a growing number of social pioneers, a cellular knowing was activated and a mythic tale from an ancient time was remembered.

As seedlings emerging from fertile soil, there burst forth in the spring of our evolutionary journey a great tapestry of hope and possibility. Just as a butterfly delicately leaves behind its cocoon and unfolds into flight, the Universal Human has emerged as a fully conscious embodiment of Spirit's expression in matter. Humanity has opened its collective eyes and has been born anew.

APPENDIX

Sample Closing Exercises

SINGING

Stand in a circle and join hands as you sing "We are the World", "Let There Be Peace on Earth" or another familiar and appropriate song. Background music is optional. If there is a musician in your group, that person could share his gift and the group could accompany him. Allow your eyes to move from person to person and take in the beauty of each member of your group.

THE QUAKER CIRCLE

Hold hands and stand or sit in a circle. Radiate your love in silence to each person. If any inspired insights emerge, speak them softly into the center of the circle. Allow yourself to be guided by Spirit and do not feel that you must speak if you are not inspired to do so. When everyone has had an opportunity to express himself, the facilitator can close the session by saying, "So be it," or any words that seem appropriate to signal the end of the meeting.

BLESSING HUMANITY AND THE EARTH

Stand in a circle and, one by one, say anything from your heart that you need to express to feel complete for this session. Reach down to the Earth and then up to the sky, sending your love and energy to all of humanity and to the planet.

CHANTING OR "OMING"

Close your eyes and center yourselves. Allow your voices to blend in a chant, moving from quiet sounds to louder ones. Imagine that you are expressing your feelings for each other and for the Creator. If you use the sound "om," feel the sound moving through your body and find the tone that brings your body into perfect balance and resonance. Continue with the chanting or oming until you come to a natural conclusion.

LOVING ONE ANOTHER

Holds hands in a circle as you take a minute to reflect on the opportunity you have been given to play, grow and create together. Close your eyes and open your heart to each person in the circle. The facilitator can speak the name of each member of your group, as you send love to that person. Then, put the name of anyone you wish into the circle and send love to that person.

RESOURCES

Global Family: How to Stay Connected

Global Family, founded in 1986, is a non-profit, international network of individuals and groups who are dedicated to experiencing unconditional love and the birth of a new co-creative society. We know that the numerous environmental, social, economic, and human problems now facing us have as their root cause a sense of separation. Therefore, our purpose is to support a shift in consciousness from separation and fear to unity, love, and cooperation, so that each of us can more fully express our life purpose and join with others in compassionate action for the benefit of all.

WHAT YOUR SUPPORT MEANS

People activate their membership in Global Family and support its work because they find themselves in alignment with our values and purpose. Global Family provides special opportunities for both personal and group empowerment. We:

- Encourage the formation of supportive Core Groups to connect people at the heart and activate their creativity

- Promote global peace events that demonstrate new ways of celebrating and working together

- Provide special processes for group alignment and social cooperation to build a resonant field of love and a unified field of action

- Offer trainings in the Core Group Process and the Circles of Co-Creation

- Link people and projects to effect positive change in the world.

Funded by tax-deductible membership gifts, private donations, and sales of services and products, Global Family serves as an important communications hub and catalyst for the changes we most deeply desire in the world. Adding your energy, unique talents, and gifts to this work will bring us that much closer to realizing our collective vision of a world reunited in Spirit as one living system. Please join us in reuniting the global family!

LINK UP!

Global family's web site can be accessed at http://www.globalfamily.net. Information about all of the programs and activities of Global Family can be found there. To join Global Family's network of social pioneers, we invite you to activate your membership, by filling in the form on our web site or on page 264 and making a contribution of $33.00, $66.00, $99.00 or more per year to support this important vision and work. (If finances are limited, please contribute what you can. We acknowledge everyone as part of Global Family, but we would like to hear from you.)

Please write or call for information:

Global Family, 11689 Lowhills Rd. Nevada City, CA 95959 USA
(530) 470-9280 fax. (805) 456-0640
E-mail: connect@globalfamily.net

Through Global Family You Can:

ACTUALIZE YOUR LIFE PURPOSE!

Become part of a Core Group to experience your deep soul connection to others. By linking up with friends, family and co-workers, you can accelerate your spiritual growth, create community, and gain support to discover and fulfill your life's purpose.

Bring greater meaning, joy, and productivity to your projects through our workshops and trainings. These valuable educational experiences apply the Core Group Process and co-creative techniques to empower teams in their work together.

Respond to the numerous environmental and social problems now facing the planet by expressing your unique gifts and talents and taking responsible action with other members of our global family.

BE EMPOWERED AND SUPPORTED!

Connect with other members by participating in regional gatherings and international conferences that foster community, enhance personal transformation, and catalyze joint projects for positive change. **The annual Global Family Advance** and other gatherings are an opportunity to meet for a number of days with other members—to be nurtured, healed, supported and empowered in the full actualization of your life purpose.

Stay in touch with the "good news" and breakthroughs of our evolving world family by checking in at Global Family's website (www.globalfamily.net).

Be empowered by linking with others to co-create activities and celebrations for global peace such as Earth Day and the December 31st World Peace Meditation.

MAKE A DIFFERENCE!

Experience the important difference that your contribution makes. To support our collective vision, we invite you to fund the ongoing work of Global Family with a donation, a membership gift or a monthly pledge.

WE WOULD LOVE TO SUPPORT YOU

Global Family provides a range of training programs in the Core Group Process and the Circles of Co-Creation, as well as conference facilitation services. Let us know how we can best serve you!

**Duplicate this page and fax it to: (805) 456-0640 or
Go online and join at www.globalfamily.net**

Opportunities for Participation
Ongoing Support for You and Your Core Group

YES, *I am a partner with Global Family. I am personally committed to modeling unity and love in my daily life, to caring for the Earth, and to supporting the well-being of all members of my global family. I will do my part by:*

☐ Sharing Global Family information with family, friends, and colleagues.

☐ Being part of a Core Group in my area.

   ☐ I am willing to join with at least two others and form a supportive Core Group.

   ☐ I am currently in a Core Group and will continue the process.

   ☐ Please send me additional Co-Creator's Handbooks @ $22.00 plus $4.00 shipping and handling. # _____   Enclosed $ _____ .

   ☐ Actualizing my full potential. Please send me more information on trainings, workshops and gatherings.

   ☐ Participating in international conferences.

Following my inner guidance, I'm grateful for the opportunity to contribute financially to support the shift in global consciousness from separation and fear to unity and love.

   ☐ Enclosed is my tax deductible gift of $ _____ to fund this vision.

   ☐ Enclosed is my donation of $ _____ for a one year gift membership for the person(s) listed below. (Please include their name, address, and phone number.)

   ☐ Please include me as a member of the Pledge Family as a special opportunity to fund world peace. I will contribute $ _____ monthly for the next twelve months, beginning with the month of _____. ($10 per month minimum.)

   ☐ Check enclosed totaling $ _____ Charge my: __VISA   __MasterCard

   Card # _____

   Expiry date: _____

Name: _____   Phone # H (_____)_____

Address: _____   W (_____)_____

City: _____   State/Prov. _____

Zip/Postal Code: _____   E-mail Address: _____

RECOMMENDED RESOURCES

Circle 1: Awakening the Co-creative Self

Books

Advanced Contemplation: The Peace Within You by Paul Brunton
Awakening the Buddha Within by Lama Surya Das
Be Here Now by Ram Dass
Change Your Mind, Change Your Body by Suzie Prudden
Chop Wood, Carry Water by Rick Fields and Peggy Taylor
Consciousness Speaks by Ramesh S. Balsekar
Cry in the Desert by Byron Katie
Diamond Heart: Being and the Meaning of Life by A.H. Almass
Embracing the Beloved by Stephen and Ondrea Levine
Emergence by Barbara Marx Hubbard
From Seekers to Finders by Satyam Nadeen
Gratefulness, The Heart of Prayer by Brother David Steindl-Rast
How About Now; Relaxing into Clear Seeing by Arjuna Nick Ardagh

Circle 2: Connecting at the Heart

Books

A Heart as Wide as the World by Sharon Salzberg
Creating Love by John Bradshaw
Love; Living, Loving and Learning by Leo Buscaglia
Lovingkindness by Sharon Salzberg
Peace, Love, and Healing by Bernie Siegal, M.D.
Teach Only Love; Love is Letting Go of Fear by Gerald Jampolsky, M.D.
The Art and Practice of Loving by Frank Andrews
The Enlightened Heart by Stephen Mitchell
The Long Road Turns to Joy by Thich Nhat Hanh
The Only Diet There Is; Loving Relationships by Sondra Ray
The Prophet (on Love) by Kahlil Gibran

Circle 3: Overcoming the Illusion of Separation

Books

A Book for Couples by Hugh and Gayle Prather
Anger: The Misunderstood Emotion by Carol Tavris
Conscious Loving by Gay and Kathlyn Hendricks
Creative Visualization by Shakti Gawain
Embracing the Beloved by Stephen and Ondrea Levine
Emotional Intelligence by Daniel Goleman
Getting to Peace by William L.Ury

Making it Safe to Love by Heidi Fox and Fred J. Keyser
The Shared Heart by Joyce and Barry Vissell
The Tao of Negotiation by Joel Edelman and Mary Beth Crain
Twenty Communication Tips for Couples by Doyle Barnett

Circle 4: Accessing Our Collective Wisdom

Books

A Course in Miracles
Discover the Power Within You by Eric Butterworth
Listening by Lee Coit
New Teachings for an Awakened Humanity by Virginia Essene
The Art of Meditation by Joel Goldsmith
The Seat of the Soul; Soul Stories by Gary Zukav

Circle 5: Honoring the Sacred: Ceremony, Ritual & Celebration

Books

Calling the Circle by Christina Baldwin
Call to Connection by Carole Kammen and Jodi Gold
Festivals, Family and Food by Diana Carey and Judy Large
Festivals in the New Age by David Spangler
Hearing Everyone's Voice edited by Susan Hopkins
Illuminata by Marianne Williamson
Natural Learning Rhythms by Josette and Sambhava Luvmour
New Games for the Whole Family by Dale N. LeFevre
Playing by Heart by O. Fred Donaldson
Sacred Living: A Daily Guide by Robin Heerens Lysne
The Sacred: Ways of Knowledge, Sources of Life by Peggy Beck, Anna Lee, and Nia Francisco

Additional Resources

Cooperative Games
Many different co-operative games for families, children, groups and communities are available from Family Pastimes. See their web site @ www.familypastimes.com.

Circle 6: Discovering Our Soul's Purpose

Books

Anatomy of the Spirit by Caroline Myss

Callings by Gregg Levoy
Care of the Soul by Thomas Moore
Do What You Love, the Money Will Follow by Marsha Sinetar
Finding a Path with a Heart by Beverly A. Potter, Ph.D.
Finding Your Life's Calling by Greg Bogart, Ph.D.
Follow Your Career Star: A Career Quest Based on Inner Values by Jon Snodgrass, Ph.D.
Fulfill Your Soul's Purpose by Naomi Stephan, Ph.D.
The Alchemist: A Fable about Following Your Dream by Paulo Coelho
The Artist's Way by Julia Cameron
The Call of God by Robert Shaw
The Kin of Ata by Dorothy Bryant
The Life You Were Born to Live by Dan Millman
The Path with Heart by Jack Kornfield
The Reinvention of Work by Matthew Fox
The Road Less Traveled by M. Scott Peck
The Soul's Code: In Search of Character and Calling by James Hillman
The Tenth Insight by James Redfield
Transformation by Robert Johnson
Vision River Guide compiled by Gary R. Smith
Work with Passion by Nancy Anderson

Circle 7: Exploring Our Shared Destiny

Books

A Passion for the Possible; The Possible Human; and other works by Jean Houston
Living in Balance by Joel and Michelle Levey
Living with Passion by Peter L. Hirsch
Teamworks; Wishcraft, by Barbara Sher with Annie Gottlieb

Circle 8: Attuning to the Design of Creation

Books

Manual for a Perfect Government by John Hagelin
Quantum Leaps by Charlotte Shelton
The Way of Council by Jack Zimmerman with Virginia Coyle
Thinking Like a Mountain by John Seed and Joanna Macy

Circle 9: Giving Back to the Whole

Books

A World Waiting to be Born by M. Scott Peck, M.D.

Beyond Globalization; Building a Win-Win World; Creating Alternative Futures by Hazel Henderson

Birth of the Chaordic Age by Dee Hock

Clicking by Faith Popcorn

Creating Community Anywhere by Carolyn Shaffer and Kristin Anundsen

Designing Effective Organizations by David K. Banner and T. Elaine Gagne

First Things First by Stephen Covey

How Can I Help? Stories and Reflections on Service by Ram Dass and Paul Gorman

Investing from the Heart by Jack A. Brill and Alan Reder (The appendix of this book offers lists of socially responsible companies in which to invest and the 100 best companies to work for.)

Living Legacies by Duane Elgin and Coleen Ledrew

Money is Love by Barbara Wilder

Natural Capitalism by Paul Hawken and Amory and Hunter Lovins

Rebuilding Community in America by Ken Norwood

Revolution of the Heart by Bill Shore

Simple Abundance by Sarah Ban Breathnach

Spirit Matters by Michael Lerner

Spiritual Politics by Gordon Davidson and Corinne McLaughlin

The Consumer's Guide to Effective Environmental Choices by Michael Brower, PhD and Warren Leon, PhD

The Ecology of Commerce; Growing a Business; The Next Economy by Paul Hawken

The E-Myth Revisited by Michael Gerber

The End of Work by Jeremy Rifkin

The Fifth Discipline by Peter Senge

The One Page Business Plan® by Jim Horan, http:

The Post-Corporate World by David Korten

The Sacred Depths of Nature by Ursula Goodenough

The Tenth Insight: An Experiential Guide by James Redfield

Visionary Business by Marc Allen

Voluntary Simplicity by Duane Elgin

Circle 10: Birthing a Co-creative Culture

Books
A World United Where All Live Together as Family by John Shevlin
And We are Doing It! Building an Ecovillage Future by Ross Jackson
Civilization and the Transformation of Power by Jim Garrison
Communities Directory: a Guide to Intentional Communities and Cooperative Living, edited by the Fellowship of Intentional Communities
Conscious Evolution; The Revelation by Barbara Marx Hubbard
Consciousness: The Bridge from Science to God by Peter Russell
Creating Community Anywhere by Carolyn Shaffer and Kristin Anundsen
Ecologue: The Environmental Catalogue and Consumer's Guide for a Safe Earth by Bruce N. Anderson, editor
Eco-villages and Sustainable Communities, Models for 21st Century Living, edited by Findhorn Press
Earth Awakening: Promise Ahead by Duane Elgin
Earth in the Balance by Al Gore
Getting to Peace by William L. Ury
Healing the Soul of America by Marianne Williamson
Imagine edited by Marianne Williamson
Jump Time by Jean Houston
Mid-Course Correction by Ray Anderson
Navigating the Tides of Change by David La Chapelle
New World, New Mind by Robert Ornstein and Paul Erlich
Sacred Circles by Sally Craig and Robin Carnes
Shared Visions, Shared Lives: Communal Living around the Globe by Bill Metcalf
The Chalice and the Blade by Riane Eisler
The Cultural Creatives by Paul H. Ray, PhD and Sherry Ruth Anderson, PhD
The Dream of the Earth by Thomas Berry
The Fabric of the Future edited by M.J. Ryan
The Global Brain Awakens; Waking Up in Time; From Science to God by Peter Russell
The Great Turning by Craig Schindler and Gary Lapid
The Last Hours of Ancient Sunlight by Thom Hartmann, Neale Donald Walsch, Joseph Chilton Pearce
The Moral Architecture of World Peace compiled by Helena Cobban
The Phenomenon of Man by Pierre Teilhard de Chardin
The Quantum Society by Dana and Marshall Zohar
The Soul of Education by Rachelle Kesseler
The Tenth Insight by James Redfield
The Tipping Point: How Little Things Can Make a Big Difference by Malcolm Gladwell
Tomorrow's Children by Riane Eisler
Unknown Man by Yatri
Wisdom Circles by Charles Garfield

RECOMMENDED MUSIC

Heartful, Inspirational, or Meditative Selections

A Day without Rain ; The Celts; The Memory of Trees; Watermark; Shepherd Moons by Enya
All music by David White Dove
Angel Love by Aeoliah
Brother Sun, Sister Moon by Buddy Comfort
Canon in D by Pachabel
Chariots of Fire by Vangelis
Color of Light; Sounds of the Heart by Karunesh
Deep Peace by Bill Douglas
Essence and all other music by Peter Kater
Fumbling toward Ecstasy; Solace; Surfacing by Sarah McLaughlin
Golden Bowls by Karma Moffett
Golden Heart by Mark Knoffler
Heart of Perfect Wisdom; Wings of Song by Robert Gass
In Love; Open to Grace by Peter Makena
In Search of Angels on Windham Hill label
Ingenue by k.d. lang
Island by David Arkenstone
Karma by Delirium
Lama's Chant songs of Lama Gyurme
Lazaris Remembers Lemuria
Love Songs by Elton John
Meditation by Fumio
The Mission by Ennio Morricone
Music by Yanni
Music to Disappear In by Rafael
Novus Magnificat by Constance Demby
Om Namaha Shivaya by Robert Gass
Ophelia by Natalie Merchant
Prayer for Peace from Silver Wave Records
Secret Garden by White Stones
Spirit by Jewel
Strength of a Rose by Miten and Premal
Sudhananda on Earth Spirit Music
The Essence; Vision; Love is Space by Deva Premal
The Fairy Ring and other titles by Mike Rowland
The Lost Chord by Jonathan Goldman
The Mask and the Mirror; The Visit; Parallel Dreams by Loreena McKennitt
The Velocity of Love by Suzanne Ciani
Two Rooms by Elton John and Bernie Taupin
Universal Mother by Sinead O'Connor

Lively, Upbeat, Dance Selections

Awakenings by Irshad Khan
Beggars and Saints by Jai Uttal
Comparsa by Deep Forest
Dirty Dancing - Soundtrack from the Movie
Dynamic Dancing by Power of Movement
Feet in the Soil; Tigers of the Raj by James Asher
Flashdance
Jump by Casey Macill
Magical Mystery Tour; Let it Be by The Beatles
One World One People by XCultures
Release by Afro Celtic Sound System
Shaman's Breath by Professor Trance and the Energizers
Spirit of the Forest by Baka Beyond
Supernatural by Carlos Santana
The Best of World Music
The Singles by David Bowie
Tibetiya; Seven Times Seven by Oliver Shanti

Ritual, Ceremonial, Exotic Selections

Monkey by Jai Uttal
Braveheart by James Horner
Chant by Benedictine Monks
Chants of India by Ravi Shankar
Conscience by The Beloved
Deep Forest by Deep Forest
Drums of Passion: The Invocation by Babatunde Olatunji
Intoxicated Spirit by Nusrat Fateh Ali Khan
Jiva Mukti by Nada Shakti
Kama Sutra by Michael Dama
Kundun by Philip Glass
Monsoon by Sheila Chandra
Mudra by Prem Joshua
Nightsong by Nusrat Fatel Khan
One Track Heart by Krishna Das
Passages by Shankar and Glass
Pilgrim Heart by Krishna Das
Sacred Buddha by Sina Vodjani
Sacred Ceremonies by Dip Tse Chok Ling
Tai Chi by Oliver Shanti
The Sacred Fire by Nicholas Gunn
Voices of Spheres by Ustad Salamat Ali Khan

About the Authors

Carolyn Anderson is a co-founder and the co-director of Global Family and a founding partner of Hummingbird Community in northern New Mexico. Speaker, author, seminar leader, and global networker, Carolyn is committed to shifting consciousness to unity and love and to awakening humanity to its full potential. Her passion is living and sharing the principles of co-creation and exploring the frontiers of evolutionary spirituality.

She has coordinated activities for numerous global events, assisted with the creation of social cooperation trainings, and facilitated a number of international conferences. Through the Core Group Process, she has empowered individuals all over the world to discover and fulfill their life purpose. As a successful business woman, she is passionate about shifting economics from fear, greed and scarcity to love, service and abundance by fostering cooperative entrepreneurship. Carolyn serves on the Council of WE, Women's Empowerment, and lives in northern California with her husband John Zwerver.

Katharine Roske, social pioneer, author, educator, minister and grandmother is committed to the realization of a co-creative planetary culture that is a living embodiment of our spiritual essence. During the past three decades, Katharine, together with her husband, Makasha, has devoted her life to the raising of 8 children; pioneering innovative social models; co-facilitating international youth leadership programs; organizing global events and link-ups for peace; facilitating programs supporting spiritual growth; and establishing networking convergence centers in both urban and rural settings.

Katharine resides at Hummingbird Community in northern New Mexico where she is a founding partner and active steward of the community. As Program Director of Hummingbird Living School, she is particularly impassioned to support young leaders in fulfilling their destiny. Katharine is also co-founder of the Path of Ceremonial Arts for Women, a program of All Season's Chalice in Boulder, Colorado.